Born in Buckingha[m] [...] a builder, Jean Shr[...] famous model by t[he...] extensively for *Vog[ue...]* *Vanity Fair* and wit[h...] here and in Americ[a...] one son and with her husband runs an enchanting old hotel in Cornwall.

C000176545

JEAN SHRIMPTON
An Autobiography

with Unity Hall

SPHERE BOOKS LIMITED

A Sphere Book

First published in Great Britain by Ebury Press, an imprint of the
Random Century Group 1990
Published by Sphere Books Ltd 1991

Copyright © Jean Shrimpton 1990

The right of Jean Shrimpton to be identified as author of this
work has been asserted by her in accordance with the Copyright,
Designs and Patents Act 1988.

All rights reserved.
No part of this publication may be reproduced,
stored in a retrieval system, or transmitted, in any
form or by any means without the prior
permission in writing of the publisher, nor be
otherwise circulated in any form of binding or
cover other than that in which it is published and
without a similar condition including this
condition being imposed on the subsequent purchaser.

Printed and bound in Great Britain by
BPCC Hazell Books
Aylesbury, Bucks, England
Member of BPCC Ltd.

ISBN 0 7474 0962 5

Sphere Books Ltd
A Division of
Macdonald & Co (Publishers) Ltd
165 Great Dover Street
London SE1 4YA
A member of Maxwell Macmillan Publishing Corporation

Prologue

One of the last professional jobs I did was to go to Sicily in 1983 as a guest at a congress of women involved in the world of fashion. I was there to answer their questions. Someone asked what I would have wanted to be if I hadn't been a model. Without a moment's hesitation, I said I would have liked to be a gardener. This brought about a cheer from the audience. But it was an honest answer. I would very much have enjoyed being a gardener. I was never smitten with a burning ambition to succeed. It was something that just happened.

It is still a puzzle to me that I ever became a model. I am an excessively private person and I do not have the temperament for fame: I spent those years when I was well known trying to hide away. I think I was rather ashamed of this trivial way of earning a living – it never seemed right to make so much money for doing something so unimportant.

Reliving my life through the pages of this book has made me reconsider things I have not thought about for years. I see now that I was in an enormously privileged position for the ten years (1960–70) that I was modelling. I earned a great deal of money that I never bothered to spend, and lived what most people would consider to be a glamorous life of travel and meeting famous people. But I also discovered that fame precludes friendship and is of no help when love affairs do not go smoothly. I have not had a straightforward life, mainly because I was often presented with such unusual choices. In my private life I was too passive in what were dire situations. For years I was a waif astray.

For me, writing this book has laid a ghost or two. Today I realize that, apart from my family, the two people who were important were David Bailey, the photographer, who made me famous, and Michael, my husband, who gave me something that for so many years proved elusive.

Michael has given me happiness.

— 1 —

When I was four, Bessie Barnes, an artist who lived in our village, approached my mother and asked if she could draw me. Flattered to be asked, my mother gave permission and I was regularly taken off to Miss Barnes's home for sittings. I wore a pastel-striped smocked dress that my mother had made for me.

I loved these portrait sittings, mainly because I was fascinated by Bessie Barnes. She was a dark, rather mysterious, arty lady with a cloud of black, fuzzy hair. Her home was filled with pictures and fascinating bits and pieces of old china and objects that each held some special memory for her. Her surroundings were quite different from those of my family. We were conventional; she was not. She was my introduction to the attractions of a less ordered, cluttered style of life that I was to embrace myself when I was older.

Years later, when I was in my thirties, I saw in a junk shop a second-hand forties' frock made of almost the identical striped fabric that my mother had used for my dress. Just the sight of it brought back an instant picture of Bessie Barnes and childhood. I bought the dress.

As I get older I find it is childhood I refer to, and it is that period of my life which has the most influence over me. Tiny, unwittingly stored and half-remembered vignettes from the time when I was small create a response in me. If I see an old, wrinkled stocking and a funny little haircut, in my mind it is suddenly just after the war and I experience a feeling of warmth and safety. A fabric printed with small rosebuds recalls the pretty underwear women wore in the

7

late thirties and early forties. When I see this kind of fabric I am reminded of returning unwillingly to school on Monday mornings, past the flower-scattered washing blowing on the line. When these pretty garments could be worn no more, my mother cut them up to make smocked dresses for the teddy bear I still treasure.

I like old things. I can be in a saleroom and pick up a jug or a piece of china that reminds me of my grandmother's home and I am filled with nostalgia. Sounds, smells, the texture of an old Harris tweed coat please me: they recall earlier days.

Physical attraction can be stirred in the same way. There was a time when the movement of a stranger's eyebrow could trigger the memory of someone I once cared about and lull me into believing I could care again. For me the past is always present.

I think my son, Thaddeus, will be the same. When he was a baby I owned an ancient silky blue nightdress that age had made soft to the touch. It, too, I found in a junk shop. It was an odd thing to buy since the front was full of holes that someone had carefully mended by button-holing round each one. These days it is rare to find darned clothing, but people were poorer when that nightgown was first worn and garments had to last. When a mother nursed her children on her lap it was the front of her clothing that wore out. I bought the nightgown because it evinced for me one of those small human touches in life that reach the heart.

Because of its softness, I, too, wore the nightgown a great deal when I was breast-feeding my son. Eventually it became impossibly tatty, but, still reluctant to throw it away, I put it in a drawer. One day I couldn't find a clean nightgown and put the old one back into temporary service. Thaddeus was then about six. I was on the stairs wearing the nightgown when he came out of his bedroom and saw me, put his arms around me and buried his face in the soft fabric. Then he quickly drew back, slightly self-conscious at the strength of his reaction. After that, I could not bring myself to discard it. I have it still.

It was another blue garment, a striped blue and white dress, that I wore for my first modelling session. I was two years old and my mother asked a local amateur photographer to call and take some pictures of me. Our ginger cat, Peter, was used as an accessory.

This first photographic session turned out well, though I have no recollection of it. We were a family who took snapshots all the time, so I was not in the least self-conscious and quite accustomed to smiling for my father's camera. The photographer's pictures were good enough for him to ask if he could enter one for a child study competition. Whether his picture ever won I have no idea, but my mother was thrilled just that it was entered. Like any parent, she believes I was a pretty child and very special, and today is convinced that I was destined to be a model.

I was born in November 1942, right in the middle of the war. My parents had been married for three years when my father had to go into the Royal Air Force in October 1942, just a few weeks before I arrived. The war was at such a critical stage that it looked as if Britain might not win. Men like my father, who had previously been deferred, were now being called up. He received his conscription papers in that desperate September when Britain's morale was at its lowest. My mother was eight months pregnant with me and he had been given a further month's deferment in order to be at home for the birth. This was meant to be on 4 October. Unfortunately I arrived very late, a habit that fortunately has not persisted. Not unnaturally the War Office decided they could not wait indefinitely, so my father had to leave home for Alton Camp in Hampshire before I arrived. I kept Mother waiting until 6 November. As luck would have it, I was so very late that my birth coincided with my father's first weekend pass, and he was at home when I finally made an appearance at 8.30 in the morning at The Shrubbery, the local nursing home in High Wycombe, Buckinghamshire. I was a big baby weighing 8lb 5oz, and according to my mother it was a normal birth.

My mother tells me that in my early days I thought of my father merely as a photograph. There were two pictures of him in the house, one on the mantelpiece and another on the chest of drawers in Mum's bedroom, and I would dutifully say 'Daddy' when asked who this dark man in RAF uniform was. But when he did come home on leave, I never made the connection between the picture and the man. In the flesh I did not choose to recognize this interloper in the family. My mother tells me that I was not at all friendly and even gave the impression that I did not like him very much.

Sad as it must have been for him, I was apparently no more friendly when he came home for good. Six months later my sister, Chrissie, was born, yet I can remember hardly anything of these two traumatic changes in my life.

Clearly, my father's homecoming and Chrissie's birth had disrupted the wonderfully sheltered life I had enjoyed until then. Immediately after I was born my mother, not wanting to live on her own with me in wartime, moved back to live with my maternal grandmother in the Buckinghamshire village of Lane End, not far from High Wycombe. Also living in the house was Granny's son, my sweet-natured but mentally handicapped Uncle Ernie. It was the happiest household imaginable. I was a very wanted child and my mother and grandmother idolized me. I am convinced that one's expectations are defined by the patterns set in those crucial early years, and my expectations were for a spotlight unshared. My father's homecoming from the RAF meant that Mother and I moved back with him to the house he had built for her before they married. When suddenly I was wrenched from Granny and Ernie to this strange place I was naturally less indulged. Furthermore, I had to share my mother with my father. I was still very loved, but I am afraid I was certainly not as happy as I had been. Father had stolen some of Mother's attention – and I had been used to having all that to myself.

I have no recollection of Mother being pregnant, and I have no recollection of seeing my little sister when she was first born. I obviously blocked her out of my consciousness.

I had always been a perfectly normal, happy child, but the arrival of a new baby naturally took up a lot of everyone's attention. I began to withdraw into myself and became rather shy and solemn. After Chrissie was born I lost even more of my mother's attention. This trauma, following so quickly on the heels of the others, had a crucial effect on me. They say that children often act out their anxieties with their dolls. I had a poor, unfortunate creature called Lizzie and I used to beat her as hard as I could with a wooden spoon, shouting: 'Lizzie, Lizzie, Lizzie.' I've often wondered since who I was really angry with. I had become rather introverted, and it was to take some years before I was as happy again as I had been at my grandmother's.

When Mother and Granny took Chrissie and me out and people came up to us in the street I remember my grandmother saying to them: 'Speak to the one outside the pram first . . . speak to the one outside the pram.' I was 'the one outside the pram' and I felt that no one was interested in me now there was this cheerful, smiling baby inside it. My mother was still as loving, but as far as I was concerned, everything had changed. I had to share, and a lot of the individual attention I was used to quite naturally went. Even when I was that young I was an extreme person, and I registered the changes as a rejection. That early conviction that I had been rejected by those whom I loved best created an insecurity and a sense of isolation which have persisted throughout most of my life.

Today my childhood memories are good, but for a long time I mourned what I felt I had lost. It had been so lovely with Granny and Ernie and Mum in that peaceful household where I was queen. Village people used to pop in to see me being bathed. I was quite an event in the little community where we lived. I was the village baby – they adored me and thought I was wonderful.

I was easily overexcited, and if anyone gave me anything I would clench my fists and hold my breath in a great, long gasp that would frighten my mother to death. I was always thrilled to be shown a flower, and would gasp

11

with amazement and wonder. I still have it in me to be moved by beauty – though I have now learned to repress my emotions since I do not like people to know what I am feeling. But many of the things which gave me pleasure as a child are still favourites. There are old-fashioned roses which I love, and the sight and scent of them continue to bring me tremendous pleasure.

My mother is one of those people who is loved by everybody. An optimist with a wonderfully positive outlook on life, she is not – and never has been – a moaner. Her first priority was always to keep the family together. We were everything to her. It was not easy for her – my father was difficult, and all three of her children have turned out to be faintly eccentric. I love her very much and I know she loves me, but I have always been something of a puzzle to her.

I doubt if she realized how much I missed living with my grandmother, a small, red-headed, spirited lady who lived in a pair of ordinary brick village cottages. My granny was poor but she was a wonderful woman. Her husband had been killed in a motorcycle accident when my mother was eight, and Granny had been left to bring up my mum, her sister, who was then ten, and twelve-year-old Ernie all on her own.

As a child I loved going back to stay with her. I slept in a great squashy feather bed that kept out the cold and she sat by my side and told me fairy stories until I went to sleep. Everyone in the village came to her for help. She would be called in when there was a birth, and more often than not it was Granny who laid out the village's dead.

She kept Uncle Ernie with her all her life. He was a gentle soul, rather more simple-minded than seriously mentally deficient – his tongue was attached to the roof of his mouth and he could not speak properly. I loved him very much and still do. We were told he would die when he was about thirty, but he is still with us, living in an old people's home, aged seventy-eight. I was never frightened by him. I accepted him totally and was always quite at home with him. He wasn't very pretty to look at, but as far as

12

I was concerned he was simply Uncle Ernie who talked a bit funny but was good company. For me it was like having another child about the place. Uncle Ernie was part of my growing-up days and when I was a little older we used to sit together for hours doing jigsaws.

I often think it strange that the first imprint I had of a man was my mentally handicapped uncle. With my father away, he was the only man of the family, but mentally we were much the same age. People were more tolerant then, and everyone in the village treated him wonderfully well. Sometimes he must have been irritating, but Uncle Ernie never irritated me and the experience of having been brought up with him has given me a natural sympathy towards people who are disadvantaged. But my early conceptions were coloured by the fact that the first man I knew well and believed to be the archetypal male was not my difficult and highly complicated father but nice, simple Uncle Ernie.

When my father did come home, I was aware that Mother reacted completely differently to this new male person. My father had so much family power and a positive impact on all our lives, whereas the other male I was used to was never forceful and completely non-threatening. It took a while, but I did eventually come to terms with having this dark-haired, good-looking father about the place. One of my first memories is riding on a seat attached to the crossbar of his bicycle. We were going over to see his sister Beryl at Downley. She always had Tizer in the larder, that fizzy orange-coloured drink that British children loved before Coca Cola came from the States to supersede it. Like my contemporaries I had a passion for Tizer which, like so many other things, was not easily come by in those days just after the war.

I remember us cycling to Auntie Beryl's so clearly because I was just beginning to enjoy having my father around. He did pay us children a lot of attention in the early days, and though it took a while, he eventually won me round. The bike did its share, and so did the fact that Dad let me ride the local farmer's two Shire horses, Peter and

Prince, who lived peaceably in the field behind our house. They were huge, gentle fellows and I was never afraid when Father lifted me on to one of their broad backs.

Both Father and Mother came from much the same working-class background. My father had left school at the age of fourteen and become a plumber's mate. Uneducated he might have been, but he was ambitious. Just before the war, when he was only twenty-three, he managed to start his own building business and he put up a bungalow. But this was not a prosperous time in Britain. It remained unsold and looked like remaining that way in our sleepy part of the country.

But with the outbreak of war and the threat of bombing, town dwellers wanted to escape to the country. No bombs fell in our part of Buckinghamshire – except one or two by mistake. The only visible signs of conflict were the tanks which rumbled through the village on practice manoeuvres. The terrible noise they made sent mothers scuttling for shelter with their prams so that the children would not be frightened. So the war helped my father's business, as well as keeping him out of the services in the early days. He sold the bungalow to a family from London and almost instantly was given orders for three more – as long as he could build them quickly for the escapees from the bombing.

On the strength of this success my parents moved into the fourth house he built, and that was where we were living when I was born at the local nursing home. But the business went into abeyance when Dad was called up.

In the two years he spent in the RAF my father rose to the dizzy heights of corporal. Since his health was bad, this was more of an achievement than it sounds. He was stationed most of the time at Alton in Hampshire, but like most servicemen moved around a lot. He was never posted abroad, so he was able to get home fairly often. Eventually he was discharged because he quietly passed out at the sight of blood!

Since my father was a neurotic man the RAF put him on tranquillizers, and he stayed on them for another thirty years before he was eventually weaned off them. He was tall and thin, with a long narrow head, and had striking, intense green eyes. He would have been a more interesting person if he had had a proper education – there was a truly original spark in him. The pity was that this originality and drive had been channelled by a possessive, domineering mother into work.

His father, whom I called Granpy, was a sweet man but meek. He grew his own tobacco, cured it himself and then smoked it in his pipe, giving out an air of remarkable contentment. There was a little garden shed where he would hang the big, brown leaves to dry. I loved the garden. Granpy had cut privet hedges into little bowers where you could sit and breathe in the distinctive, not entirely pleasant, smell of the privet and the little white flowers that infrequently appeared. There were also two ponds full of newts and tadpoles, which started in me a lifelong affection for frogs. It was a long garden where my self-sufficient grandparents grew all their vegetables, plus strawberries and raspberries, redcurrants and blackcurrants. I was intrigued by the pale, unfocussed pink of the new rhubarb when it pushed through the straw that Granpy had wrapped around it to keep off the frost. Logs for the fire were kept in a perfect little black coach which must have once been owned by a lady in a Gainsborough hat. It was impossible to sit inside it as the logs took up all the room. This was a source of childhood frustration. Best for me was the honeysuckle, for its wonderful smell – a smell that can still transport me mentally to warm, still evenings in Granpy's magic garden.

My paternal grandmother was more intelligent than Granpy, which made her frustrated, bored and a total hypochondriac. Every day she took a pharmacopoeia of pills against imaginary ailments. She persuaded my father to wear a stomach belt for the sake of his health, and he faithfully did so until the day when a doctor managed to convince him that it was doing him more harm than good. She was a truly obsessive woman who never threw anything away. It must have been she who taught my father to worship money. He began earning by helping on the farms when he was still a schoolboy, and he saved. When he built the first of his houses he never borrowed a penny. And he never borrowed in his life. His whole pleasure came from making money, but he hated to spend it. He never bought any clothes – a trait I inherited. Like him, I do not buy things for the sake of buying, and I am not at all susceptible to shop windows. My father kept a coat for twenty years and had it altered when necessary. He would have applauded the fact that throughout most of my modelling career I existed on one evening dress. We had a Bentley in the garage but he always drove around in an old pick-up truck. Like him I have never owned flash cars, though my husband, Michael, gets a lot of pleasure from big, over-the-top American cars and sells them through a small company called Dream Machines.

My father had no social pretensions – something else I inherited. He was very understated. He also happened to be extremely good at business and was quite popular around the town – High Wycombe was a much smaller and tighter community in those days. He was well known for always putting in a tender lower than the other builders, and conversely when buying land his offer would be higher. It might only have been a few shillings lower or higher, but it ensured that he got what he wanted. He always had a rough idea of what things cost, and he would refit small items free of charge for his customers if they went wrong. He was shrewd and he always kept his word.

He was undoubtedly an unusual man, highly intuitive and with the courage to back his own hunches. Life with him was not easy for my mother. The atmosphere changed when he came home at night, and we were all anxious not to disturb him. He tried to do too much and as a result was always exhausted; so my mother, trying to save him further stress, was left to make decisions about us children which she would have preferred to discuss with him. There was an underlying tension in the house which I felt, though Mum tried to hide it from us. I hate rows; they unsettle me and so I am very slow to provoke one. My sister is quite the opposite; she quite enjoys a good dust-up. But then, people always react one way or the other to friction. To my mother it was a matter of pride to keep up appearances. She would not even confide her difficulties to her own mother.

Being a loyal soul she would never have thought of leaving my father. She had never known any other kind of marriage and, as many women did in those days, she accepted his behaviour as the masculine way of going on. He worked hard and eventually he got rich and gave us a wonderful home. He was popular with his friends but we had to live *his* way, which I suppose was normal then. Women's Lib was unheard of. My mother never worked – Father wouldn't have tolerated that – but then she would never have wanted to. Her job was the family and keeping Chrissie and me out of Dad's way, particularly if his friends were about. He thought he adored us, but his work came before his children.

Our greater good fortune was that our mother was a perfect mother at many, many levels. She made sure that Chrissie and I had an idyllic childhood. Father provided the wherewithal; Mother sustained us emotionally. The result was that our childhood days were happy ones.

My mother always wanted to do the best she possibly could for her children. She wanted us to be more middle class than she and my father were, but she was not ambitious for any great future for either me, my sister or our brother, who came much later. She just wanted us to be happy. She would never have considered sending me to boarding school, though if I had wanted to go – which I certainly did not – she would have done something about it. In her mind the next best thing to boarding school for anyone aspiring to become middle class was a convent education. So that was where I, and Chrissie in her turn, went. My father wasn't that interested. His view was the short-sighted one. He would have sent us to the state school if he'd had his way. 'Bloody waste of money!' he used to mutter when it was time for school fees to be paid. He had had hardly any education himself and he was doing all right, so to his mind education was useless.

I was reluctantly taken off for my first day at St Bernard's Convent, High Wycombe, in September 1947, just before my fifth birthday. I didn't want to go to school. Home life at Naphill, the village where we lived, was truly idyllic in many ways. I loved my mother and father and I had all my animals for company. For a long time when I was young, I was obsessed with animals. My father, who also was fond of animals, was always coming home with a kitten or a duckling in a box for me. He always kept a pig or two at the bottom of the garden which eventually, with lamentations from me, had to be killed for my mother to salt. He had space on a field up the road where he kept a few more pigs, and these he bred to sell. It was well after the war, but food was still scarce. My father would grumble that we might as well still be fighting Hitler for all the difference beating him had made to shortages.

Not that we suffered. We, like his parents, were self-sufficient. We had chickens that were treated more as pets than as farmyard animals, but at least they laid eggs. I enjoyed the daily search for the next morning's breakfast, carrying the egg basket and grubbing in the undergrowth where the hens laid. One of the chickens, my favourite, I used take out with me, wedging her firmly under my arm. She was called Pecky because she would peck at people's teeth. She would pull her head back, fix her victim with her beady little eyes, and then lunge with deadly accuracy straight for the teeth. It was a habit which made neither her nor me popular. We also had a black labrador, called Danny, who had been trained by my father. Danny had the softest mouth. He would collect the eggs in his mouth and bring them to the kitchen without breaking them. Dad, who had enormous patience with animals, had trained him to sit with one chick on his head and one on his nose.

Danny was a remarkable dog. Father took him to the pig field one afternoon and left him outside, instructing him to stay. And forgot him. Dad left by a different gate and came back home. It wasn't until about six hours later that he realized the dog was not with him. Obedient Danny was still patiently waiting exactly where he had been told to wait.

My father also taught Danny another novel trick – taking off people's hats. This caused Mum many problems when she and I were out with the dog, particularly on a bus. She would take care not to sit behind anyone wearing a hat, but if a hat-wearer came aboard and sat in front of us Danny went into action, determined to perform. My pink and flustered mother would try to control him, apologizing to the surprised person in front, while at the same time desperately trying to keep her skirt in place as Danny scrabbled for his target.

Danny had also been trained to pick things up, which was a considerably more useful trick and less embarrassing. When Chrissie threw her blanket or a toy out of her pram, Danny would retrieve it and follow her along with it. Passers-by were always pointing out that the dog had something in its mouth.

I loved Danny and I was fascinated by the pigs and all my pets. My days were full. With all these really nice things going on at home, why should I want to go to school? My mother explained that I had to. I accepted what she said, but it still didn't seem a good enough reason to me.

I remember that first morning all too well. Mother and I had to go on the bus to High Wycombe to get to the convent she had chosen for me. The town was nowhere near as big as it is today, but it was still not easy to get on the bus. We lived near a Bomber Command station and, though the war was over, a great many servicemen were stationed there and the buses were always full. Mum and I waited for ours, me clinging to her hand, and when it came we pushed our way on. As it bounced and rattled along I was full of unspoken terror and I didn't want the journey to finish.

In High Wycombe we disgorged ourselves from the press of servicemen and made the short walk to St Bernard's. It loomed into view, looking like a big house. That might have been reassuring if it hadn't been for the railings that surrounded the building, presumably to keep little children inside. I remember my mother standing behind those railings to wave goodbye as I went cautiously into the unknown, upper lip stiff, my hand in the large hand of some strange woman who was called the teacher.

Going to school was yet another terrible trauma for me. Other children settled down quickly, but I was very apprehensive and trying not to show it. Even at five years old I understood there was no point in fighting what had to be. I knew how to bow to the inevitable and was already aware that the inevitable was more than likely going to be unpleasant. Optimist I was not. But, like everyone else I had to go to school and so I went, quaking with fear.

Every single, miserable day of that awful first term I wet my knickers, simply because I was too nervous to ask the teacher if I could go to the lavatory. Undoubtedly the teacher would have preferred me to ask rather than hear the other children sniggering at the nasty sound of trickling water on the wood floor at the back of the classroom where I sat. I always managed to find somewhere private to go and take my knickers off, and I would then try to hide them somewhere until home time. Every day I came home clutching this shaming wet package. It was both ridiculous and amazing to be that nervous. At playtime I stood in the playground with my shoulders tense, face screwed up, eyes shut tight, elbows in and hands over shrinking ears while the awful noise of boisterous, less inhibited children thundered around me. I found school totally bruising and it took me a long time to become accustomed to it. Even now I am uncomfortable in large groups of people. There's nothing to be done about it; this dislike of crowds is obviously part of my nature. Goodness knows why I let myself drift into becoming famous. At school I never wanted to be part of any gang, and later I never enjoyed being well known.

My mother said I never let myself appear unhappy, but she was well aware of just how upset I was by this frightening new experience. After a week or so, and for the rest of the first term, she sent me to school only in the mornings. The knowledge that she would be waiting outside the school for me at lunchtime was about the only thing that got me through those mornings.

Getting the bus to school every day was a problem, on top of the fact that my mother had my sister to look after. For a while Dad used to take me to school on his motorbike, and that was wonderful. I loved the sense of speed and rushing wind and the *frisson* of danger as I clung to his waist.

As I grew a little more confident about school and life in general, my father stopped taking me on the bike and I was sent off on the bus with the slightly older children from across the road. The bus stop was opposite our house, and while we waited for the grunting old thing to arrive I spent my whole time dangerously running back and forth across the road and calling to my mother: 'You are quite sure you'll be there?'

I needed to be absolutely certain that she would bring me home again. In the perfect world which I was already aware did not exist, she would have stood outside the school for the entire day so that I could look up from lessons occasionally and be reassured by her presence. As it was, as the end of the lessontime drew near, the teacher lost my attention completely. I was watching the window. If my mother wasn't standing there, behind those hated railings, at exactly the spot where I could see her and a good fifteen minutes before the bell went, I would start to panic. She never once let me down, even though she had Chrissie to consider and she had to catch that dratted crowded bus.

I found the convent strange. Nuns are peculiar beings to a young child, and all they did for me was instill in me a huge sense of guilt from which I will never be free. It seemed to me they spoke in riddles. I never knew what they were on about with the 'fruit of the womb', and the 'stain of original sin' which, as far as I could gather, came about just from being born – which seemed most unfair. 'The quick and the dead' was another puzzle, as were 'the sins of the fathers'. We children used to go around parroting

21

these phrases without the faintest idea of what they meant. In fact, it is only recently that I discovered that 'the quick and the dead' meant nothing more dramatic than just the living and the dead.

I found all this biblical jargon very confusing, particularly as I did not come from a religious household. Granny had been a reasonably staunch Methodist and my mother was Church of England, probably because that was what most people were and by swopping chapel for church we all came up a bit in the world. Father believed that God helps him who helps himself.

As I wasn't a Catholic at the convent, I was separated along with the other C of Es when it came to religious instruction, so I never got hooked on the Virgin Mary and I never wanted to be a nun like so many girls who are sent to convents. I suppose there were enough ordinary teachers to dilute the influence of the nuns, and it didn't seem as if I were susceptible to any of those things. My mother was as religious as she considered necessary – I was confirmed eventually – but any interest I had in church slowly withered and died away for lack of nourishment. I didn't need it then, and I don't appear to now.

Though I don't have anything against nuns, I do think convent school was another slightly unsettling experience for me. I found the nuns themselves a little scary – all that black flapping cloth haunting the school corridors. The drama of it may well have had some deep effect on me. Today I am often inclined to dress in 'black flapping' style myself. My husband often tells me that I look like six bats on a hanger!

We wore proper little English schoolgirls' uniform at both convent schools I went to. At the first one it was short grey gymslips and maroon blazers and in the summer a grey dress. When I went to what we called 'grown-up school' it changed to a navy blue gymslip with a light blue dress in the summer, and of course the regulation tie. I didn't mind wearing uniform, and I still like the look of it. I wasn't one of those 1950s' schoolgirls who wore full frilly petticoats underneath their gymslips. But I did notice later that it

22

was always the girls who had had the petticoats and who were terribly flirty when young who seemed to grow up to be frumpy. I was a tomboy until late, and uninterested in petticoats and boys. It was animals, particularly horses, that were taking all my attention by the time I went to the big school.

I was a conscientious little schoolgirl, buckling down to work and living with all the pressure of making sure I did well – which of course I did. I could keep up, but it was quite a strain, though I don't think it ever showed in me. Terrified of failing, I was always in the top five or eight in class when it came to examination times. I worked really hard, so much so that my mother told me to stop. I would study all through the night, taking a torch and working on my school books under the bedclothes. There was no necessity to do this: my mother never pushed me, and there were no stresses or pressures at home. I was an odd child – intellectually striving, bright and curious. I wanted to learn. This worried my mother.

'Jean,' she would say, when she came into my room late at night and found me still awake and grappling with homework, 'don't drive yourself so hard. Your daddy and I don't care if you don't pass the exams.'

But I cared. I had to succeed. It was a need that went back to the time when I was two years old and suffered the miserable feeling of rejection. I was still striving to show that I was worth approval. Even when I became famous I feared the pain of rejection. It seems to me that most famous people strive for fame because they are desperate for approval. But they never get it – not in the form that they look for. It doesn't exist.

Looking back, I realize that because I was so afraid of failure I learned nothing properly at school. I just parroted all I needed to know to get me through, and forgot the lot a week after the exams were over. Studying became such a relentless chore that I finished up hating literature, hating English composition and unable to write even a letter with any pleasure. This was not the school's fault and it was certainly nothing to do with either my parents or my teachers. It was something within me – a personal drive; my own pushing.

There was also a tendency in me to be a goody-goody, and I disliked this about myself. My sister was truly naughty and rebellious at school; I admired her for it and half-wished I could be the same. Being the good one of the family seemed such a dull role to play – though in my heart I couldn't really see any point in being a nuisance for the sake of it. I secretly thought that those who were a nuisance were – a nuisance! Yet for some reason the naughty ones, the disrupters, seemed to be the popular ones with the other girls.

I worked it out. Ten per cent of the time I would be naughty, so that the girls wouldn't label me a goody-goody. I wasn't seriously disruptive. I only chattered in class and set up the giggle syndrome, a much milder form of naughtiness than that of my sister, who didn't give a damn for authority. I was just a rather boring nuisance. My school reports always complained that I talked too much, and it was true. I was fortunate enough to be able to do the work and chatter as well.

School wasn't all bad. For someone who has difficulty in making friends, I wasn't unpopular. I liked games a lot and was quite good at them, which probably helped.

While I was struggling through schooldays my father was struggling to improve our lot. His ambition was to have a farm, and when I was about eight or nine he bought one. For a while, until he retrenched, that took all the money he had. He sold off the beautiful main house of Rose Hill Farm so that he would not be in debt, and we moved into one of the smaller houses on the property. Even so, owning the farm created financial strain and he began working even more than he had before. My father was a workaholic all his life. When he came home from his building business, he would go straight out on the farm to put in more effort. The building business always took a lot of time. At night he had to do his 'bookings'. He would come home, have his supper and watch the nine o'clock news (once we had television), and then settle down to work out where his workmen would be deployed the next day. He always took sandwiches for lunch so as not to waste time and money, and would eat them out in the field sheltered by a hedge. But even on Saturdays he would still have a lunch of sandwiches – and eat them in the sitting room. He never changed his ways and never accommodated anyone, though he did deign to join us for Sunday lunch.

He had always worked to make sure we had a good life, but when we acquired Rose Hill Farm our lives were even better. The farm was at Burnham, a particularly lovely Buckinghamshire village not far from Cliveden. I loved it. Life on a farm was the perfect childhood for me. Once we had settled in, Dad started to breed pigs on a larger scale than before and he became quite well known in the agricultural world.

He started off with a Scandinavian pig, the Landrace. He bought a boar, and it cost a frightening amount of money; Dad intended to mate it with a Large White sow. He was taking a chance, because at that time the Landrace was a very rare pig. The breed has since become much better known and is popular because it yields very lean meat. Unfortunately the animal he bought was not in very good health. The first time we tried to breed from the Large White and the Landrace, the boar collapsed on the job and died.

There was an element of black comedy about the incident, but it wasn't at all funny at the time. My father had not really been able to afford the boar, and its death was a terrible blow. But it took a lot to defeat my father. He bought another, with the result that this time I finished up being allowed to help deliver the first litter.

Because everything he took up he did so well, in no time he was winning prizes with his pigs at all the big agricultural shows. I loved going round the shows with him. Our slowly forged bonding had everything to do with animals – the animals he brought me when I was a small child, and then sharing the excitement of the shows with him. It was there that I got to know him. At home he was too obsessed by work: he worked all the time, and yet he never wanted anything that money could buy. Now that he had seventy acres of land my father was able to indulge his passion for animals. Ours was not a cold-hearted farm, dedicated to making money. The farm was Dad's dream, and he still had his building business to keep some money coming in to finance the dream. We had a few of every kind of livestock at first; they were all treated as pets and had their own names. I had this wonderful pig who used to follow me round like a dog. My names for them reflected the totally unimaginative person that I then was. My pig was called Tiggy, my sheep was called Woolly, my chinchilla rabbit was called Chilla and my hamster was called Hamp. My pony fared a little better – I named him Ricky.

Once we were living on the farm I began to go through the stage that attacks most little girls who are brought up in the country, I became mad about riding. I rode a lot, but I was never good because I always felt sorry for Ricky. I was always leading him home because I thought he must be tired and I couldn't bring myself to kick him on. He was a rig, meaning that he hadn't been properly castrated, so he still had a lot of stallion about him. Ricky was not a quiet, gentle animal: he used to give me hell because I was a bit frightened of him, and he sensed it and threw me many times. Dad would send me out to ride him, but I used to lead him most of the way. Even so I was passionate about this contrary beast, and leaving him was like being torn from a lover. I remember my dismay when my parents decided that we would go to Switzerland for a holiday. They had friends who ran a coach tour company and we were to go as their guests with all the privileges that being guests implies.

'The best thing you can say about this tour,' I grumbled, 'is that at least we'll be the last to be picked up and the first to be dropped home.' In a straight choice between Ricky and a holiday in Switzerland, Ricky won hands down.

I was out one day with him when I first met Margaret and Adrienne Berlei, two bigger girls who were much better riders than I was and who were related to the Berlei bra family. They shared one pony between them and they agreed to help me out with Ricky.

'Tire him out and he'll be easier to ride,' Margaret, the elder girl, informed me.

She would ride him for me, and it was a funny sight. She was really too big for him – her legs nearly reached the ground when she was on his back. She rode him at the local gymkhana and he bucked so much that he broke the girth. Margaret stayed on because of her weight. I'd have been off.

He was a dangerous little beast. At a gymkhana at Maidenhead there was to be a fancy-dress competition and we decided to enter for it. We had all watched the Coronation on TV and, along with the rest of the nation, been entranced by the enormous, laughing Queen Salote of Tonga, sitting in her carriage in the pouring rain with the tiny Haile Selassie, Emperor of Abyssinia, at her side. We made a banner which we pinned along the side of our pony and trap; it read 'Linga longa, Queen of Tonga'. Margaret, who had a fine pair of bosoms, was to be Queen Salote, her face blacked with boot polish. Adrienne was to be Haile Selassie and I was to be the postillion on the back of the coach, holding an umbrella and wearing a top hat and trousers.

It was difficult enough getting Ricky to Maidenhead the day before the gymkhana. We took him, hitched to the trap, along the main road and with relief left him in a friendly farmer's field for the night. He was still playing up the next day. In our costumes we managed to get him and the trap together and then ourselves into position for our entrance. We didn't even get into the collecting ring. Ricky bucked until he finally kicked the whole lot, including us, over backwards.

It was from riding that I began to see more of the seamy side of life. High Wycombe was growing larger, leaving behind as it expanded those small, vague pieces of land that escape the developers but are of no more use to the farmers. This type of terrain, be it wooded or scrub, seems to develop an odd, menacing character of its own. These wastelands make the countryside less safe. People dump rubbish there and children use it for play. I'm sure our area was no different from any other, but while I was at school it seemed that there were unpleasant men about and the wastelands were their hunting ground. These men with their nasty habits merely made some of the girls embarrassed and giggly. I was uneasy and wanted to get away.

I always seemed to encounter what I now understand to be these rather pathetic males when I was on my pony. I suppose young girls are vulnerable to such encounters when they ride. Happily no one ever touched me, but they did scare me. I became used to seeing one particular man who hovered in the woods where we used to ride. He wore nothing but a G-string. Perhaps he was just a harmless naturist, but I can tell you he frightened the hell out of me.

The Berlei girls' father was in the police force and he had told his daughters that if they ever saw anything 'like that' they must try to get the man's car number by either noting it down or remembering it. The girls passed on this alarming instruction to me, and one afternoon after school when Adrienne and I were riding we were passed by a rather unpleasant-looking man in his car. He stopped a bit further up the road and turned his engine off. When we caught him up he was sitting in the front seat, watching us in the rear mirror riding towards him. He was also masturbating. This man was not the first I had seen doing this, but previously I had been alone. I had always instinctively realized that what they were doing was wrong, and hurried away.

Adrienne insisted that we must get the number of his car. So we did. She went home and told her father what had happened. Obviously her relationship with her mother and father was more open than mine. I had not mentioned any of this to my parents.

The awful thing was that, after a few days, the police rang my home. Since I had not told my mother about the incident the call shocked and embarrassed her. The police had decided to take the matter to court because the man would not plead guilty, probably because he had a wife and daughter and also because he was receiving psychiatric help at a Windsor hospital. It transpired that he was well known for masturbating in front of young girls. This time it was his bad luck that he chose to do so in front of the daughter of a policeman.

It was also my bad luck. Aged twelve, I had to go to the little court at Burnham where I was put in the waiting room outside. Adrienne and I were not allowed to be together. My mother was not permitted to come with me and I was left in the care of a policewoman. Also in the waiting room was the motorist's pregnant wife, with another woman who owned a riding stable. She was giving evidence on the motorist's behalf.

It was horrific. The wife hated me. I could feel that she hated me as we all sat in a desperate antagonistic silence trying not to look at each other. I finally had to go into court and there he was. He wore heavy, crêpe-soled shoes, ugly thick, pebble glasses and had crinkly, oily hair. He looked the part. I just stared at the electric fire which was attempting to warm the courtroom and avoided looking at him. The worst of it was that I was not allowed to say I had seen 'his thing'. I had been told that I must pronounce that awfully rude (to most twelve-year-olds) word, 'penis', and relate what he had been doing with it. This was horribly embarrassing and traumatic. The woman witness from the riding school said it would be impossible to see into the car from a horse, when I knew perfectly well that you could. I was made to feel that everyone thought I was lying. I couldn't understand why no one seemed to believe me.

He was found guilty and given a small fine. It really was not worth the misery it caused everyone involved. My mother would certainly never have put me through the ordeal had it been left to her, but once the prosecution had been set in motion, there was nothing she could do to prevent it. I had no idea of how to handle the situation, but I do know that today I am against making a big thing of these incidents where children are concerned. Without that courtroom appearance I would probably have forgotten all about it. I had managed to convince myself before the court case that it was his thumb he was playing with, but I could not tell myself that once it was over. As it was, I used to think he was under my bed at night with his horrible pebble glasses, waiting to jump out at me. Night after night I lay there terrified, too frightened even to breathe.

I never told my mother about these lingering fears because I instinctively felt she would not have been able to cope with them anyway. And besides, every cold light of morning I realized that my fears were stupid. He could not possibly be under the bed. I was not the type to make a fuss about my nightly terrors – I was a reserved child, not given to unnecessary drama.

Today I am a reserved woman, not given to unnecessary drama. We do not change a great deal. The child always lingers within the adult.

B ecause of the way I lived my life for animals, it seemed to take me longer to grow up. I did not see myself as being particularly good at making friends, and never felt at ease within the gang. I saw myself as ordinary. There were only two or three girls at school that I felt comfortable with. It wasn't until I was a lot older that I realized I was actually quite popular.

I continued to believe that I was not liked until I had gone past caring about whether I was or not. But that took a long time. I do not believe that I even began to think about anything seriously until I was twenty-six or so. There was no reason for deep thought, and life just swept me along. But when I was twenty-six life stopped being so accommodating and I was forced to consider events rather than just let them occur.

In the meantime, I never seemed to be on quite the same wavelength as anyone else. Unlike my contemporaries at school I was never much interested in boys, nor did I have crushes on pop singers. I am not given to being a fan, though I have to admit I did quite like Elvis Presley. I can remember standing in a record booth when I was about fifteen and listening enraptured to him singing 'Teddy Bear'. He was the only man I dreamed about when I was young. In the dream Elvis was riding a big, black stallion up to Taplow Station. I was behind him, my arms tight around his waist as we galloped along. That was my one and only romantic dream. I suppose I was a Presley fan, as were most girls of my age. He had a wonderful voice, a profile like a Greek god and that dangerous look of a handsome hoodlum.

I was about fifteen when along came another of those incidents that convinced my mother (if only in retrospect) that I was born to be a model. We went to a holiday camp and I was just the right age to enjoy it. I was keen on trying everything that was on offer – the tennis, the swimming, the cycling and the dancing. At the end of the week all the happy snaps that had been taken by the camp photographer were put up on a big board for the campers to make their selection. To my astonishment they were mostly of me. I had not been aware of the photographer following me, but there was the evidence up on the board that he had. I have to admit to being flattered and my mother, of course, was delighted.

It wasn't until I was sixteen that I finally discovered boys. I had taken my GCEs at the convent and, having done my usual pre-examination slogging, managed to do quite well. The nuns wanted me to stay on and eventually go to university, but I had other ideas. I just wanted to leave school as soon as possible. As soon as possible was aged sixteen, so at sixteen I left. My parents did not object, but said I must be trained for a job of some kind.

I had been friendly with two other girls, Dale and Sasa Perkins, since I was fourteen. They lived in the house where Terry Wogan lives today. I thought the Perkins family were absolutely wonderful. Life at their home was casual and unstructured – they lived exactly the way they wanted to live, with no regulations. It seemed to me that they never did anything boring like having meals at regular times, which was surely the height of freedom. Their habits were quite different from my family's. They had alcohol in the house. And they kept it on a silver tray. The Perkinses were much more upper-class and worldly than my family. Mrs Perkins always had red nails (that were chipped), and looking back I understand why I was intrigued by her and her family. Like the artist Bessie Barnes, they too were different in their own way from my norm. I can see now that they were just like any horsey household in Britain, but I had not

32

come across this species before. Though we had horses on the farm my mother did not ride and she was a little bit frightened of them. We were not what you would call truly horsey. Mrs Perkins was – she went in for eventing and won rosettes.

Mr Perkins worked in the City, and Mrs Perkins bred labradors. The whole family was as potty about animals as I was. There were dozens of tortoises, rabbits, and cats having kittens in the bed with nobody seeming to mind. They had a docile old pony which would pull you along by its tail if you hung on tight enough. They also had a stable with several horses which I was allowed to ride, and that also attracted me to them. I could ride their ponies for a change, and they could ride mine. Mrs Perkins could cope with Ricky. When he was playing up one day she turfed me out of the saddle, got up on him, and rode him up and down until he was worn out.

'Now you can get on him,' she said, handing me the reins.

I rode with Dale and Sasa and spent a lot of time at their home. It was Dale who more or less introduced me to the delights of boys. She was quite forward for her age and I used to go riding with her with the specific intention of meeting the local lads. This initiated a series of invites to teenage dances, which posed a problem. Sasa and Dale's friends gave much smarter dances than the ones I would normally have gone to at that age. My sort of girl went to the hop at the youth club or the church hall, but I seemed to have left the youth club and the church hall behind without even having sampled them. I was impressed when I realized that the season's debutantes attended the dances I went to with Sasa and Dale. This was not really surprising since the Thames Valley and rural Buckinghamshire shelter a great deal of wealth and privilege.

I would have enjoyed all this more if my parents had had the money to dress me as well as these upper-class young ladies with whom I was consorting. I remember the humiliation of noticing that they always wore satin shoes specially dyed to match their evening dresses. Mine were always double-duty dark-coloured leather. My mother used to make my dresses for these occasions. I was convinced that this was obvious and that everyone could tell at a glance I was in a home-made outfit. The truth was that I was a bit ashamed of my mum at this time, and embarrassed because she and my father came from a different background to that of my new friends. Looking back, I blush to remember what a horrid little snob I was.

While I was discovering this other world I began to notice that my mother had taken to going to bed early, leaving my father to do the washing up after supper. This was such an unlikely event that I finally said to him: 'What's going on, Dad? What's the matter with Mum?'

My father looked desperately uncomfortable. He was silent for a moment and appeared to be looking round for escape. Then he blurted out: 'Your mother's having a baby.'

I was astonished, but my immediate reaction was to say cheekily: 'That'll teach you to be more careful.'

I could not have said a worse thing, and I still don't know why I said it. He was furious with me. He and my mother were quite embarrassed enough by the situation without me adding to it. I was going on seventeen and Chrissie was fourteen. My father was upset and worried. The pregnancy was certainly not a planned one, and both of them were having difficulty in accepting that it could have happened. My father's anxiety was that my mother was getting to the age when it was unwise to have a baby. She had been given all the tests available, but these were not then as advanced as they are today. They both had Uncle Ernie in mind, and so they worried.

Apart from the fact that Mum seemed awfully old to be getting pregnant, Chrissie and I didn't mind a bit. Chrissie, who is much more maternal than me, was quite excited; I wasn't terribly interested one way or the other. The thought of this third baby was no threat to me, such as Chrissie's arrival had been. My wings were spreading and I was ready

34

to fly the nest: I longed to get to London. The baby seemed remote from my own expanding life.

I'm afraid I never was very interested in Danny when he was little. Not long after he was born, Mum once asked me to look after him. I popped him under my arm and went on reading in bed.

Apart from boys and parties and riding, I hadn't the faintest idea what to do with my life. Eventually it was decided by family committee that I should go to a secretarial college. My mother and I went up to London to look at a couple of schools, and I had interviews at both of them. Not that the interviews were particularly important. If you could pay, they took you!

We finally settled on the Langham Secretarial College which was at Marble Arch. Oxford Street was familiar ground to me. When I was at school Mum and I would occasionally come up to London around Christmastime to get me a new winter coat. This was usually purchased from Selfridge's, which seemed to me then to be the biggest and most exciting shop in the world. Our London trips were always down Oxford Street. Mum would not have dreamed of going to Harrods or to Regent Street – much too expensive, and besides, Oxford Street was nearer to Paddington and the old Great Western Railway which took us home.

I must have gained some confidence from somewhere, because going to the secretarial college caused me no anxiety at all. I was a little nervous the first day as I milled around with all the other new girls, but then so were they. Unfortunately I proved to be terribly bad at typing, which we should have guessed as I had always been a clumsy child, unable to do anything with my hands. It didn't worry me that I wasn't particularly good, and that was strange since I had been so driven to succeed at the convent schools. Something must have been giving me a sense of security, or maybe I instinctively knew that the life of a typist was not for me.

I was not too bad at shorthand, but when it came to typing I could never manage to hit the right keys, and I did not seem to have any strength in my fingers. The school had a mixture of manual and electric typewriters. Neither improved my ability. The electric ones ran away with me, and even by bashing as hard as I could on the manual I couldn't make any impression because my fingers are so weak. I did stay behind at nights to practise, to see if I could crack this thing, but I might just as well have gone home for all the difference it made. However, I stuck it out because I did not know what else to do with my life. But then how many people do on first leaving school?

In any event, secretarial college was unimportant against the background of my blossoming social life in rural Buckinghamshire. While the Perkins girls and I were out riding we had met a boy called Billy whose mother, Helga Moray, was that glamorous being, a well-known authoress. Mrs Moray was marvellously exotic. She had taken Marlene Dietrich as her role model and she was all red lips and wispy hair and mules with feathers round them. Her husband enjoyed throwing parties for his children and their friends. We never gave parties at Rose Hill Farm. I was moving in a different world, the world of minor public schoolboys who knew their way around the West End clubs of the day like Winston's and Churchill's. We all met in coffee bars, we went 'up West', we drifted as a group from party to party looking for the next outing. This was a positive social life which my parents, though a touch uneasy, accepted, reasoning that it was better for me than being down at the pub with the village boys.

Ian, one of the boys on this circuit, was one of my first boyfriends but, to use today's terminology, it was never a relationship. In 1958 most sixteen-year-old girls were a great deal more cautious than nowadays about what we called 'letting a boy go too far'. One weekend Ian took me to see a polo match at Windsor Great Park. We had been there before to watch Prince Philip playing, but it was this weekend when I met my first dirty old man.

I was wearing a grey silky dress that I had bought at
C & A's across the road from the college. I had only just
discovered the comparatively new cheap and cheerful C & A
and Selfridge's no longer enjoyed my custom. I felt I
looked good, and Ian and I were wandering around feeling
rather pleased with ourselves for being in such distinguished
company when this squat, swarthy man with swept-back
dark hair came up to me. Smoothly he introduced himself
as Colonel Voynovitch and in the same breath asked if I
wanted to model.

'I've never thought about it,' I said cautiously.

'But you should,' he told me. 'You really should.'

He stood chatting to us for a moment, and then
suddenly said: 'Would you both like to come into the Royal
Enclosure?'

Ian and I looked at each other. We didn't say anything,
but we both knew we would like to go into the Royal
Enclosure. Ian thanked him, and the Colonel led the way.
The attendants seemed to know him and we were let in
without any fuss. Inside, we were both a little nervous at
being on such hallowed ground; but everyone seemed to
know the Colonel, which made us feel more secure. The
Queen Mother, who was wearing one of her amazing hats,
was just a few feet away, and I was trying not to stare at
her when the Colonel, charm itself, said.' You must meet
Norman Hartnell. You know who Norman Hartnell is, of
course?'

Impressed, I blurted out: 'The Queen's dressmaker?'

He nodded, looking pleased that I had given the right
answer, and led us both across the Enclosure to where
Norman Hartnell stood, appearing exactly as he did in his
pictures – dapper, marvellously smooth and looking as if he
had bathed in asses' milk.

Mr Hartnell greeted us graciously and spoke a few kind
words and then we were led away – presumably before we
could become tiresome.

'You know you really should model,' the Colonel said
again as we walked towards the Enclosure gates. 'I'd like

very much to take some photographs of you. Let me give you my card, and if you like the idea I'll come and talk to your parents about it.'

The mention of talking to my parents lulled me into a false sense of security and I found myself nodding. The Colonel nodded back.

'Why doesn't young Ian here wait for us while I take you to my car and give you my card?' he suggested.

I looked at Ian.

'Do you mind?' I asked.

Ian didn't mind, and the Colonel took me off to the car park, where I noted that he was driving an Aston Martin DB4. He told me to sit in the front seat while he looked in the glove compartment for his card. As we sat there in this sudden enforced intimacy I was appalled to realize that he was stroking my legs. As I shied away, he said soothingly: 'You do have marvellously smooth skin.'

I could think of no answer to this and, realizing my disquiet, he said quickly: 'You will let me talk to your parents, won't you? You could have a great career as a model. I'd like to help you.'

I didn't know what to say. Modelling sounded a great deal more interesting than shorthand and typing, and I was flattered. I gave him my telephone number and agreed that he could come and see my parents.

Sure enough he phoned, turned up at the farm and asked them if he could photograph me. He explained that he worked for *Everywoman*, a glossy magazine of the day for middle-class housewives. My mother, who normally read *Woman*, thought he was quite charming and was highly impressed when he offered to pay me £5 for an afternoon's work. That was a lot of money thirty years ago, and she thought it a wonderfully easy way to earn a fiver. He seemed so above-board that she and my father agreed and the following weekend he came to the farm, picked me up and drove me out to somewhere near Sunningdale where he lived. It was a large house, probably built at the turn of the century, and I had the impression that he only owned

38

the bottom half. I noticed someone else in the grounds, a man walking a labrador. The Colonel offered me tea and then showed me pictures of the debs of the day. I remember there were some *Tatler*-style photographs of some of the very same girls I had seen at one of the dances with the Perkins girls. This impressed me. I was definitely a bit snobby in those days, and realizing he had connections made me feel more secure. He also showed me some straightforward model-girl pictures that he had taken, and told me that he used the name John Scott professionally. And all the while he kept touching my legs and going on about my smooth skin.

'To have skin like that you must be very well bred,' he said when I had shied away yet again.

'I'm not well bred,' I said flatly. 'You saw my parents.'

'No, no, your skin is so soft you have to have breeding,' he insisted, and it was so silly I didn't bother to answer.

The soft skin line was merely an excuse to keep touching. Even as young and green as I was, I understood that – but it was making me restless. Realizing this, he suddenly became businesslike and said that we should take some photographs.

'But perhaps you'd better have a bath first,' he said. 'It will relax you.'

'I've already had a bath today,' I told him, indignant that he should think I needed one.

'For relaxation,' he insisted.

Reluctantly I went into his rather basic bathroom and started to run the water. I was dismayed to find that there was no lock on the door. There was, however, a chair, and I had the wit to jam it under the door handle. I let the bath run but sat on the edge without bothering to undress, and after a while he rattled the door and tried to get in.

'I have some strawberries and champagne here for you,' he called coaxingly from outside.

'I don't want any,' I shouted over the noise of the running water. 'And you can't come in.'

I sat there for as long as I thought a bath and drying myself would reasonably take, and then emerged.

'Now we'll start,' he said, 'but I think you still need loosening up. Why don't you take your bra off?' He was handing me a couple of blouses. 'It'll give a softer line.'

Taking my bra off worried me, but I didn't know how to avoid it. I went into a bedroom, shut the door firmly and took off my bra before putting on one of the blouses. Again he rattled the handle, and again I shouted that he couldn't come in. And then we went outside into his garden where he took a few shots by a lilac tree and that seemed to be that for the day. He handed me a five-pound note and drove me home. On the way he said: 'You're not a virgin, are you?'

'I am,' I said. He looked as if he didn't believe me and making a ring of his thumb and index finger, he then suggestively pushed his other index finger through the centre of the ring several times and said: 'This.'

I didn't fully understand the gesture, but there was something so ugly about it that I pretended not to notice.

As naïve as I was, I was uneasy about Colonel Voyno-vitch. Nevertheless I agreed to go again the following Saturday afternoon, basically because I didn't know how to get out of it. I couldn't bring myself to explain my anxieties to my parents, and I felt miserable and trapped.

The following week he took me to Kew Gardens – he always made it above-board first – and then back to his home in Sunningdale, where we went through the same performance of changing my blouse and taking off the bra. He then said he wanted to photograph me lying down on the bed. Having arranged me there, he went away for a moment or two and then came back in again wearing a dressing gown which he had left hanging open. I was trying not to look, but I could see that he still had pants on, which looked like binding or bandages. Ugly again, like the gesture in the car, and dreadfully off-putting.

'I just want to touch your breasts,' he said, as I lay there on the bed freezing, wondering how on earth I was going to get home if this all went wrong. I worked out that there were other people about – the man in the garden with the labrador must live above. If I yelled loudly enough, would they hear? The Colonel sat down beside me and touched my breasts, and it seemed to me that that was all he wanted. If I let him do that he wouldn't hurt me and I'd get home safely. I knew I was on dangerous ground, and I had a strong feeling that I had to give him something. Then he tried to touch my thighs but I sat bolt upright and said: 'No.' He immediately stopped, took some pictures and eventually took me home. He never actually pressurized me all that much. I wonder now if perhaps he was impotent and just needed to touch young girls. But then I did not understand such things. I was a retarded sixteen-year-old, and it all seemed OK because of Norman Hartnell, the pictures of the debutantes and the fashion shots.

I never went again. I told my mother bluntly: 'I'm not going again, he's a dirty old man. He keeps trying to touch me.' She didn't know what to say. I don't think my parents understood either, and they had been flattered that this man should think I could be a model. My mother was as naïve as I was. I didn't explain any further, and my parents didn't push it. The truth was that they didn't want to know and were terribly embarrassed. Yet, when he rang up again, my mother dealt with it rather well. She said firmly that I wasn't meeting him again; I had to get back to college and get on with my work.

Amazingly, one of the pictures he took appeared in *Woman's Own* – me hanging on to a piece of lilac standing by the lilac tree. He did ring once more and I answered the phone. He said he was at the Dorchester Hotel and asked me to go there as he would like to do some more pictures of me. I told him that I couldn't, and hung up. He had also given me an introduction to someone on *Everywoman* magazine, which I decided to take up. At their offices in Covent Garden the man the Colonel had told me to talk to also wanted to look at my legs. I remember having to lift up my skirt in an untidy little office. He was obviously another member of the dirty old men brigade.

It was years later, long after his death, that I found out who Colonel Voynovitch or John Scott really was. His main claim to fame was photographing the Royal Family, and there are hundreds of pictures in existence that he took of the Queen and of Prince Charles and Princess Anne when they were little. It seems he was a friend of the family – even invited for tea and the weekend.

I had several boyfriends at this time, including one called Peter Severn. Peter drove a Jaguar, which made him quite a catch. I had first spotted this good-looking young man from the train window when I was travelling up to the secretarial college – when you travel up to London every day you note what is going on outside out of boredom, and I had certainly noticed the Jaguar which he left at the station every day. He got into the same carriage one day, and we began talking. He was a nice shy young man, the son of wealthy parents, and he was studying something in London. I was still a virgin then – and he wasn't a forward young man anyway. I liked him very much, but he wasn't important in my life except for one small thing that happened that again seemed to be pushing me towards a modelling career.

Predictably, Peter was a Young Conservative, and he took me to the Conservative ball. I was quite thrilled by this and took some effort with my appearance. I flipped my hair up at the sides, borrowed my mother's black evening dress which had a discreet boat neckline, and applied my new make-up carefully.

We had been in the dance hall at Maidenhead for only a few minutes when an official came up to us and said to Peter: 'Is it all right if we enter your young lady for the Conservative beauty queen contest?'

I was enormously flattered and Peter was pleased. Later on in the evening I had to parade around the hall with the other girls who had been picked, and I really rather enjoyed it all. It was a confident time in my life. I was mildly disappointed that I did not win – I came third. But it was me the photographers chose to photograph, and it was my picture that appeared in the local paper.

Colonel Voynovitch having quite put me off the idea of being a model, I was still slogging away without much enthusiasm at the secretarial college. I had made two girlfriends. One, Valerie, was another of those upper-class girls who always seemed to attract me. She was marvellously glamorous with the most perfect beehive hairdo and long, shapely legs appearing from beneath a tight, pencil skirt. I used to watch her going up the area steps from the basement where we left our coats at the college, clattering on her high heels, tight skirt straining above wonderful legs, and feeling full of envy for all that sophistication. The other friend was a big, rounded lass called Liz whom I suspected to be quite a girl. There were lots of boys in her life, and even I figured out that they were doing more than kissing her goodnight. As for me, I was still a virgin so I felt everything was passing me by. And then to cap all these feelings of discontent, the college sent us for two weeks' work experience at Polytours' offices in Regent Street. There we were all consigned to the typing pool. It was dreadful. I could get nothing right and they kept making me do the letters over and over again until the work was at least halfway presentable. I hated Polytours. I could not believe my life would be that diminished. I felt a dismal failure all round.

It was about this time that I met my first serious boyfriend when a girlfriend of mine took me to his parents' home. His name was Simon de la Tour and he was the older brother of Frances de la Tour, who was to become a well-known actress. He was also my first lover. Simon and his faintly crazy family lived in a huge Victorian brick house on the river at Bourne End. It was so enormous they had to make it work in order to keep it, and they ran a kind of holiday school for foreigners. There were at least ten children of different nationalities, who were treated as part of the family. We all ate together, seated round an oversized table. They also hired the house out for the filming of commercials. Simon's father was Charlie de la Tour, a tall, thin, raffish man who made commercials for a living. Simon's parents had divorced some time before, and both had remarried. They all appeared to be the best of friends. It was another of those unconventional households that always appealed to me.

When I first began to spend time there Michael Winner was filming a nudist film in the house and they had put up screens along the end of the garden so that people going by in their cabin cruisers would not see what was going on. Quite casually, Winner asked me if I wanted to be in it. 'Oh, no, thank you,' I said primly. Nevertheless I was riveted by it all. There were nude people wandering around in the huge grounds all mixed up with the young foreigners who came in the summer. My parents would have been shocked to the core.

Simon was sweet but not at all like Frances, his sister, or Moya, his mother. He was a much more conventional upper-middle-class boy. His great ambition was to race cars, and the thing I remember best about him was that he had beautiful hands (another thing that I always go for). He looked like his father.

They were a funny household. The parents would be sitting up in bed together while all the kids, including me, used to traipse in and out of their bedroom, which I thought amazingly daring. They were all terribly nice and completely natural, and I found them relaxing to be with. They were always so welcoming and there was no parent/child division. They just accepted me as part of the family. Moya was a sensible woman and a wonderful mother. She was so encouraging to her children, always telling them they were fantastic.

When I first met Simon he was with a Swedish girl and I must have pinched him from her, probably attracted by his beautiful hands. When he became my first lover, Moya instantly spotted what was going on.

'I really think it's time,' she said briskly one day, 'that you and Frances got yourself some contraception. We don't want either of you getting pregnant.'

We were sent off together to get Dutch caps and I wasn't in the least embarrassed, even when the woman gynaecologist said crossly: 'What are you doing having an affair at your age? You're far too young.' Nevertheless she fitted me up. I was seventeen, nearly eighteen – not that young by today's standards.

I was so grateful to Moya, and am to this day. It was a remarkably enlightened attitude for that era. She took a chance, because my own parents could have been angry with her, but she did what she thought was sensible. There is little worse in life than an unwanted pregnancy. It is no doubt down to her that I never got pregnant until the day many years later when I chose to do so.

I was still at secretarial college at the beginning of the affair. Simon, who was a couple of months younger than me, used to drive me up to town most days, coming to the farm to pick me up. It was a perfectly straightforward courtship which was absolutely fine until I met David Bailey.

I was fortunate that there was never any sense of disapproval from Simon's parents. Moya used to come into his bedroom sometimes while we were in his little single bed, but it all seemed perfectly natural. This first foray into an affair caused me no hang-ups, but when my poor mother found out she was devastated. I had not told her: she guessed. I am afraid the thought of me sleeping with a boy caused my mother enormous pain. It was not that long after the war, and moral standards were much the same as they had ever been. It was not until the late sixties that parents were finally forced to become resigned to their young having sexual adventures.

I do not recollect ever being told the facts of life, though I had a reasonable idea from the day that the old boar collapsed on the job. You cannot spend all your time around animals as I did without having some awareness of the reproductive process. Many years later my sister and I nagged Mother that she really must be more open with our brother, Dan. She tried terribly hard and picked one teatime to attempt to explain the facts of life to him. He

45

was about thirteen. Chrissie and I decided that she did not do a very good job. He listened aghast for a while, and finally pushed his plate and cup and saucer away. 'You've put me right off my tea,' he said indignantly. 'Honestly! You'd think God would think of a better way.' And he got up from the table and stomped upstairs to recover.

—3—

I had loved my childhood, but in my adolescence I just wanted to get to London and out into the world. There was nothing to hold me at home – not my parents, not even the animals and the riding. The horses were part of my childhood. I had once considered them the most important thing in my life, and yet I stopped riding when I went to modelling school and I have hardly mounted a horse since.

In spite of my mother's anxieties about me, I was not really a difficult daughter. I dutifully ploughed on with the secretarial college, though I was becoming more and more convinced that I would never make a secretary. But I graduated. I managed to get 140 words a minute for shorthand and 70 for typing, just about scraping through. But before those final exams, there came a further incident that seemed to be pushing me towards a career dependent on my looks.

When the weather was good I used to go with Valerie and Liz at lunchtime to the Lyons tea shop round the corner from C & A. There we bought sandwiches which we took into Hyde Park, near Speaker's Corner, enjoying our freedom from the dusty classrooms of the college. Lunchtime lasted an hour and then, dragging our feet, we would head back for Langham Place. We were dawdling to the college one afternoon when a man stopped his car to let us cross at a zebra crossing. I wasn't aware of it, but the driver then contrived to follow us round to the college. It could not have been easy for him, but he managed not to lose us.

We were just going down the area steps at the side of the building to leave our things in the basement when a head and a face half-hidden by big owl-like glasses appeared over the railings. An American voice called out: 'Hey, miss, I'm terribly sorry about this, but can I talk to you?'

We all stopped dead, uncertain which of us he was addressing. We stared upwards as he stared down. We were beginning to giggle.

'You,' he said, pointing directly at me.

I hesitated. He looked respectable enough. He was clean and tidy and properly dressed – but so had Colonel Voynovitch been. Liz nudged me. Still a bit suspicious, I went back up the steps to where he was standing. He was already pulling out a card from the pocket of his slightly loud jacket. He thrust it into my hand.

'I'm Cy Enfield,' he said without any preamble. 'I'm a film director. I'm making a film and there's a part in it that would be just right for you.'

Startled, I stared at him while he explained that the film was to be called *Mysterious Island*. He said he felt I was perfect for one of the roles, and he wanted me to go to see the producer of the film.

'But I'm not an actress,' I said.

'That doesn't matter,' he said, a touch impatiently. 'What's your name? Shrimpton? Jean Shrimpton.' He registered it. 'You'll be great,' he assured me, full of enthusiasm and pushing another card, this time the producer's, into my hand. Baffled, I stared at the two small pieces of white card without saying a word.

He clapped his hand to his forehead. 'Oh, my God, my car!' he said, looking behind him and beginning to back away. 'Now you will get in touch, won't you?' he shouted back as he scurried off to where he had abandoned his car.

My friends, agog, waited below, full of questions. When I showed them the two important-looking cards they were thrilled, recalling how Lana Turner had been discovered in a drugstore.

'Now *you've* been discovered on a zebra crossing,' Valerie said, awestruck. 'You are going to ring him, aren't you?'

I examined the two business cards. Memories of the Polytours typing pool were all too horribly fresh in my mind.

'Why not?' I said. 'It's got to be better than typing.' And later that day I did.

Cy Enfield had been serious. He had already prepared the ground and the producer had been expecting my call. He told me to come and see him at his office.

Unfortunately, when I got there he was nowhere near as enthusiastic about me as Mr Enfield had been. I wasn't what he had in mind at all. Beth Rogan, a Rank starlet who was pretty and perfectly groomed, took the part in the end. As a type she could not have been more different from me. She was dark with short hair, and pertly pretty. Perhaps the producer had already mentally cast her. He looked me up and down as I stood before him on the carpet in his smart office, and politely but firmly told me I would not do for his film.

I left crushed and, perhaps hoping to change the decision, I went to see Mr Enfield at the address on his card and gave him the bad news. He already knew, but managed to make me feel that he was genuinely disappointed by the producer's decision.

'I really would like to have used you,' he said, very kindly not telling me that the producer's assessment of me was that I looked like a horse. I learned that years later when Cy had become a good friend and I had become too famous for the judgement to hurt. Cy never lost his enthusiasm for the way I looked. He used to say that Terence Stamp and I were the two most beautiful people in London. 'But you should try modelling,' he persisted in his office that day. 'You really have got something. Why don't you go to Lucie Clayton's and take a modelling course?'

Heaven knows what he saw in me that appealed to him then. I suppose it must have been the same thing that David Bailey spotted. I was waifish, coltish and cack-handed – I still

49

am, even though I don't break many things. I have always been a bit of a mess. Yet somehow there are people who seem to warm to this messiness. Being a bit of a mess is, I suppose, more endearing than being perfect. I always think of it as the Margaret Rutherford syndrome. She was endearing, and people loved her because she was quaint and funny but mostly because she was human.

In those early days, at a time when model girls and young actresses were bandbox perfect, I had little flair for fashion. I had started to use make-up rather late (found, of course, in the make-up department at C & A) and hadn't quite got the hang of it. I wore too much. Lipstick did not suit me. I have always looked peculiar with red lips, even when I was modelling. The only cosmetic I really needed, and now need more than ever, is my eye make-up. I feel undressed without it. In those days I haunted C & A in rainy lunch hours, rooting through the inexpensive, tackily fashionable merchandise. I bought this terrible pale blue raincoat with a rabbit collar which I wore with very shiny black patent leather shoes, and I thought I was the cat's whiskers.

But though I couldn't really understand why Cy Enfield thought I should model, it would have been spitting into the wind to ignore the number of occasions – right back to when I was two years old – when people had said the same thing. His suggestion about Lucie Clayton stuck in my mind. I told my mother what had happened, and we both recognized his name as being a known one. Cy Enfield was a far cry from Colonel Voynovitch. He was legitimate. He was a talented man who had spotted a girl with potential and tried to do something about it. There was no funny business involved, and because of this I decided his advice was worth taking. I borrowed £30 from my mother and enrolled for the Lucie Clayton modelling course. It was the last time that anyone, dubious or otherwise, approached me in that way. I suppose that once I began working, because of Bailey, I hit the legitimate vein very quickly.

Like the Langham Secretarial College, Lucie Clayton was prepared to take you on as long as you could pay, and I had my mother's £30 to do that. I cannot remember learning much there; all I remember we charm school pupils doing is walking around with books on our heads and learning how to cover our faces in pancake make-up. However, it does give the confidence and poise that young girls need and it all felt important and glamorous. The charm course took only a month and those of us who were any good went on the books of the model agency attached to the school. I was one of these chosen to go on the books and I was thrilled. It was better than Polytours any day. Passing-out pictures were taken to make up a portfolio and we had to have a 'composite' – a sheet of different pictures to prove how different we could look. My composite pictures were taken by a photographer called Larry Neal who later reported that I was 'the most gawky, awkward thing he had ever met'. Armed with the passing-out pictures and our composites we chosen, fledgeling models then made the round of London's hundreds of photographers, hoping for a booking.

Three of us graduated from Lucie Clayton's at once and could truly call ourselves models. One was Fiona Laidlaw Thompson, a really beautiful girl, better than any of us, more soignée, more elegant. She was neat and always did things right, and yet for some reason she gave up modelling quite soon. There was also the stunningly beautiful blonde Celia Hammond, always my nearest rival, who today has devoted her life to saving cats. In those days she was a wonderfully sexy girl and such fun that everyone loved her. Her only problem was that she was a bit overweight. That did not matter when the marvellous photographer Norman Parkinson – 'Parks' – found her and made her his model.

Celia and I were sort of friends, but I was always a little apprehensive when she was about. She was so sexy and terribly attractive, and I never saw myself that way. Once I had become involved with David Bailey, every time he was going to photograph her I felt uneasy in case he found her more attractive than he did me. At the beginning of my career I was not very special and had no gift for making clothes look good. It was Bailey who was to teach me how to do that. Today's models are more concerned with money. We were not. We never earned very much.

At first photographers booked me because I tried to be conscientious. In those days models were expected to arrive on time with their hair properly done and pancake make-up in place. We took our own accessories. I was laden down with bags full of shoes, make-up, hairpieces and gloves all jumbled up with my lunchtime sandwiches. I was always in a muddle. Unlike today, there were no hairdressers and make-up artists on the sessions; it was many years later before they were hired as a matter of course for most photographic sessions. Sometimes in those early days *Vogue* did bring in a hairdresser, but make-up was the model girl's own problem. It was the era of false eyelashes. We bought them in long strips, cut off a length and stuck the strip above our own lashes. If you were not careful there was a nasty, gummy line of white glue showing on the eyelid, which was torture to get off. Left lying about the dressing table, the lashes could be quite alarming – they looked like enormous spiders. Some models had eyelashes stuck on one by one at beauty salons with something that acted like super-glue. They would stay on for about a fortnight and it was probably well worth having done, but I could never be bothered.

When I was not working for *Vogue* I had to do my own hair. Unfortunately I was never very good at it. I used to rush round London with my hair in rollers under a scarf, or try my best with the ratty hairpieces that were fashionable at the time. Not surprisingly, I wasn't doing too well until Bailey created the Jean Shrimpton look, which needs hardly any hairdressing or make-up. After that I wasn't called upon to do much to my hair except comb it. (Sometimes not even that.) I put it up or would pull it into a tarty ponytail as an alternative, but it was never what you would call a style. Once I became known I did much better. I didn't have to change my looks all the time. Previously I had had to be versatile and make myself look different, and that was a problem for me.

Becoming famous created difficulties of another kind altogether. I dislike having attention paid to me and I can't bear being looked at. I'm much more comfortable placed cosily in the background. When I used to complain about being stared at people would ask: 'But how can you be a model if you don't like being looked at?'

A good question, but in the studio you work with the same people most of the time: they know you. It becomes a one-to-one encounter between model and photographer, and I'm always easier in a one-to-one situation. I hated being photographed in the street, but the studio was never a problem. I could work there without that awful feeling of embarrassment. On locations I was always sure that people were looking at me because I looked funny. That probably came about because I didn't much like what I saw when I looked in the mirror. People don't believe me when I say that either. But it is true. Few of us really admire our own looks.

One way or another I was hardly cut out to be a model, but I persisted and Simon continued to drive me up to London most mornings. My working day was spent calling at photographic studios from a list supplied by Lucie Clayton. It was, quite simply, presenting yourself and touting for work. Most of the model girls disliked parading themselves, hoping for a job. I certainly was not keen on that part of it and could not bring myself to do it today, but I never minded wandering around all the quaint, sometimes not too salubrious areas where the photographers had their studios. I enjoyed exploring the back streets, the alleys and those unexpected little corners where old-fashioned craftsmen had their premises. It was then that I started a love affair (that still persists) with an alternative London.

At first I used to get work posing for mail-order catalogues – every young model's standby – and some catalogue jobs were better than others. One of them was shot in Tangier and I went with four other girls. It was my first overseas job. We were put up at the El Minzah Hotel, which had once been the home of American millionaires; it had a wonderful swimming pool and there were peacocks on the terraces. It was the first time I had ever heard the curious screeching of a peacock. The hotel was cool, with marvellous Moorish-tiled courtyards. 'This is the life,' I thought – particularly when I was the only one of the five of us who managed to avoid diarrhoea.

Another standby was modelling knitting patterns, a not particularly exciting job but one which keeps a lot of young models solvent even today. The booking was usually for an hour during which, in order to keep costs down, I had to scramble in and out of as many itchy knitted jumpers as possible. These sessions were usually shot in a small studio belonging to Peter Clarke – a photographer who did a great deal of commercial work as well as these commissions for the more homely women's magazines.

The most important of the photographers Lucie Clayton sent us to was John French. He was the doyen of the small group of photographers for whom every modelling agency wanted their girls to work. If French booked you, you were on your way. I was fortunate enough to work for him quite early on and, since Bailey began as one of his assistants, he had a lot to do with both Bailey's career and mine.

French, along with others like Cecil Beaton, Angus McBean and Parkinson, was among the last of the grand photographers. When these men were at their height the working-class fashion photographer was unheard of – the species did not exist. Even the models were grand, well-bred, well-brought-up young ladies, like Fiona Campbell Walter, who mostly married very well and then gave it all up. Fiona became the Baroness Thyssen. *Vogue*, *Harper's* and *Vanity Fair* would have been most unlikely to hire a girl without a cut-glass accent and that positive stamp of breeding that the nanny-trained always have. But it was mostly due to the elegant John French that the East End boys battered their way into what was a rarefied profession. All the crop of Cockney lads of the day – David Bailey, Terence Donovan, Brian Duffy – who aspired to be photographers wanted to work with him and learn from him. Many of the top photographers in London in the early sixties learned their trade from John French. Yet none of them copied him. They all went on to produce their own more virile style of work.

French adored women and made them look marvellous. No one could touch him when it came to lighting. The intricately placed spotlights and the big old plate cameras in his studio in unfashionable Clerkenwell could wipe years off a woman's face. Lines, bags, sags just vanished. His photography was rather mannered and very much of the period and older ladies clamoured to be photographed by him.

The young would-be photographers who worked as his assistants all loved him. He in turn loved them. He had a great affection for all the pretty yet tough East End boys who worked at his studio, even though they embodied everything that he was not.

French was a one-off. We girls always had to affect a coy string of pearls around the neck and place obligatory little stud earrings in our ears. He would not take a photograph until these, and the white gloves he liked in his pictures, were in place. He was terribly correct with the models. We were all treated like Victorian young ladies (a habit that Bailey, Donovan and their ilk did not adopt). French himself wore thin ties and grey slacks with a lambswool cardigan over a striped shirt. He was married to Vere, a deep-voiced woman who was one of the first to cut her hair into spikey bits pulled around the face. She had her own career in advertising, and she was very modern for the period. She is still with us – aged over eighty and living in Brighton. Sadly John died in 1966. He was only fifty-nine.

Being photographed by him was an experience. Languid, effete and ever correct, he would pose the model – he called us all 'darling' – while standing behind his big plate camera. He never touched the girls to arrange them as the younger photographers were inclined to do – and certainly as the Colonel had been inclined to do. Then the thin, long-fingered hand would lift, palm facing out. 'S-t-i-l-l', he would say in his high-pitched voice, turning the word into a long sigh. Then someone else, one of his assistants, would press the button on the camera.

I remember being in Victoria Park in London's Hackney with him on one occasion when we were shooting a feature for *Vanity Fair*. We were working by the side of the lake in the middle of the park when some boys messing about in boats got in the way of the shot. Like a fussy old woman, John was waving with excited gestures to get them to move.

'It's all right! Keep your 'air on, John,' one of them shouted. John, who was not familiar with the East End habit of calling everyone John, was terribly flattered and thought they knew who he was. His fussiness turned to expansiveness. 'Stay a little longer, boys. Please don't hurry,' he called back, and waited, quite content, until they were out of the way.

The first of my modelling jobs I remember really clearly was the one where I first saw Bailey. He had already spotted me when I was working for Duffy in the *Vogue* studio. This time I was working at Studio Five – one of the studio complexes which houses probably as many as half-a-dozen photographers' studios – again for Duffy. We were shooting an advertisement for Kellogg's cornflakes. I was surprised he had booked me again, since previously he had grumbled that I was stiff and awkward. But this time Kellogg's wanted an ordinary girl who looked as if she might come from the country, and Duffy had chosen me because I was the epitome of ordinariness. I looked like every other young girl of my age; my hair was shoulder-length and flipped-up at the ends; I hadn't yet quite mastered the eye make-up which was to become a sort of trademark; and I was stiff and uneasy before the camera. Word had got around that I had the most amazingly blue eyes, but other than that all I did with any degree of success was to embody ordinariness – which is, of course, a hugely marketable quality.

I was terrified as I stood there in a blue dress chosen by Duffy to bring out the colour of my eyes. Later I would come to enjoy my work, but at the beginning I was always

56

petrified when I was modelling and the session wasn't going well.

'Relax!' Duffy kept saying. 'Come on, relax.'

The more I tried to relax, the stiffer I became.

In desperation he said: 'Recite "Humpty Dumpty" for me. See if that helps.'

Feeling an absolute fool, I stood there saying: 'Humpty Dumpty sat on a wall, Humpty Dumpty had a great fall. All the King's horses and all the King's men, couldn't put Humpty together again.'

The slave driver behind the camera shouted: 'Say it again.'

'Humpty Dumpty . . .'

'And again.'

I was on about the fifth recital when Bailey popped his head around the curtain. He had come to check if my eyes were as blue as they were supposed to be. I was far too nervous to take much notice, and too busy reciting 'Humpty Dumpty', but I did register that the owner of this little head with long, black hair (pre-Beatles), black, suspicious eyes and a wary expression was very attractive. He never said a word, just stared at me and grimaced. It was such a stern little face that I thought: 'Ooh, he doesn't think much of me.' And then the face vanished.

Not surprisingly, Duffy did not book me again in a hurry – not until Bailey had loosened me up, let me look like myself and turned me into the slightly more exotic waif that became famous.

But that didn't happen immediately. Bailey was still with John French. He had stayed for the security while he tried to get started on his own. And then he got his first break while he was still working for French. He was booked by *Vogue* to shoot Shop Hound – a feature at the front of the magazine which gave information about merchandise available in different cities round Britain. It was not a particularly exciting assignment, but it was one that *Vogue* offered to unknown young photographers to try them out. The job was important to Bailey and he booked me as his model – not, I suspect, for my modelling ability, but because he rather fancied me and my long legs.

That was the first job we did together. I liked him the instant I arrived in his cluttered studio. I was much taller than him – all our relationship was high heels for him and low heels for me – but he was different and appealing and I found him very attractive.

'I'm Bailey,' he said when I arrived.

'Just Bailey?' I asked.

'Just Bailey.' And that was all I ever called him.

He was wearing high-heeled boots and he had a funny little self-important walk that was very endearing. We were dreadfully nervous. The job was important for both of us and it went well. After that he started to get more of his own work, and he kept on booking me. French was very generous about letting his lads fly the coop. Bailey, ambitious and darkly intense, was intent on making a career as a photographer. Every job was vital, and he had to prove himself every time. He had little confidence then; that came later.

We were instantly attracted to each other. Whenever we worked together this attraction created a strong sexual atmosphere. I didn't want the sittings to end, and I felt he didn't either. There was a pull between us, an awareness. But he was married and I lived in the country. There was, I felt, no reason to move too fast. I knew he wanted to make love to me, but I was uneasy about it. I kept reminding myself that he was married and I was still with Simon, and therefore neither of us was really available.

Because I had been running around with all these public school boys, my accent moved all over the place in those days and Bailey thought I was 'posh'. He was wrong. I wasn't. We were both working class. It was just that we came from different settings, and as I had been privately educated I had already begun moving up the scale. He had played truant, left school as early as possible and had briefly been a tallyman – a sort of debt collector. His education was minimal – but he was, of course, much more streetwise than I. At that point he was slightly out of his depth with the whole *Vogue* setup, but

58

he was serious about his career and believed he would make it one day. I never expected to make it. I had no reason to think that I was going to be so successful.

Bailey was twenty-three, five years older than me. He had married very young – when he was twenty – but there were no children. At first I had guilt feelings about his wife, but as time went on I selfishly lost them. I made a conscious decision that it was not my fault that his marriage had broken up. I never saw her, nor ever met her. But I was shocked by my own behaviour. Virginity still just about counted for something in 1960. I had been 'deflowered', so to speak, by Simon de la Tour and it was now becoming quite clear to me that I had not even been in love with him. I did not want my next sexual encounter to be with a married man. Bailey was pressurizing me and I remember crying my eyes out in the *Vogue* dressing room. He had been trying to kiss me, and I was full of apprehension because I knew I would eventually give in and that I was going to ditch Simon. I felt trapped. It was inevitable that Bailey and I would become lovers. I sensed he was going to be important in my life and that we wanted to be with each other. But there was his wife: she would be hurt.

I have always worried about decisions before I make them – not after. But that does not stop the guilt feelings. Today I have come to terms with the harsh truth that it is not possible to go through life without causing pain to someone. Bailey and I were going to cause pain.

On the first evening he took me out we had been working on Wimbledon Common on a spread for the magazine *Man About Town*. When the job was done, we got into the car and he kissed me. I liked it, but I wouldn't let him make love to me. With both of us living at home, we had nowhere to go where we could be alone except the car. I was not averse to this as, frustrating as it was for us both, there we would stay, cosily alone, steaming up the windows – but only going so far. Bailey was very patient and sweet and I held out for about a month while he took me out every evening and we got to know each other.

He had to go home to his wife most nights, so we never went anywhere in particular. 'Wanna come down the East End?' he would say casually. Or, 'Feel like something to eat?'

Unlike the public school boys, he never asked me out in advance. It was always a spontaneous invitation, usually after we had finished work. We generally went to the East End, where he felt at home – I didn't need to be wined and dined. I have never needed romantic gestures. Which was just as well: Bailey could not go into a restaurant in the West End at that time; he did not have the faintest idea of how to order a meal. He was not at all macho, so it would not have offended him if I had ordered for him. He wasn't defined by his sex. The problem was simply one of insecurity for both of us – I would not have known what to order either! Avoiding the high life, we used to go to Chang's in East Ham High Street and eat chicken chow mein all the time.

I was a naïve girl from the country and he was the streetwise Cockney. I was perfectly content with this. I was fascinated by Bailey's background, which was so different from my own. I used to love going down the East End. Brick Lane, a long, narrow street of noisome buildings which was truly rough and really quite dangerous in those days, fascinated me.

'Let's drive down Brick Lane,' I would say.

'OK,' he'd agree. 'But lock the car doors.'

Bailey did not entirely understand this interest in a street bordering Jack the Ripper and Kray brothers' territory, where razor gangs hung out. It was always night when we drove there and all that was to be seen were shadowy, mysterious figures hovering by dimly lit, crumbling buildings. It seemed to me to be a street of danger and excitement.

I loved Bailey's territory. I loved the energy and the warmth of the people. They had resilience and a quick sense of humour, unlike country people who are slower and say very little. East Enders in those days were different. It was unlike any other part of London.

Occasionally when we had been down East we would sleep at Bailey's parents' house. I had met them early on when Bailey had taken me home to their semi-detached Edwardian house in East Ham. It was a typical dwelling of London's respectable poor: solid, plain brick, the polished but unused living room in front with the kitchen and scullery at the rear. The kitchen was the heart of the house where the family congregated. Behind was the handkerchief-sized yard. Bailey's dad, Bert, grew sunflowers out there, great splashes of marvellously exotic yellow and black against the grey of East Ham.

The first time Bailey took me there I was not unwelcome, but it was uncomfortable. He was married, after all, and he really should have gone home to his wife. His mother, Gladys, always known as Glad, was smallish and fierce with jet-black hair and very dark eyes. Bailey's father was a tailor, a great big man with a great big scar that ran around his chin like a runnel.

It was Glad who kept the family together. She was the tough one. For all his size and dark, dangerous looks Bert was pretty ineffectual. Glad wasn't easy, but I liked her in spite of her difficult manner and I came to see that Bailey was an even-handed mixture of the two.

Bert quite liked me. Glad obviously had her reservations. Nevertheless she did not mind me sleeping in Bailey's bed while he slept on the floor in the living room. The first time I stayed, being a well-brought-up girl, I started to make the bed in the morning. I could only find one sheet. Not being very imaginative I couldn't work this out at all, so I went downstairs to where Glad was in the back kitchen getting breakfast.

'I'm awfully sorry, Glad,' I said. 'I've tried to make the bed but I can only find one sheet.'

Glad turned from the stove, her face red and indignant. 'We're not all posh like you and have two sheets on our bed!' she snapped.

I could have died.

While all of this was going on, officially I was still with Simon, but as Bailey was taking me out every night I was obviously not seeing a lot of him. I never knew if Simon was upset when the affair finally finished. There was no discussion

– we just drifted apart. He had probably found someone else too. It ended in the way that many young romances end – with no more than a bored whimper.

I just fell in love with Bailey. It was not difficult. Bailey was naturally lovable. Everyone loved him – women, children and men. He was not in the least gay, but it never worried or offended him when homosexual men made it clear that they fancied him; he did not find their interest at all threatening. Bailey was in touch with his own feminine side. He genuinely understood fashion and had a feeling for clothes and trends. He was naturally artistic. We went to art movies – films like *Last Year in Marienbad* and *Jules et Jim*. He loved Jacques Tati movies – he had that same quirky sense of humour. Unexpectedly, he had a strong cultural curiosity which indirectly influenced his work. His enthusiasms rubbed off very strongly on me. Between us we were discovering a whole culture and awareness. I found this exciting. Bailey was never commonplace. Basically there were few people whose opinion mattered to him. He had a great laugh and this extraordinary, unforgettable giggle. People heard his laugh and wanted to laugh with him. His entire personality was infectious and became more so as his success grew. My life with Bailey, once I had decided to throw my lot in with him, was the greatest fun.

As far as I was concerned he was endearing and adorable in the little grey bum-freezer jacket and black polo-necked sweaters he wore all the time. Just after our affair began I remember him picking me up from John French's studio. In drab Clerkenwell he was wearing his grey suit and his boots with Cuban heels (again, long before the Beatles); he was carrying a bunch of flowers for me and had Phantom, his sleek Afghan hound, at his side. It was the way he held the bouquet that touched me. Straight out in front, very Anthony Newley. He was into Newley and Judy Garland and Dietrich and jazz. He might have been a Cockney lad but he had style with his old Morgan car and his hound. I can still see this little figure coming across the street with the Afghan and holding the flowers, totally unembarrassed, even though it was not a time when men were seen carrying flowers.

He never minded a joke against himself. It was a shock when I first saw his legs. For a small man he has awfully large legs, like a ballet dancer's, with big calves. When I first saw them I giggled. Later, while we were working in Egypt, he wore a pair of ancient shorts. What with the shorts, the legs and his little self-important walk he looked so funny that I could not stop laughing. But he did not take offence.

As both of us had homes to go to, our early courtship was difficult. A couple of times I booked a lonely little room at the Strand Palace Hotel. We never went into the hotel together – we were not brave enough. In those days hotels didn't like unmarried couples sharing rooms, and I always had visions of the awful humiliation of being caught out. Most nights, since I now had my own car – an old Morris Traveller with lots of wood on the bodywork – I would drive myself thirty miles home to Mother.

It had been on one of these occasions that I had finally succumbed. He had followed me from town in his car and we made love for the first time on Littleworth Common up the road from my home. It was late, in the dark, on the grass and quite awful. I was miserable, protesting all the time that I did not want to do it, and complaining that he was pressuring me. It was not much fun for either of us. Happily, our love life improved considerably after that. Bailey was cheerfully randy – lusty, one could say – and basically I had no hang-ups about sex, perhaps thanks to Mrs de la Tour. Yet that night I went home distraught, thinking how I had already had one affair and now I had started another – and that with a married man. I felt dreadful. I felt guilty. But our lives seemed to be inexorably entwined. I was becoming his model and part of his life.

I had been modelling for about a year when I realized I was becoming famous. People were recognizing me in the street – though not as often as one might expect, as I looked so different in real life. I started to get requests for interviews from the media, as indeed did Bailey.

Everything was conspiring to push us together. Our friends were other photographers and models. With only a minimum of rivalry the photographers used to go round to each other's studios, watching each other work and giving each other ideas. There was always something happening after the day's work was done. None of the photographers went home to their wives. One, who had better be nameless, kept his wife safely tucked away at home by making sure she was constantly pregnant. It was said he used to push a pin gently through her Dutch cap.

Men's and women's lives were very polarized at that time, especially among the working classes. A lot of male show-off, aren't-we-tough talk went on while the girls were expected to sit in front of the mirror primping and being the accessory when required. It was starting to irritate me. One of Bailey's Cockney assistants had a nice young girlfriend called Janet. We were having a drink one night in a pub near the studio when I noticed that Janet was missing.

'Isn't Janet about tonight?' I asked in all innocence.

'She's waiting for me in the car,' Bailey's assistant told me.

I didn't understand. 'You mean she doesn't want a drink?'

He looked at me as if I were stupid. 'I don't know. She's waiting for me in the car,' he repeated.

It dawned. I gave him a dirty look and, without asking for his yea or nay, went out and brought her in to join us.

The East End might have been matriarchal, with the men earning the money and giving it to their women, but their women had to know their place. Bailey and I were unusual in that, once we had joined forces, we were together all the time. He rarely went anywhere without me, and when we were out it was usually just the two of us. But his background precluded him from being aware of or coming to terms with my emotional needs. His own emotions were occupied, focussed on his career. Bailey's work was his biggest preoccupation. Our strength was that for a long time I was part of that work. In that aspect of our lives we could not have had more in common.

Our little group consisted of Bailey, Brian Duffy and Eric Swain, another photographer who was Patti Boyd's first boyfriend before she left him for Beatle George Harrison. Sometimes Terence Donovan, who was a bit older, would come around with us. The group we went around with was dictated by who was on the loose when work finished about seven or seven-thirty. Sometimes later; never earlier: those boys were always working.

We did go nightclubbing, but since I felt stupid on a dancefloor nightclubbing bored me. I was no good at any of the current dances, and attempting to gyrate about in time with the rhythm held no pleasure for me. People had once complained that I was awkward as a model. They should have seen me dancing! This was the time when nightclubs were turning into discos – dark caverns full of flashing lights where the noise was horrendous. The waltz and the foxtrot were no longer seen. As far as I was concerned, the disco was a subtle form of torture even in the grandest of places, like Hélène Cordet's Saddle Room, though I did actually manage to learn to twist there along with the rest of swinging London. The attractively toothy Hélène, once a girlfriend of Prince Philip's, made it her task to instruct everyone in this new dance. We also used to go to the Ad Lib, another noisy haunt of those who believed themselves to be the jet set. I am not a person who is comfortable in many situations, and there were times when I must have been something of a killjoy. As I did not care for dancing, and since it was quite impossible to hold a conversation in that noise, I took my knitting to the Ad Lib. I took my knitting to a lot of places. It used to drive Bailey mad.

Not that I was much better at knitting than dancing, but it was something to do in situations where I was not 100 per cent comfortable. Because my skills were so limited, I chose very big needles and very thick wool and knitted a skirt that was made in panels. When I finally wore it it kept stretching. It got longer and longer until I had to throw it away.

Our taste in entertainment was catholic. As well as the Ad Lib, drag acts, which were just becoming acceptable, were a favourite. Bailey had camp connections and most of the alternative comedians were friends of his. We used to venture to Hackney in the seedier part of northeast London to see the comedian Ray Martine performing in a large and smoky pub. His act was very dirty. I only understood half of what he was saying, but this did not matter since I liked the atmosphere. Scruffy, alive with Dickensian faces, Hackney and its inhabitants were a far cry from minor public school boys and Conservative balls.

We spent a lot of time on what was considered the wrong side of the tracks. When we went East we had to give the local kids money or they would scratch the car. If you paid up generously they made sure no one else did either.

We were all young and successful. We worked hard, we earned good money and we had every reason to enjoy ourselves. Bailey and Co. were always gee-ing people up. Even at work the model girls were gee-ed up rotten. One of Donovan's games was to tickle the girls around the legs with a feather duster. It was all a touch suggestive, but while the photographers giggled with their assistants, a lot of hard work went on. They knew how to have fun while they were working. The model girls had to keep on their toes. The sexist teasing and touching up that went on were enough to give a feminist the vapours, and no doubt a feminist would make a big thing about how disgusting it all was. But none of us saw life like that then. The gee-ing up was neither serious nor ill intentioned. It was nothing personal, and model girls soon learned how to dodge the passes and spot the tricks. If they wanted to, that was. The lads were just having fun, though sometimes it was not much fun being on the end of it. Generally speaking, the girls could look after themselves and the photographers' misdemeanours were all in a day's work.

On one occasion, rather courageously by the standards of the day, *Vogue* used me with nude models. I was to pose – dressed – in front of these girls, and I was feeling rather uncomfortable about it. They were all going to be standing behind me, naked. I was sure they would be bitchy, thinking that I was going to be standoffish and stuck up. Not at all. They were sweet. They were so cheerful and cosy as they walked down to the studio from the dressing room with absolutely nothing on under their coats. As they waited for the shot to be lined up they were all twittering away, discussing one particular photographer.

'Oh, you have to watch him,' one said darkly. 'He's always trying to get round the back.'

Admittedly at times these East End lensmen who had found fame so quickly were a bit tiresome, but I never got on my high horse, not even when for an entire session Donovan had me posing with a milk bottle clutched between my knees.

But life would have been duller without all the shenanigans. We were silly and young and a pain in the neck. We did stupid things. One night about one in the morning a great crowd of us, in three different cars, went in convoy to London Airport and drove the wrong way around all the roundabouts. Duffy, Bailey and Tom Wolsey, who started *Man About Town* magazine, were the drivers. Fortunately there was hardly any traffic about and so there were no disasters.

Another of these spontaneous nights, however, did have a disastrous ending. It was Friday night, very late, and I didn't fancy staying at the Strand Palace on my own again. Sometimes carrying on an illicit affair was not much fun. We were with Bailey's mate Charlie, a friend from his East End past.

'We'll drive you home,' Bailey said.

I was doubtful – and it was a long way back to town from Burnham. 'I suppose you could sleep in the hayloft,' I suggested, after some thought.

'Great!' said Bailey, always ready to enjoy a new experience.

It was after midnight when we arrived at the farm where I showed these two archetypal town boys to the hayloft, left them there and went indoors to creep into bed. Everyone in the house was asleep and had no idea that I had come home with company.

In the morning I went down early looking for Mum. She was already in the kitchen, setting the table for breakfast. By then my mother knew that I was going around with Bailey and I said to her cautiously: 'Mum, Bailey's here.'

'Oh,' she said, putting down the knives and forks. 'Where?'

'In the hayloft.' Suddenly I was decidedly nervous. 'I don't know whether I should tell Dad or not. Bailey's with his friend. They're both over there.'

Mum appeared unperturbed by the news. It took a lot to perturb my mother, but I have no doubt that she was very worried about what Dad's reaction would be.

'They can't have had a very good night,' she said. 'Not sleeping up there. I'll cook them some breakfast. They'll be hungry.'

Relieved that one hurdle was over, I thought I had better find Bailey and Charlie. I looked from the kitchen window across to the barn, but the only person in sight was the pig man carting a bucket of swill. What I had forgotten to mention was that we kept our pigs in the barn under the hayloft. The pigs had been sound asleep the night before and had not made any noise when the boys bedded down. But it was a different story when the man went in with their food. The dreadful noise that pigs make when confronted with their swill is like something out of a horror movie for those who have never heard it before. Bailey and Charlie, so rudely awakened, and never having heard one pig, let alone a herd, were frightened to death by all the terrible snorting.

Standing at the kitchen window I saw them emerge from the hayloft, running for safety. At first I could not think why they were running – but whatever was causing the panic, safety eluded them. Their escape route led them into a field where Dad grazed his horses. Horses can look very big to town people who are not used to them. Already helpless with laughter I saw how Bailey, propelled by fear, moved the fastest and got himself over the fence to safety. Charlie, handicapped by his Cuban heels, set off more cautiously before realizing that a particularly large horse was walking towards him. The horse was only being friendly, but Charlie did not know that. He started to run. The horse ran too, as horses do in such circumstances. Charlie was terrorized, convinced this enormous animal was chasing him. Bailey, safely out of danger, was standing at the far side of the fence shrieking: 'Run, Charlie, run.' Charlie ran, but the horse put on speed as well. Charlie won by a nose. Shattered, he reached the fence and vaulted it to join Bailey on the other side.

The boys were beginning to congratulate each other on their narrow escape when, having composed my features suitably, I went to get them. It was still hard not to laugh. They were so completely out of place in the country, alarmed by it, and looking like scarecrows with bits of straw from the loft sticking in their trendy clothes. Yet, though it took a while, Bailey came to love being at the farm.

That Saturday morning I gathered them both up, shaken but unharmed, took them into the house and introduced them to my mother. She was warm and welcoming, as she always was to my friends. I sat at the table in our tiny kitchen, making conversation. I was too worried about what Dad's reaction would be to eat anything myself.

Mum was just about to serve them bacon and eggs when Dad came in. When he saw the two boys sitting there, he stared at them with deep suspicion. I started to make introductions, but the name Bailey brought about an explosion. Dad had a habit of exploding.

'Get out!' he shouted. 'Get out! All of you!'

There was a frozen moment, followed by a great noisy scramble as we all leaped to our feet. I did not bother to argue. I knew my father well enough to know that it would be a waste of time. We all fled the kitchen, me leading the way, leaving the uneaten breakfasts and my mother to cope with my father's wrath.

We stood outside looking at each other.

'I'm sorry, Bailey,' I said. 'That was awful.'

'Big chap, your dad, isn't he?' he said, inconsequentially, and Charlie started to laugh, probably as much out of embarrassment as anything else.

They were both pretty shaken by the morning's various adventures, but being young they found a funny side to it as we drove back to London. I went back home that evening, a touch nervous, but not as nervous as I ought to have been.

I found Mum in a terrible state. She had had a very bad day indeed with my father, who was waiting to give me his verdict on my behaviour. Sitting in the lounge in his leather chair, in which no one else ever sat, he went straight to the point.

'You're not going to live here if you're going out with a married man,' he said. 'Either you never see him again, or you don't come back here.'

'I'm not going to stop seeing him,' I said defiantly. 'Whether you like it or not. I'm eighteen. I can do what I like.'

'Very well,' said my father coldly. 'Then you'd better go.'

I went, full of bravado, and only realized as I drove back down Western Avenue that I had nowhere to go to. Finally I turned up on the doorstep of Eric Swain's flat in Hampstead, and he and his wife generously took me in.

That weekend Bailey and I did some serious talking.

'I think we ought to live together,' he said.

There was nothing that would please me more, but I said: 'What about Rosemary?'

Rosemary was his wife.

He grimaced. 'I'll have to tell her.'

'Won't she have already guessed?'

'Probably,' he said. 'But it's not the same as knowing for sure.'

I do not know when or how he told her. We maintained a sort of delicacy in matters relating to his wife. I never asked many questions and he didn't tell me much, and the unspoken arrangement seemed to work reasonably well. I felt my usual guilt. Yet it seemed to me that if the marriage had been good I would not have been able to break it up, so I did not consider that I *had* broken it up. He and his wife hardly saw each other. I believe she was a rather stylish girl but they had married young in the East End – probably too young. They had no children.

70

The break-up must have been hard for her and I am sure she was angry, but I knew little about it. It was Bailey's decision, and he said he wanted to be with me.

I went back to the farm as soon as I thought I could see my mother without my father being there. I wanted to see that she was all right and to talk things over with her. I also needed to pick up some clothes. I had been in no hurry to tell her when I started to sleep with Bailey, and I was not ready to tell her that we were now going to live together.

'This is really all for the best, Mum,' I said. 'I need to live in London and have my own flat. I couldn't keep up with all that travelling every day.'

She agreed that living in London made sense.

She had already known for a long time that we were lovers, and the fact that Bailey was a married man made it even harder for her to accept. She was devastated when she found out he had a wife. I did not want to hurt her any more, so for years I kept up the pretence that I was living on my own. I remember she once visited the flat Bailey and I were sharing and there were great panics to hide all signs of dual occupancy. Of course, she was not fooled. But she said nothing.

I am afraid I have given my mother a bad time over the years. At the time of the Bailey blow-up I said to her: 'Look, I'm eighteen now and for the next twelve years or so, until I'm thirty, I have to lead my own life. I will always come and see you. We'll always be friends. But I'm going to do things that I won't be able to help – things you'll find difficult to accept.'

The truth was that, by then, I had already done a lot of things that Mum was finding difficult to accept, but I was never foolish enough to try to live my life someone else's way. I was tough, as the young are. It was hard for her, but in the end my mother forgave me – and my sister, Chrissie, who went her own wayward way – everything. She was not one to cry over us. She must have shed the odd tear, but she did not use her tears – she was not given to emotional blackmail. Somehow she never made me feel guilty – and I suppose that is why I have always been so close to her. But it was still fortunate that at this difficult time when I was banished

71

from Rose Hill Farm she had the new baby to keep her busy, while I did what I wanted to do.

My father did not speak to me for a year. I had to go to see my mother in the week and at times when I knew he would be out. She was deeply hurt by this rift in the family at a time when she had her own problems. She had my little brother to consider, and at her age she found a small baby tiring. My sister, fascinated by the rock world, was beginning to become as recalcitrant as I. Not long after the drama with Bailey, Mum found Mick Jagger sleeping in Chrissie's bed one morning when she went in with the tea. Chrissie was not with him – she was sleeping in my unused room. Fortunately, the Rolling Stones were not yet famous, but even so Dad was not happy – though, unlike Bailey, Mick Jagger was at least single then.

Leaving home really did not trouble me all that much. I had realized much earlier that I could not lead my parents' life. I was not like them and did not want the same things. I sensed that what they wanted for me was a nice husband and a family, while what I wanted for myself was something quite different. To some extent they had lost me by educating me. I did not want to hurt them, but I did. I had gone too far into a different world ever to live at home again.

For the time being, while Bailey and I started looking for a flat, we both moved into Eric's place. The pair of us shared a tiny spare room and a tiny single bed. At least we *attempted* to share the bed, but poor Bailey always landed up in a sleeping bag on the floor. We were young enough for it not to matter, and Eric and his wife were good friends to us in that time when we had nowhere to go.

The flat was far too small for four people but we stayed there for a month. Sometimes Bailey was sad. I think he felt guilty about Rosemary, but it was far too late for us even to attempt to halt the rollercoaster we were on. We loved each other.

Bailey heard of a flat going and we took it without even bothering to look at it, so urgently did we need a place to go. It was in Primrose Hill, and when the wind was in the

72

right direction at night we could hear the lions roar and the seals bark at London Zoo. The flat was a scruffy, unfurnished basement. There was a bedroom, a living room, hanging space in the hallway, a crummy kitchen with a table and chair, and a bathroom. We went off to a warehouse in Camden Town and bought a bed, a G-plan Harris tweed sofa and a few more bits and pieces. We chose them together, carefully deferring to each other's taste. When we got it all home, the flat was still very sparsely furnished.

We moved in along with Phantom, the Afghan hound, the only possession Bailey took from his previous home. Unfortunately Phantom was a problem. He was a mad kind of dog, as most Afghans are. They do not make good pets. It was my job to walk the dog and I always did my darnedest to get Bailey to come with me. With good reason Bailey would try to avoid it. Phantom was taken to Primrose Hill every morning before we went to work – and it was the worst possible start to the day. Once off the lead he ran for freedom, and Primrose Hill was alive to the sound of a demented model and a furious photographer screaming for Phantom to come home. At night, we went through the same pantomime. We could be chasing this wretched dog for two or three hours, and I could see all too clearly why Bailey's wife did not mind parting with him.

Poor old Phantom! He did not want to be with us and we should not have had him with us. He never wanted to go back to the flat. When we came home after leaving him all day, as we had to at times, he would just lift one miserable eyelid and go back to sleep. The poor dog was so sad that we eventually gave him to Tania Mallett, a model friend who lived in the country. There he settled down much more happily.

When Phantom had to go, Bailey bought me a little Yorkshire terrier. Yorkshire terriers are not really my style. I don't care for pretty little lap dogs; I prefer a good sturdy dog with some body to it. But I called the Yorkshire Bertie and, in spite of his deficiencies, became very fond of him. Then the butcher's bitch across the road had an unexpected and unwanted litter which the butcher tried to convince me were Yorkshire terriers. I knew jolly well they were not – I was not brought up on a farm for nothing. But rather than see the puppies homeless I had one and he turned out to be the sweetest, most wonderful mongrel. I christened him (would you believe!) Mongie.

My first big chance came when Bailey wanted to use me for one of *Vogue*'s important features, The Young Idea. It was something *Vogue* would not have dreamed of running five years before, but it was 1961 and the swinging sixties and the youth cult were nudging their way in. London was actually starting to become a fashion influence, showing the rest of the world that girls did not have to dress like their mothers; it was the OK thing to look young. *Vogue* decided that it should start a young section in the magazine, using less sophisticated clothes and younger models, photographed in a more modern style. Photographers were beginning to use the Rolleiflex camera and 35mm film to get movement and life into their pictures. Sometimes, on location work, the camera was even hand-held. The days of the big, unwieldy plate camera were running out.

The Young Idea that Bailey had been given to photograph involved famous young men. The intention was to use the same model in different outfits for a series of pictures with men who had made some impact of their own towards the new sixties' style, humour and thinking. *Vogue* was using David Frost, Peter Cook, Dudley Moore, Terry Donovan, Stirling Moss and Vidal Sassoon in the pictures.

Bailey wanted the plum job of the model girl in these pictures to go to me. There was one snag. Lady Rendlesham, *Vogue*'s fashion editor, was masterminding the series and she did not want me as the model. She wanted to use a French girl who worked a lot for *Elle*. As the photographer, Bailey had some say in the matter, but when it came to the crunch Clare Rendlesham had every right to overrule him. She was a brilliant fashion editor, very chic and, in our young eyes, quite elderly and for some people rather frightening. Bailey and I were not frightened of her. Because we were a duo we gave each other support. She might have scared me if I had had to deal with her on my own. But Bailey, who with his Cockney

74

background could not have been more different from Lady Rendlesham, most certainly was not alarmed by her. But he was never alarmed by anyone or anything.

He had to fight like mad to get me the job, and I admired him enormously for the courageous stand he took. As a new young photographer he was being given a great opportunity, and he could have spoilt things for himself by insisting on using me. Whereas most people would have bowed to Lady Rendlesham's decision, Bailey did not. He stuck to his guns. Looking back, I can see that Clare Rendlesham had good reason for not wanting to use me. It was still early days and I had not yet acquired that indefinable something that makes a top model – in truth, I was a bit of a mess.

Eventually Clare gave in. She agreed Bailey could use me. But she got her own back: she made me have my hair cut.

I was sent to Vidal Sassoon and off came my hair. I hated the results. It wasn't the Vidal asymmetrical or club-cut hairstyle that he later became known for – it was merely neatly and tidily cut short. To me it was the feminine equivalent of a short back and sides. Maybe Clare was right to do it, but I was not happy. I just kept telling myself it would grow.

The job seemed to occupy Bailey's and my life for months. It took ages to set up. Getting the celebrities booked was not easy, and once they had agreed the sessions were short because, to a man, they were always pressed for time. And that put Bailey and me under pressure. I do not remember anything about the men I was photographed with except that Dudley Moore was so much smaller than me, but Peter Cooke balanced it out. At the time, as far as I was concerned, it was a job, an important job, and I was intent on delivering the goods and doing it well for Bailey's sake. I wanted to prove Lady Rendlesham wrong.

The finished feature was well received and did both Bailey and me a great deal of good. The result was that, when it was decided that *Vogue* would make a trip to New York for The Young Idea, Bailey landed the job. He wanted us to discover New York together, and this time there was not so much argument about him using me. We were thrilled to bits, even if a resigned Lady Rendlesham was none too happy. The assignment was for English *Vogue*, and New York had merely been chosen as a backcloth for British clothing manufacturers, like Jaeger and Susan Small. Fashion was not so international in those days: it was possible to guess someone's nationality by the way they dressed, and it seemed rather innovative to photograph British clothing in the United States.

We did little in the way of preparation for the trip. My mother always remembers that when we went off all I took with me was a plastic bag holdings a few odds and ends.

'What about a suitcase?' she asked. 'What about your clothes?'

'Oh, it won't matter,' I said blithely. 'I don't need many clothes. *Vogue* will have the clothes for the job.'

The truth was I had very few clothes. Modelling them for a living had put me off wearing them for fun. I also dressed to please Bailey, and he liked me in the most peculiar leather gear. I had this terrible black leather coat, a black leather pinafore dress and some hideous black boots that I had had specially made. They laced up the front and were enormous. My feet are large anyway, and the boots made me look as if I had club feet. Dressed in this bizarre costume, I climbed on the plane with just my plastic carrier bag for luggage. Bailey was equally visual with his black eyes and black pudding basin haircut, encased in his black leather jacket, black polo-neck sweater and high-heeled boots. We had adopted this style long before the Beatles came on the scene and we did not look like anyone else. It was hardly surprising that the New York customs officers went through what little luggage we had with a toothcomb, convinced we must be carrying drugs.

We were amazed at their thoroughness. They found some worm pills for the dogs that I had forgotten to take out of my handbag. I always kept them in my handbag so that I knew where to find them. A customs man carefully broke each one of them open. They even dug around in my face creams and tore my Tampax apart before, baffled and clearly disappointed, they handed me back my plastic bag and

76

my handbag. There was nothing for them to find. We were very young and not into drugs, though we knew what they were. Anyone who worked as hard as Bailey did had quite enough adrenalin flowing without needing hard drugs. Bailey could get high just from holding a camera.

We were enthralled by New York. We stayed at the St Regis Hotel, but we were up top in the maids' quarters while Lady Rendlesham had a very grand suite down below. We were taken to the American *Vogue* offices and the editor, Diana Vreeland, the high priestess of fashion, instantly took to us because we were odd, fresh and different. 'But they are adorable!' she declaimed dramatically, embarrassing us both to death. 'England has arrived.' In a milieu where everyone was so smart we were unconventionally scruffy. She instantly said we must do some work for her – which, I thought, was one in the eye for Lady Rendlesham.

On that first New York trip Bailey and I had such fun but we drove Lady Rendlesham mad. We would never do anything that she considered interesting.

'They just go and eat hamburgers at the same place every night,' she complained. It was true. We had fallen in love with the Primeburger and ate day and night in this hamburger joint. But Lady R. was not quite right about the hamburger. Bailey was on a diet of egg and chips. And we thought we did a great many things. We went round the jazz clubs, we saw Ella Fitzgerald at one of the big hotels, we looked at museums, photographic books and buildings and we did what we had come to do. We photographed The Young Idea. Some of those pictures were taken in Harlem. There is in existence a wonderful photograph of a small black boy on some broken-down street, standing all cheek and brass, putting his tongue out at us. Even then Harlem was not particularly safe, but we were young and confident and we did not think of danger. It was February and Bailey photographed me in a Jaeger camel spring outfit with an apple-green blouse and suit standing on the dizzy heights of Brooklyn Bridge. The wind had to be coming from Alaska. I thought I would freeze. I was crying with the cold.

Most of the top model girls will not do location work in the winter, and who can blame them? Bailey preferred location work, so I went along with it. There was one occasion in January when we were working in Paris for the *Sunday Times* with their fashion editor, Bridget Keenan. It was a feature on evening dresses, and Bailey wanted to photograph them in the grounds of the Palace of Versailles. Bridget borrowed all these beautiful dresses – one, in pleated chiffon, still sticks in my mind. We took them out to Versailles and it was freezing cold, damp and wet. I had to change in the car – there was nowhere else – and the cold was bitter. I stood for three hours in nothing but a series of ballgowns, and again I was in tears with the cold. My teeth started to chatter, my skin was blue and my nose went red. Thank God Bailey wasn't shooting colour! That session had an unfortunate ending. It was impossible to keep these wonderful dresses out of the mud and the damp, so they went back to the couturier in a bad condition and poor Bridget was in trouble.

Bailey's big thrill was when we met Salvador Dali in the lift on that first New York trip. The artist was also staying at the St Regis, and made enquiries to find out who we were – he was intrigued by us because we looked so different. As a matter of fact, we were pretty intrigued by him. He looked even odder than we did. He was wearing a hat that looked like a bald head with a little doll perched on the top that spun around as he moved. Dali was a hero of Bailey's, and Bailey got to photograph him.

The trip was wonderful. We came home still in our terrible leather gear, happy and triumphant. We both knew we had it made.

— 4 —

Back in Britain, Bailey and I never stopped working – mostly as a duo. Though I was becoming well known I was not making a great deal of money, nor did I particularly want to. *Vogue* paid me approximately £10 a day, which seemed fair enough to me. I did some advertising, which was better paid, but we were selective. Bailey was masterminding my career and it was successful because he kept me exclusive. When I was offered work that he thought was unsuitable, he would say: 'Don't do it. That job isn't good enough.' I could afford to turn down work that I did not find attractive because I had the security of knowing I could work for him. One year I turned down more money than I made.

It was 1960 and with Bailey behind the camera I had learned my job. He showed me how to move, how to react and how to respond to the lens. I was no better-looking than many of the other models around, but Bailey brought out something in me that was different and exceptional.

Very quickly I was the top model and Bailey was the top photographer. We made a formidable team. It was wonderful for me: being high up in my profession gave me the opportunity of doing the better work. I was given the best clothes to wear and the most interesting assignments. Fame was only a small problem socially at this time. I did not mind being recognized, but I was not that enamoured by it. If I was in a nightclub I would never dance, because I felt people were watching me.

We were successful because we worked hard and we did a good job. Much of the competition at that time was slightly older than me. In the States the wonderfully glamorous Suzy Parker was in her thirties, already had one child and was to have another. In Britain there was elegant Tania Mallett, who made a James Bond film before retiring. Sandra Paul of the pussy-cat smile, now the wife of government minister Michael Howard, was still very much at the top, but she was groomed, classy and nothing like me. The girls who were about my age were also different types. Paulene Stone was a big name, but she and I were not remotely alike. Paulene was wonderfully, heathily good-looking. She was a girl who glowed. Sue Lloyd, who went on to fame in *Crossroads*, was also on the scene. Tall, again classy and elegant, she was always in work despite having to cope with diabetes. Today she is a talented painter working and living in Hollywood. None of us were close friends; we really only met at work if we were booked for the same session. We did not mix socially a great deal.

Most of my work with Bailey was for *Vogue*. The magazine was like a big family, so I was quite happy to work for it even for a low rate. Money was not a motivating force in our lives – we had enough, and so we did not need to think about it. I never really made any money until I was with Terence Stamp.

Bailey and I lived in this scruffy basement surrounded by animals and birds. Bailey, not surprisingly, was the bird fancier. The whole sitting room was full of bloody birds – about twenty-four tiny little things, mostly finches and lovebirds. Every Saturday he would go down the pet shop in Camden Town and come back with yet another box with yet another bird in it. The noise! And the smell! The place did not get cleaned very often. We had Mongie and Bertie as well, and we made a token gesture of putting rush matting down on the floor and giving it an occasional shake. We were a squalid lot.

All these pets and birds were a great pleasure for us, but not so much fun for the poor lady who lived in the flat above. Bertie and Mongie made indiscriminate use of the yard, and she was always throwing buckets of water out of the window to remind us it was time to clean up. She must have had a miserable time. I either walked the dogs morning and night, or we had to take them to work with us. *Vogue* was astonishingly tolerant of these animals – it was fortunate they were house-trained. I was back in my old routine of having pets, which always adds to my contentment. The only problem was that Bailey and I worked so hard that the dogs did not get as much attention as they should have.

We were hardly ever at home and we ate at restaurants nearly all the time. The only thing I could cook was a Vesta beef curry out of a packet, so it was eat out or starve. Bailey was almost a vegetarian. He would eat chicken but he survived mostly on egg and chips. We never were into the grand lifestyle.

We sat around the flat a lot at weekends, and Duffy usually came round and entertained Bailey while I made some attempt to clean up. It never occurred to us to get a cleaner, so Saturday mornings always found *Vogue's* top model scrubbing the floors and doing the washing.

I sometimes thought Duffy resented me. I got in the way. Also, Bailey and I were more successful as a couple both professionally and personally. Duffy didn't have the equivalent of me: he was older and married, with lots of children.

They used to go off together, and I am sure that while I was getting the ironing done they were pulling birds. The pair of them used to swagger off together in Bailey's car, heading back home to the East End on Saturdays. I was never able to prove that they were up to mischief, and I did not apply my mind to it overmuch because I knew Bailey cared about me. In a curious way I did not really mind what he did – I was glad of the chance to be on my own and do a bit of housework. But I still had this strong feeling that they were picking up girls, and if I had known for sure I would have been terribly jealous.

It is possible he was doing just that, but only if an opportunity presented itself: it was a case of boys being boys. I sensed that whatever happened, Bailey would be back. I was still very innocent, and I think he liked that. I can see now that Bailey made me as he wanted me to be. That was why in the end I had to go.

I have changed so much since those days, but I do not think Bailey has. Long after we had split up he told me a story about two women on a plane, both of whom were trying to pick him up. One was an old harridan, and the other a good-looking young girl. He decided, as he put it, 'to go for the old bag' because he thought he would have a better time with her. She looked a bit leathery, but she also looked as if she would know her way around a bed. He was right. She almost nipped a lump out of his vital equipment and frightened him to death. But he had made his choice – youth or experience. Bailey never took life seriously. He had a rare, jaunty exuberance and the ability to be light-hearted. Most of all, he snatched an opportunity whenever one arose.

It was obvious to everyone, even to my family, that Bailey and I were serious; and so after a year my father relented – no doubt under constant pressure from Mum! Bailey was allowed home, and my dad took to him. But then it was impossible not to like Bailey. It became very cosy. Bailey took photographs around the farm, in particular of the white doves we had. And he quite fancied my mum, which I thought was charming. She was a pretty woman, younger then than I am now, so he was not averse to giving her the odd cuddle. They had a sweet relationship: Peg, he called her. He met her again two years after my father died; cheeky as ever, he gave her a nudge and said: 'Got a lover, then, Peg?'

My mother went quite pink.

Sometimes our relationship was stormy. As he became more famous and under greater pressure he was sometimes nervous and he took out all his anxieties on me. People were always saying that he treated me badly, and occasionally he did, but only when we were working. Then he could be aggressive and totally impossible. I understood the insecurity that caused the aggression, and most of the time I could take it. A couple of times I did land up in tears if I was feeling a bit rough myself or if it was the wrong time of the month.

I remember one day he was really dreadful and it was all caused by the bags under my eyes. We always had a problem with what are known as 'my bags'. They have always been huge. Even when I was young I could look like an exhausted panda. When I was modelling my bags had to be blotted out by careful lighting. I was fine with the right light but with the wrong light I was no good at all – which, of course, made me rather difficult to photograph. If Bailey was feeling a bit fed up and he wanted to be awkward, I knew that if he drew the ceiling blind away from the skylight in the roof I was in dead trouble. Daylight would flood down from above, emphasizing my bags.

On this particular day he was crotchety, and to make matters worse I was looking dreadful. He pulled the blind back and down flooded the light. Then he started photographing.

I thought he had finished the roll. Then he said, glowering at me, 'This time we'll put some film in the camera.'

He was destroying my confidence, but I said nothing. All I did was to keep my head as high as possible for the next reel, trying to minimize the highlighted shadows under my eyes. He clicked through the reel and reloaded the camera.

'This time we'll put your head in,' he said nastily.

It was his not-so-subtle method of telling me that, because I looked so rough, he had cropped my head out of the pictures. It was a terrible and demoralizing thing to say to a model.

'Then why don't you blank out the top light?' I said, near to tears. He just snarled something at me, and then I did go off to the loo in floods of tears.

Unity Barnes, the fashion editor we were working with, was furious with Bailey.

While people were right when they said he was hard on me, it was not as simple as that. I understood how much pressure his job put on him. Any photographer is only as good as his last photograph, and the results of every session must appear fresh and innovative. When we were working well, both the session and the outcome could be exhilarating, but this did not happen every time. On a bad day he could make me miserable, but he would apologize later and say how truly sorry he was.

Those bags were an enormous nuisance all the time I was modelling. Fashion editors and photographers were constantly saying to me: 'You must get to bed earlier.' But it was nothing to do with lack of sleep or anything else. God had given me bags under my eyes, in the same way as he had forgotten to give me a bosom and shoulders. No one who worked with me would accept this simple fact. I was under great pressure to have them removed by cosmetic surgery, but that is something I have never believed in. Bailey did not really mind. Except when they were causing him photography problems, he quite liked my bags – he did not want me to be perfect. I might have been his model, but I am certain that he saw me first as his girlfriend and he cared about me for more than my looks.

We enjoyed each other's company and enjoyed shared discoveries. We had such a good time on the Lady Rendlesham New York trip that the following winter we decided to go back and see if we could get work there on our own. We went for a month. Bailey wanted to visit other American photographers. As usual he was trying to learn more about his job. I had found myself a top model agent in New York, Eileen Ford, who had been urging me to come over. My London agent, Lucie Clayton, was happy for me to go, since to qualify as a top model it was necessary to have worked for American *Harper's Bazaar* or *Vogue* and to have modelled the Paris collections for one of them.

Our first move on arrival was to go and see Diana Vreeland again. This amazingly chic lady, jangling with jewellery, with the carved features of an Indian squaw, welcomed us with open arms. She was much more powerful than Lady Rendlesham, and quite outrageous. In the middle of America's Depression she was advising her readers to wash their babies' hair in flat champagne, and it was she who first suggested using an old mink coat to line a raincoat. No one knew more about fashion than Diana Vreeland, and she could make or break anyone in the fashion world in the States.

She made us. She gave us both work. And to be able to say we were working for *Vogue* gave us a great advantage.

We stayed in an apartment loaned to us by Nicky Haslam, a dear friend who in those days was living in New York and interpreting the newly swinging London for New Yorkers. Nicky, one of life's characters, is an old Etonian who had his first leather suit about the same time as Bailey in 1959 and who dyed his hair blond and wore make-up. He seemed very way out in the early sixties, but I suppose he was merely ahead of his time. We were both extremely fond of him. He was, and still is, a most talented man, an ex-art director and columnist who today makes a living as an interior decorator.

When Bailey first knew him he had this wonderful little camp house in Lambeth down in south London. Set in the middle of a small, plain terrace, it was a cushioned and comfortable palace inside. The dining room had an elegant tented ceiling, dimly lit and very exotic. Entering through the door led to a completely different world. And apart from all that, what attracted me most was that Nicky kept marmosets as pets, which I thought quite delightful.

I was not quite so sure about this New York apartment, which he had rented from ballet dancers. It was on Astor Place, near the Bowery, an area of New York that really shocked me. Astor Place, apparently once smart, was going downhill. Vagrants clustered along the block and there was one poor old tramp who had set up home in our doorway. The squalor and the poverty of the Bowery, with meths drinkers collapsed under any shelter they could find and straining boot polish through rags, made Bailey's East End stamping ground look like paradise. It seemed wrong to be living in this spacious, stylish apartment while there were so many homeless outside.

Nicky took us around to a lot of gay places and parties at a time when very few queens had come out of the closet. New York seemed more open about homosexuality than London. We landed up at a party one night and I was startled to find that I was the only woman guest. All the guys were encased in leather, chains and hobnailed boots. Another time we went to a place called the Glass Door, which was a homosexual club. There were women, presumably lesbians, there as well. I was still pretty naïve and found it hilariously funny to see six-foot men carefully made up and dancing together.

The only snag was that, once the novelty had worn off, it was all rather boring.

'Bailey,' I said. 'I'd rather go home.'

He was finding it a bit much as well. 'Right,' he said, and we finished up having our usual egg and chips.

Bailey and I were very close at that time, probably at our closest ever. We were popular in New York; everyone wanted us to come to their party, and I was forced to go out and buy an evening dress. Nicky pointed me in the direction of a designer boutique in Greenwich Village where I found a black, very fine jersey dress made by Rudi Gernreich – the man who later invented the topless bathing suit. Cut in the empire line, the dress had short, tight sleeves and a deeply plunging neckline. Unfortunately I had no bosoms to spill over as the designer intended. Bailey and I got giggly, because I went out and bought this special bra to push me up to make me look as if I had some. It was always a terrible strain for me to appear to have bosoms.

Because I bought so few clothes, and only ones I really liked, I loved my one and only party dress – I have it to this day. I used to tuck a red rose in the cleavage for modesty. Bailey, Nicky and I would walk along Broadway feeling on top of the world – Nicky in formal clothes, Bailey in something black velvet he had borrowed from Nicky, and me – the pretty thing, as Nicky called me – in the middle. Evenings consisted of endless partying at some apartment with stunning views of the New York skyscrapers. These were the homes of elegant, successful and extremely rich New Yorkers who were either in the fashion world or the media. They were not celebrity seekers. We were invited because we were Nicky's friends and because we were part of their world. I remember once seeing Kirk Douglas at one of these parties, and with his Hollywood tan and his film star clothes he looked rather out of place.

I was not a bit like the American model girls of the period. I was not wholesome-looking – more pre-hippy – and I still had that gawkiness. The photographers who hired me always tried to make me look more like the norm, which always puzzled me. Why were they hiring me if they didn't want me to look like me? They invariably started a photographic session by trying to curl my fringe. It seemed to worry them if it was left straight.

I worked for one of the greatest on that trip – Irving Penn. He looked like a businessman: he was balding, wore white, short-sleeved shirts and was married to Lisa Fossangrieves, who had been a top model in the fifties. Penn was not, however, as old as he looked. He was a serious man who ran a disciplined studio. Bailey revered him; the quality of his work was astonishingly pure. Some photographers use their personality to get results; with Penn it was dedicated hard work. Sometimes working for him was a little like being back at school.

I always enjoyed being photographed by him, even if he did persistently complain that I had a green neck.

'Your neck looks greeny grey. Go put some more pancake on,' he would say, peering at me through the lens. 'I don't want to see a green neck.'

This would make me sigh. I hated putting on pancake. Bailey never made me use it.

'It's the colour of my skin,' I told him. 'I've always had what looks like a dirty neck. My mum used to scrub it with Vim and that didn't do any good either.'

'Nevertheless, go put on some more pancake,' he would say firmly, adding, 'and put some on your hands while you're at it.'

He repeatedly sent me off to put on more and more pancake. Of course I did what I was told. American *Vogue* expected much more grooming from their models than was required in Europe.

I worked with Penn a lot over the years. It was always a treat, particularly when he chose me to do the French collections with him. Once when we were working in Paris he riveted me by saying in a conversational tone: 'You know why the French bread smells so good?' and without waiting for an answer explained his theory. 'It's because the French carry it home under their armpits.'

He would chat away when we were working, making little jokes. I remember him asking me about my childhood. I told him about the farm, and I laughed and said: 'Oh, yes, I carried a lot of egg buckets in my youth.'

We had been talking previously about Marisa Berenson, a top model who later became an actress. She was known in the model world for being rather grand.

'Unlike Marisa Berenson,' he said drily. 'All she carried was a powder puff!'

Penn is a great photographer and a sweet man. I asked him to sign one of his photographs for me. He did. He drew a little heart with 'I.P.' in it. I thought that charming from this master of his profession for the little model that I then was.

I had been a little anxious when *Vogue* booked me for Penn the first time – I did not want to hurt Bailey's feelings. But though I almost always worked for Bailey, he never minded me working for the really great photographers. He was as ambitious for me as he was for himself, and there was no rivalry in our relationship. Bailey would push for me, as he had with Lady Rendlesham. He was delighted that I got the job in Paris working for American *Vogue* and that I had been photographed by Penn. On his own territory, back in Britain, he was anxious for me to be photographed by the

Dad, me, Mum and
Chrissie in 1945

Mum, Chrissie,
Granny and me on
holiday in Cliftonville
in 1947

At St Bernard's Convent in 1955

Below: With friends at Winston's nightclub in 1959

Fiona Laidlaw Thompson, Celia Hammond and myself on the day we left Lucie Clayton's Modelling School in 1960 *(Mail Newspapers plc)*

Below: An early assignment modelling knitting patterns for *Woman's Own* *(Woman's Own)*

In the studio with Bailey *(Terry O'Neill)*

Photographed by John French for *Woman's Own* in 1962
(Woman's Own)

With Peter Cook for Bailey's *Vogue* 'Young Idea'
photograph in 1961 *(David Bailey)*

In New York for *Vogue*'s 'Young Idea' series *(David Bailey)*

Photographed by Cecil Beaton for *Vogue* in 1964

(Courtesy Vogue. *Copyright © 1964 by The Condé Nast*
Publications Ltd)

Vogue cover girl 1963–70

(top left: Photograph David Bailey. Courtesy Vogue © 1963 by Les Editions Condé Nast SA; top right: Photograph William Klein. Courtesy Vogue. Copyright © 1963 by The Condé Nast Publications Inc; bottom left: Photograph Gianni Penati. Courtesy Vogue. Copyright © 1969 by The Condé Nast Publications Inc; bottom right: Photograph David Bailey. Courtesy Vogue. Copyright © 1970 by The Condé Nast Publications Ltd)

late Cecil Beaton. To be photographed by Beaton was the ultimate accolade for a model.

'If you're going to be a great model,' Bailey would instruct me, 'you must work with all the great photographers of the day.'

Bailey himself had photographed Beaton and Nureyev together – two of his idols in one go. Beaton had taken to Bailey, and on the strength of this Bailey asked him to photograph me. Surprisingly, Beaton agreed.

It was all set up in the *Vogue* studios, but the session did not go well. I wasn't feeling good – it was the wrong time of the month – and Beaton didn't like me. He had no time for me, which I do understand. He was used to photographing grand ladies, preferably with titles and patrician features. I was not titled, I had a turned-up nose and I was not much good at conversation. I had nothing to offer Cecil Beaton, just as he had nothing to offer me. He would never have thought of using me if he had not been interested in Bailey. He photographed me in a Scottish kilt, sporran and all, and in a huge white Pompadour wig. I wasn't comfortable in either, but I do appreciate now that the wig picture is rather special. At the time the sense that he disliked me suspended my critical faculties. And to my astonishment, three years later, I read that he had said of me: 'She's the unicorn, the rare, almost mythical thing.'

Bailey and I were starting to jet-set around the world, all expenses paid – sometimes first-class if the magazine had done a deal with the airline. More often than not, however, the fashion editor got the first-class ticket and we were in the back with the rest of the hoi polloi. American *Glamour* magazine sent Bailey and me to Japan, where I had the uncomfortable experience of finding myself head and shoulders above everyone else. Also the country was far too formal for my temperament and so crowded, though I think I would appreciate it more today. But the water gardens where we did much of the photography were exotic and peaceful, and I liked them. I also acquired a taste for Sumo wrestling. We were taken to see a match and

I was fascinated by the structure of the bouts, and the wonderfully chic, tall ripples of the traditional hairstyles that somehow survive all the activity. Those enormous men have extraordinary dignity and composure.

Very early on *Glamour* magazine also sent us to Miami to photograph swimsuits. The fashion editor working with us, like Lady Rendlesham before her, complained that we sat in our hotel room all day, eating club sandwiches and cheesecake with strawberries. This seemed perfectly reasonable to us, as on our one foray to the beach we had found the sea full of jellyfish.

Most of our work was for *Vogue*, and on that second trip to New York they flew us down to Mexico. Only two things spoiled Mexico for me – the Mexicans were so cruel to their animals, and I got a terrible sun blister on my lip. Like an idiot I put Vick on it, which didn't improve matters. For two days Bailey could not shoot any covers or full-face pictures of me.

When we went on *Vogue* trips Bailey always had to photograph a couple of local celebrities to go with an interview, with the idea of giving some weight and reading matter to the feature. In Mexico, Dolores del Rio was one of the chosen. I never went to the session, but when Bailey came back he said she seemed artificial. He was disappointed.

The second celebrity, Luis Barrigan, was much more interesting. A distinguished Mexican architect, he lived in a strange and wonderful house right in the middle of a poor quarter of Mexico City. He was tall, balding and elegant and spoke only a little English. This did not matter since Bailey had an extraordinary ability to communicate with anyone, regardless of language. The spacious house was enclosed behind high walls and there was a small, beautiful garden where the architect put out food for the wild birds. He had a strange, round, wooden table like a column which revolved, with magazines scattered round it. I remember the incongruity of the covers on the magazines – Sue Lyon, Marilyn Monroe, all pouting blondes looking out of place in this oasis of good taste.

Barrigan was an extremely attractive man and, though well into his sixties, amazingly seductive. He was a man of class and originality. I mention him because he was unlike any other I had known, and it was from that meeting with him that I began to understand that age does not kill attraction.

On that same trip we also worked with the Italian film-maker Fellini and his star, Marcello Mastroianni. Again the session, in a New York studio, was set up by American *Vogue*. Bailey was excited and nervous and so was I. We were fans: we had seen *La Dolce Vita* over and over again.

The session was not exactly a disaster, but nor was it a huge success. We had the feeling that Fellini and Mastroianni had no great desire to be photographed for *Vogue*. We had little advantage with them since, unlike most other people, they did not find us particularly interesting or unusual. Fellini's films were all so exotic that our own personal sixties' style paled into insignificance.

Bailey wanted me to stand between the two men, one on each arm, and then the three of us were to run towards the camera. Quite simply, they didn't want to do it. They did not speak English, and Bailey was so nervous that his powers of communication vanished and that gave them an unfair advantage.

Eventually they agreed to run, but it was all dreadfully embarrassing. I had to keep leading them back into shot on the studio floor, making them run time and time again while Bailey tried to get the picture he wanted. It would have been a lot easier if we had been on location and not cramped by the studio, but as it was these two highly sophisticated and elegant Italians thought all the running backwards and forwards downright silly, which on reflection it probably was. The pictures, unfortunately, showed that it had not gone all that well.

Bailey and I travelled all the time, sometimes under our own steam. If we had no work in England we went looking for it abroad. On one occasion we went to Paris with Duffy and had not realized that it was the week of the Paris Motor Show. We couldn't get into a hotel anywhere in the eighth *arrondissement* and finished up in a real fleabag of a place in the Algerian quarter near Belleville. It couldn't have been less like our usual watering holes. Not that we were bothered. Where we stayed never concerned us overmuch. I found the *quartier* fascinating. I was hanging out of the window, trying to work out how the prostitutes got their beehive hairdos all of two feet high, when I saw a crowd of angry Algerian men swarming down the street, overturning cars on their way. When they reached Duffy's car – a little Mini – they began jumping up and down on it.

'Hey, Duffy, they're wrecking your car!' I called out.

Duffy came running and hung out of the other window. He and Bailey looked down, shouting 'Oi! Oi!' from the safety of three floors up. As much as Bailey and Duffy liked a dust-up, the odds weren't on.

It was at the time of the Algerian troubles, and we were wise enough to stay discreetly in the hotel until the police arrived and, with cold and probably painful efficiency, dealt with those of the rioters who were unwise enough not to disappear. Only then did we go down to inspect the damage. Happily there was not much.

Back in Britain we had become such a well-known twosome that not unnaturally Bailey's wife had decided she wanted a divorce. She telephoned him at *Vogue* and told him her decision.

When we met up that evening he said baldly: 'Rosemary wants a divorce.'

My first reaction was relief. Our situation was not ideal.

'Do you mind?' I asked cautiously.

He shrugged. 'No, of course not. But it'll get in the newspapers.'

'Oh, hell!' I said, suddenly thinking of my family and how they would feel. 'Will she bring me into it?'

'I'd be surprised if she didn't.'

He was right. Why should she keep me out of it? She had nothing to thank me for. These were the days when evidence had to be supplied for a divorce: there had to be a guilty party and there had to be a co-respondent. The guilty party was obviously going to be Bailey, and the co-respondent me.

'There's one good thing about it,' he said cheerfully. 'We'll be able to get married.'

'Yes, we will, won't we,' I said – but the quick, sharp look he gave me indicated that perhaps I had not responded with quite the enthusiasm he expected.

In those days I was good at putting things to the back of my mind and forgetting them. That was what I did with the thought of Bailey's divorce until it dawned on us that the seedy-looking man wearing the obligatory raincoat who had been hanging around outside the house for weeks was a private detective. His role in all this was to find evidence that we were living together – which was hardly difficult. More difficult was the fact that he had to serve the divorce papers on Bailey. They had to be thrust into Bailey's hands; at that time the post was not legally acceptable for such documents.

We were rarely in. We came home late and we were gone again early in the morning, so the poor man had to hang about all day and most of the night clutching his brown manilla envelope. When he did sight us Bailey used to dodge him – more out of mischief than anything else. We gave him the run-around and Bailey called him rude names. We could see no reason why we should make it easy for him. Inevitably we were caught. Bailey was left holding the divorce papers and I was named as the other woman. Which, of course, I was and had been for the past two years.

The divorce came to court on 6 December 1963. It was just about the time when I had become *really* famous. I was now known as the Shrimp – a name I hated. Shrimps are horrible pink things that get their heads pulled off. News of the divorce was all over the front page of the *Daily Mail*, and it was mentioned in most of the other papers. To be truthful, it didn't bother us very much, though obviously I would have preferred not to have been named. I could hardly deny that Bailey and I were living together, and I thought then that I would be with him for ever. I felt I loved him very much and I was happy with him. But my mother was terribly upset and she thought we should get married right away – something that was in Bailey's mind as well. Mother thought the whole thing was dreadful and she cried over it. She found it deeply embarrassing to have her daughter on the front pages in such a situation.

I am afraid she cried more when, shortly afterwards, I decided that I was not going to marry Bailey after all.

I was beginning to get a little bored with the modelling. It was all right, but nowhere near as exciting for me as it was for Bailey. He had the creative role. I was beginning to find my work very repetitious; the novelty had worn off. I was sick of seeing photographs of myself and bored with constantly having to dress and undress. Sitting in front of a mirror putting on make-up can become very tedious. I was twenty-one, and Bailey and I had been together getting on for three years. We were still working constantly. Often there was more work than we could accept, and we had to turn jobs down.

A lot of my discontent came from the fact that there was no challenge. I was sheltered under the wings of *Vogue* and Bailey. I never did the boring rounds of the advertising agents, magazines and photographers in the way most other models had to. Bailey and *Vogue* looked after me and provided all my work: I was their discovery and they protected me. I felt as if I was suspended, trapped in a time warp. I never had to make a decision. I was beginning to realize that I could not go on doing what I was doing indefinitely. I needed to pay attention to other aspects of life. Yet even when these stirrings of discontent surfaced it was a long time before I did anything about them.

Bailey and I were beginning to take separate jobs because we were in danger of becoming stale, and it so happened that we were both working in Paris, but not together. I had accepted an assignment for *Harper's Bazaar* at a location in a Paris house. The session was to be photographed by a Frenchman, Jean Loup Sieff. I had never worked for him before.

Bailey was quite happy for me to be photographed by Sieff; he knew his work and admired it. I went off to do the job as I went off to do any job. I had no reason to think that this particular sitting would prove to be different – and disturbing.

Jean Loup Sieff was waiting in his studio with another model, Tilly Tizziana. He was a lean man, with straight, blondish hair and a tanned skin. He had a habit of twirling his hair in his fingers; otherwise he was sophisticated in both looks and manner. All in all he was very different from Bailey. He drove Tilly and me, along with the fashion editor, to the location just outside of Paris. Tilly and I were in the back and we had only been driving for a short while when I noticed he was watching me in the driving mirror. This made me feel slightly uncomfortable. He continued to watch me throughout the day. Slightly surprised, I realized he was flirting with me, and I was equally surprised to find myself responding. I was attracted by him, while being perfectly aware that this gentle titillation was probably his normal behaviour.

It worried me that I had responded. It made me aware with a sort of shock that Bailey was not the only man in the world who could attract me. I had perceived that I could fancy someone else. This had not happened since we had been together. Of all the men I had encountered since I had been modelling not one had made me look twice; I had been indifferent to everyone except Bailey.

I set off back for London and, sitting on my own as the plane droned over the Channel, I pondered these disturbing new thoughts. I took time to think about my life with Bailey. It seemed to me we worked so continuously that we never seemed to talk to each other – not about anything important. If I had said that modelling was beginning to pall, his reaction would have been that I was at the top – so what was wrong with that? Working had become our life. I knew he was ambitious; he didn't realize that I wasn't. I needed a new ambition. I had worked for everyone whom I wanted to work for in England. We spent a lot of time talking about work, but we never talked about our relationship. He had no idea how I felt about anything

– but there was no reason why he should: the confidante role was not the one I played in his life. And he was too absorbed with his work for meaningful talk.

Time went on. The memory of Jean Loup Sieff faded. We lived as we had always lived, and yet I knew I was beginning to back away from the idea of marriage and I knew I did not want children. I began to feel that there must be more to life. I was, quite simply, getting bored.

It was in January 1964 that Terence Stamp came into my life, though our paths had already crossed briefly when Bailey photographed us together for *Vogue*. At the time it was just another job. The picture shows Stamp standing behind me looking at me while I, in profile, stare straight ahead. That picture reappeared on the cover of Terry's autobiography many, many years later. The more significant meeting was at Antony Norris's wedding to Paulene Stone. Tony was a rather fashionable photographer and Paulene a stunning young model who later married the actor Laurence Harvey when that first marriage went wrong. Not surprisingly, most of the guests were models and photographers. It was a rather grand do held at St James's, Piccadilly, with a reception afterwards at an expensive Soho restaurant.

Terry was on his own. Apart from Bailey and me he was the most famous person there, and he looked self-conscious, uncomfortable and slightly standoffish. He was wearing a huge cossack fur hat, whereas Bailey was his usual scruffy self. He and Bailey got on rather well – if Terry needed photographs, Bailey always took them.

I was aware of him because he was so good-looking. I had seen him in his first film, *Billy Budd*, and thought then how amazingly handsome he was. His hair had been dyed blond for the film but was now back to its normal dark shade. He was in his early twenties – three years older than me. Apart from his good looks, Terry had made no impression on me at all as a person, but at the wedding Bailey started to chat with him in the way Bailey always did with people. Because Terry was alone he had taken him under his wing. Bailey and I had planned to go on to see my parents that afternoon, and before

I knew it I was being informed that Terry was coming with us to Rose Hill Farm.

The news that we were taking him home to Mother surprised me. At the time Bailey was driving a Morgan, a small racing car. There was only one passenger seat. The invitation meant I had to sit on Terry's lap all the way to Burnham. I do not normally like touching people and dislike being touched myself. I do not like intimacy being forced upon me, and I found it horribly uncomfortable to be perched on this strange man's lap, sitting as stiffly as I possibly could, for a journey that took over an hour. And yet as Bailey navigated us through west London there was also the thought that I was locked in this intimacy with probably the two most attractive men in London.

After that, Terry seemed to become part of our crowd. We were of the age when new friends are casually added to a circle, and he and Bailey became good friends. Terry was astonishingly beautiful. That first time he came to the farm, even my father – who did not particularly notice people's looks – was taken aback when he came into our living room. Stamp is tall, and the huge cossack fur hat did a lot for his extraordinary pale blue eyes. He didn't look like anyone else, and at that time it was hard to imagine that any girl would be indifferent to him. He was the only person (apart from Jean Loup Sieff) who had made any impression on me since I met Bailey.

But I still was not taking a great deal of notice of him. I was used to going around in threesomes. Once it had always been Duffy with us; now some of the time it was Terry. The nice thing was that Bailey always wanted me with him too.

Bailey and I had planned another trip to New York in the late spring. We had sensed a certain resistance to us working together from our various employers, who were beginning to tire of us as a duo. Bailey was under pressure from *Vogue* to use other models. Realizing the implications of this, I decided to seek out more work in New York, where I was certainly not overexposed. I wanted to see if my appeal was international or if it depended on Bailey. Not unnaturally, other photographers are not keen to book a girl who is known as a rival's model. Being an exclusive model can shorten one's career. The question was, would other photographers use me if Bailey and I began to work apart? I still hadn't worked for Richard Avedon, who was considered the greatest fashion photographer in the world, and that was my ambition. I was free, Bailey had some work in London, so I decided to go to New York two weeks ahead of him. I rang my agent, Eileen Ford, and asked if she could find me some work there.

'Work!' she said. 'I can keep you busy for weeks.'

That did my confidence a power of good and that evening I said to Bailey, trying to sound as casual as possible: 'I'm going to New York on my own. Just for two weeks before you arrive.'

He looked at me, puzzled. 'Without me?'

'I need some time to myself,' I said, trying to sound reasonable.

'I don't understand.'

I took a deep breath and said: 'It's because I feel that I live totally in your shadow. I'm twenty-one, Bailey, and I don't know who I am at all. I want to see what credibility I have as a model on my own – without you.'

He obviously had no idea what I was going on about, so I left it at that. There seemed no point in saying that I was beginning to sense my life was empty and propelled by something that was very little to do with me.

So I went to New York on my own, and took a small model girl apartment in the Concorde apartment block where Eileen Ford booked in her models when they came from abroad. Surprisingly, I had a nice time. I worked a lot and I was invited out by editors from *Vogue*, and I quite enjoyed myself. Bailey, who must at last have been beginning to realize that all was not well with our relationship, rang up every evening, and I was always out. I did not go on to nightclubs because I was working – I merely went out to dinner and was home and in bed by eleven. I was certainly not involved with anyone.

99

I was just having a good time with people who invited me out.

In London Bailey was five hours ahead, so when he did manage to get hold of me I knew he was ringing me at four or five in the morning. He was an early riser, but not that early.

Sometimes the phone would be ringing as I let myself into the apartment.

'Where have you been?' was always the first question, and the tone was aggressive.

I would tell him with complete honesty, but I could sense that he was upset. He was beginning to see that things were changing, and understandably he felt threatened. I was able to ignore his state of mind. It did not trouble me. I was cold about it. Now I cannot believe how cold I was. I had decided that I did not want to go back to being Bailey's girl, working for Bailey all the time. I wanted a change, and I wanted an independent career.

In my estimation he was also treating me a little less well, taking me for granted, though I could have been making excuses for my own state of mind. Apart from the bad times when we were working, he treated me well all through our life together. He was always generous, and I knew he loved me. Like anyone else we had rows – he once booted me out of bed with an almighty kick in a fit of fury. I can't remember what it was all about, but I do recall it was only my dignity that was hurt. It wasn't traumatic.

He rang the night before he was due to arrive and asked if I would be at the apartment when he got into New York.

'I'll try,' I said, 'but I'm working.'

'Who for?'

'Mel Sokolsky. You know he always runs late.'

'Can't you cancel it?'

'Oh, I wouldn't like to do that,' I said.

I could have cancelled. I knew Sokolsky's sittings always ran late. I should have cancelled that one and also the rest of the jobs I had that week. I should have kept Bailey company, but I didn't want to. I was avoiding him. Sokolsky's sitting did run late. I got back to the hotel to find a disgruntled and weary Bailey waiting for me. It was not an auspicious start to the trip.

The trouble was that I did not want to see him. Nothing about our relationship felt right any more. I kept taking work so that I could avoid facing the situation. He was avoiding it, too. The atmosphere was a silent one – he never said anything. I think he thought that if he said nothing the problem would go away. He did not want to deal with it any more than I did. We both just wanted it to go away, but in different directions.

It was a relief for both of us when the phone rang and it was Terry ringing from California where he was filming *The Collector* with Samantha Eggar. He explained that he had ten days off from filming, and asked if he could join us. He had been in the States for some weeks. Bailey had driven him to the airport when he left London for Los Angeles and told him that we were going to be in New York. Those days not so many British people went to America. If someone you knew was in town, you got in touch.

Terry's presence took the heat off both of us. With all the bookings I had taken, he was someone for Bailey to go around with. When I wasn't working we went round in a threesome for the ten days Stamp was with us. He came to the parties we were invited to and was much sought after by the other model girls, but I was aware of his light blue eyes watching me all the time. When I was working, the two of them would pick me up from the studio and take me to dinner. They made all the arrangements. I did not mind. For three years I had lived Bailey's life – not my own. I was accustomed to going along with what the men wanted to do. And besides, at this time of discontent I was realizing in a much less dispassionate way that Terry was perhaps something more than an immensely attractive man.

And yet, looking back, it could have been anyone that caused me to break with Bailey. Being successful in my own right was changing me: I was aware of other men. I was even seeing the photographers I worked for as men, not just as figures behind a camera. Photographers do have a lure for models, and a photographic session can be a very seductive time. Locked together in a studio, a sexual buzz gets going which normally ends when the session ends. It had occurred to me that Sokolsky was attractive. So was his darkly good-looking partner Jordan Kalfus. Jordan was living with Ali McGraw (who was working at the studio and had yet to become an actress) and therefore was not available, but it did not stop me seeing him as a desirable man. I was going on twenty-two, falling out of love and casting around.

Eventually Terry had to go back to Los Angeles, and he stopped by to say goodbye. It was a Sunday morning and, not having anywhere to go, I was still in bed. I was reading the papers, my hair was in a mess and I had no make-up on. My natural vanity made me hate being seen without make-up and I ducked behind the newspaper, leaving Bailey to talk to Stamp until he left.

Things came to a head about three days after Terry's departure. There was a gaping hole that we could not fill, and we could no longer hide the fact that something had gone wrong.

'Why are you continually working?' Bailey asked eventually. 'Why no time for me?'

'It's all good work. I don't want to turn it down,' I said defensively. 'I needed to know if anyone would book me without you.'

They did – I was working for *Vogue* and *Harper's Bazaar*.

'And now you've found out.'

'I suppose I have.' The boot was on the other foot. In London I waited on his momentum. Here he was waiting on mine. With Terry gone he hadn't much to do. And he was sad. The fairy tale was coming to an end.

'I want you to book yourself out,' he said, testing me.

'I can't do that – the work is all arranged.'

He looked at me, his expression morose, and suddenly said: 'You don't want to get married, do you?'

I panicked. I stood looking at him in that scruffy little apartment I had rented, and thought: 'Oh, no! Marriage! I can't.' I was only twenty-one and I did not want it. In that split

102

second I decided that I must end the relationship right there and then. I did not want to be married, and if I did not want to be married there was no point in continuing to live with Bailey.

'I'm right?' he persisted. I just nodded, and managed to mutter that I was sorry. There was nothing more to say. Ours had been such an extraordinary relationship. We had been so happy together – we had travelled the real world and reached the top of our own world. When something is 100 per cent successful there can be no element of compromise afterwards. He and I (certainly not I) could not have settled for anything less. It had been a wonderful relationship, but it had no emotional maturity to sustain it and I was growing up. The deep sadness was that if what we had shared was not enough for me, whatever in life could be?

I began to cry from a kind of helplessness in the face of his dismay and my own. I could not help him. The decision was made. I felt a deep melancholy. He was hurt and he, too, began to cry. I knew I should comfort him, but what was the point? It would only give him false hopes. He sat with his head in his hands for a while and then said: 'I'm getting the first plane back to England.'

'You'll stay here tonight?'

He nodded.

I felt I should make some gesture, but the irony was that the apartment had twin beds. Apart, we both fell asleep exhausted.

When he got back to England he went straight to see my mother. My mother loved him, and the minute she heard the whole story she was on the phone to me. She was furious.

'After breaking his marriage, you change your mind. Jean, what have you done?' she said, and I could hear from her voice how upset she was.

I was out of love, and I had done what I thought was right for me, but it did not stop me being terribly sad. After he had gone back to England he used to ring me up in the hotel. He wrote to me. Katie Merrigan, our next-door neighbour in London and a dear friend of both of us, had to help him with the letter and the spelling. He wanted to get it right. My mum said he was devastated, and I think he was in his way. I was the fairy tale come true. I was the dream, the fantasy. He loved me. The trouble was that he had not realized that it was going wrong, and it must have been going wrong for me to be working abroad without him and taking separate jobs. We had always worked together.

In the long term it would not have worked. In the nineties Bailey's lifestyle is much the same as it was twenty-five years ago, whereas mine is completely different. He enjoys all the fame, though he has never wallowed in it. I came to be aware that I did not want the famous life. I had it with Terry, and it was dreadful. Being with Terry was *really* being famous. With Bailey it was less pressurized. Our motivation was nothing to do with fame. As the money rolled in, we still lived in the grotty surroundings we found comfortable. Fame and fortune didn't change our lives at all. But life with Terry was totally different.

It was not entirely Terry that made me leave Bailey, though perhaps the intensity of those looks – which in honesty had been nudging at me from the time we met him – had made me see him as a possibility. All through my life the cure for one man has been another. But I did not understand myself as well then as I do now.

My mother continued to be very sad, and when Bailey called I had no good news for him either. I felt tearful for a few days, but I was young and selfish. I dried my eyes, and gradually this wonderful sense of relief and an awareness of freedom wrapped around me. The fact that I could do as I liked was the uppermost thought, and for the time being what I wanted to do was stay on in New York. There was plenty of work, plenty of company and plenty of excitement. In my quieter moments I did feel the occasional bout of misery, and there were times when I missed Bailey a lot and wondered if I had done the right thing. We had been inseparable for three years, and it was odd being all alone.

And then one day the telephone rang. It was Terence Stamp, calling from Los Angeles.

'Where's Bailey?' he asked.

'Gone back to London,' I said.

'Why?'

'We've split.'

What I did not know until much later was that he already knew we had split. Bailey had phoned to pour his heart out and ask for advice.

'I'm sorry,' he said, and sounded as if he meant it.

I felt impelled to talk and tell him my side of it. 'It wasn't working out. I need my own space,' I began (in the sixties we talked a lot about our own space).

He listened, and then said he thought I should follow Bailey back to London. Patch things up.

It was not what I wanted to do, and I told him so. We talked on for a while and then said goodbye. I sat looking at the phone, thinking about him.

Terry sent me a jokey postcard, and I rang him in Los Angeles to thank him for it. He then called me a couple of times to see how I was. I did have one difficulty. The word was out that Bailey and I had broken up, and I was finding that I was getting offers I could easily refuse. As an unattached girl, suddenly I was fair game – and I was not used to that. I was complaining to Terry about the unwanted attention when he said: 'Why don't you come out here for a while – get away from it all?'

I had no need to think about it. 'Why not?' I said.

It seemed like a good idea. I was beginning to be lonely and confused, and he was someone I knew. There was the added fact that I *wanted* to go and stay with him, even though I felt it was a slightly shabby thing to do. Terry was meant to be Bailey's friend. But shabby or not, I was going.

I booked out of work without a qualm and made my preparations for the trip without thinking about the consequences. I had nothing to lose by going. I was a long way from home and I no longer had a home to go to, nor had I many friends worth speaking of. It seemed glamorous to be flying off to Los Angeles. I had never been there, and I had bought my own ticket with my own money and made my own decision. I was independent at last.

Terry was waiting at the airport, and the sight of him made me feel very self-conscious. He seemed shy, too, but went out of his way to put me at my ease – and as ever he looked wonderful. He took me back to a rented house on Doheny Drive which belonged to an actor, Lee Patterson. There we sat talking quietly. Nothing occurred, though the atmosphere between us was strong. I was happy – exhilarated at being in a totally new environment with a man whom I was finding extremely attractive. I was still at an age where physical attraction counted for a lot – though the physical attraction I felt was not entirely sexual. Beauty is powerful, and a quality not often attributed to men. Stamp's beauty was very powerful at that point in his life. He was more beautiful than I. He had a spun gold quality, and his eyes appeared to have light behind them. He seemed flawless. In the fashion world beauty was commonplace – I was accustomed to it – and yet Stamp still stood out and I could not take my eyes off him.

He treated me with enormous tact and consideration and had put a great deal of thought into making me comfortable with him. He made no demands of any kind and, as I came to know him better, I fell deeply in love.

I stayed with him for three or four days. He flew me to Las Vegas to see a show. He said it would be an experience, and it was. We stayed two platonic nights and one fascinating day at Caesar's Palace. Even for someone like me who is not given to gambling, Las Vegas was enthralling for its awfulness – so many greedy people, enticing slot machines, exotic floor shows, star names and wonderful food all crammed into one short street in the middle of a desert. It left me wide-eyed. I was relieved there was so much to hold my attention; I was saved from asking myself exactly why I was there with Terence Stamp.

I found the answer to that question when it was time for me to go back. I did not want to leave him, and he wanted me to stay. Nevertheless I went back to New York, saying that I had work to do. I wanted to assimilate everything that had happened and I was anxious not to outstay my welcome.

Some kind of premonition made me realize that it was possible to do this with Terry.

I had hardly settled back into the Concorde Hotel and begun working again when Terry called. I had been hoping that he would. He was very much in my thoughts, supplanting not only Sokolsky and Jordan but anyone else I had found momentarily attractive. Terry said he missed me. I admitted that I missed him. He asked me to come back to Los Angeles and again I went to see Eileen Ford to book myself out, this time for a month. And this time when I flew out I took a suitcase and some decent clothes. I remember I had some gingham trousers, a Polly Peck black linen suit and a pink linen dress.

He was waiting for me at the airport and took me back to the welcoming house on the hill where we had stayed before. This time, however, almost as soon as we walked through the doors we became lovers. We felt guilty because of Bailey, but the guilt changed nothing. I was in love with Terry, and that was all there was to it.

That month in Los Angeles was a curious time for me. I spent most of the day stretched out by the swimming pool, working on my tan, waiting for Terry to come home from the studios. I had nothing else to do. With only the thought of his homecoming to look forward to I was sometimes bored, but that did not matter. I was exhausted emotionally and physically after the break-up with Bailey, and that month provided me with a much-needed rest.

I learned quickly that it is necessary to drive in Los Angeles. I would have been marooned in the house if I had not forced myself to handle big American cars. I never became used to driving anything of that size and there was no pleasure in it, but at least I could drive to supermarkets and look round the shops. I spent the rest of the day primping myself up to go out to dinner. I wanted to look good for him; I wanted to be a foil for him and for him to be proud of me. Apart from when I was working, I had never before been so concerned with my own appearance.

He took me to all the glamorous places like Chasen's and Scandia that I had read about in the gossip columns – where,

I suppose, people like us were meant to be seen – but we really had more fun pottering around the huge supermarkets. These were new to me. The supermarket had not yet arrived in England, and I could not believe all this largesse. For me it was more fun to eat in, but it was important to Terry that he occupied himself with all the things that a film star was meant to. Even so, early in our affair I was aware of his preoccupation with himself. I was amused to discover that he was into health foods. Health foods, like plastic surgery, do not interest me. Terry had this whizzing machine going all the time, pulverizing wheatgerm with fruit, yogurt and God knows what else. I used to tease him that the results were disgusting – which they were.

After he finished filming in Los Angeles he took me to Nassau for a week. I should remember every moment of that first holiday we spent together, but all that remains is a blurred memory of warm sea, sugar-sand and a lot of laughter under unchanging skies as blue as his eyes. I do recall that I was wonderfully happy. He was a loving companion, doing everything to please me, but I can remember little else except an underlying anxiety about what I would do when inevitably we had to return to London. I was in a curious position. I no longer had a home. I had burned my boats. Not that I had any intention of doing so, but I could hardly go back to Primrose Hill with Bailey and the lovebirds. Even if the thought had crossed my mind it was too late. The news that Stamp and I were together had appeared in the newspapers. I had to live somewhere and I assumed that I would live with Stamp, just as I had lived with Bailey. There was no reason why we should not be together, but he had not mentioned it. The added complication was that Terry had been sharing a flat with Michael Caine before he left for California. While he was away Michael had found a new house for them. I heard Terry on the phone to Caine talking about this in both LA and Nassau, but I was not sure if there was room for me. He had not told me what had been said.

We flew back to England, and it seemed to me the further east we flew, so his mood changed. He seemed to become silent and withdrawn. It was then that I brought up the subject of what exactly was going to happen when we got back.

'I suppose I'll have to look for somewhere to live,' I began tentatively, unable to understand why I was so nervous about bringing up the subject.

Terry pursed his lips. 'Where do you have in mind?'

This conversation was not going well. 'I hadn't thought,' I said.

There was a long silence and then he said: 'You can stay with me at the new place for the time being.'

The relief! – though the suggestion did not sound like a permanent one.

'Will there be room?' I was aware of sounding humble, and was angry with myself for it.

'I should think so. Mike's with Edina Ronay, but she doesn't live there. She's just around a lot of the time. You'll be company for each other while we're both working.'

Michael was making *The Ipcress File*, his first really big film. It was this rush of good fortune that had spurred him to finding larger accommodation in a house in Albion Close off the Bayswater Road. The accommodation might have been bigger than the flat they shared previously, but Terry and I were given a tiny bedroom with a single bed that was a horror. The arrangement wasn't practical at all. I do not know what we had done to upset him, but Michael Caine did not seem to want us around. Not that we saw much of him. He left early in the morning for the studios and did not come back until late at night. But I recognized the signs of yet another Cockney lad trying to improve himself: his bedside table was creaking with reading matter.

I was working, but I had a problem. I had always been Bailey's model; but not unnaturally Bailey was not now booking me and neither was anyone else much. When I first arrived back I did work a couple of times with Bailey, but it was painful for both of us. It was not the same: the few sessions we did were traumatic; little was said; we never spoke about the past. Bailey was still in his twenties and never articulated his feelings. He had his pride. It was not for some years that Bailey and I were really comfortable together again. It was easier once I left Stamp and went off with someone else. And Bailey quickly found consolation. After me there was an eighteen-year-old model, Susan Murray, but that was not a big thing. I did feel the odd pang when Bailey first found a new model. No one likes to be replaced, but it was obviously going to happen. She was a green-eyed blonde, and she did six *Vogue* covers in six months. Bailey said she had a vaguely Indian quality and was more mysterious than I was. She also appeared in a TV documentary about me. The French actress Catherine Deneuve, whom he later married, was special. Years later I had a job in the South of France where I had dinner with Bailey and Catherine. He was not at ease, but it was nothing to do with the fact that he was with the two of us. I think he was uncomfortable in Catherine's culture. I am sure he was happier in London on his own ground. She was sophisticated and stylish, and I liked her very much.

Eventually I had to go and gather up my possessions from the Primrose Hill flat. I was careful to go at a time when I knew Bailey would be out – I could not have faced seeing him there, and no doubt he felt the same. I shut the door on the Harris tweed G-Plan sofa and the twittering birds without a pang. Mum had been looking after the dogs. Mongie was disobedient, so she had found him a new home. A few years later we saw a picture of him in the local paper; the headline was: 'Jean Shrimpton's dog wins prize for obedience'. Obviously his new owners trained him better than I had. Mum kept Bertie, for I had nowhere to take him.

As far as I was concerned nothing mattered except being with Terry, and yet I felt lost. It was not the same as it had been in Los Angeles and Nassau. Terry, who had been more aware than I of the odd atmosphere in Albion Close, announced that we were going to stay with Jimmy Woolf in his apartment in the residential section of the Grosvenor House Hotel. Woolf had very kindly agreed to us moving into the guest room and bathroom of what was a genuinely sumptuous flat. The sitting room we had to share with him.

I had never met Jimmy Woolf before then, but he was very much a fixture in Terry's life. He was an enormously wealthy man, one of two brothers who had owned Romulus films in Britain in the fifties. He was urbane, but slightly sinister with a long, thin face, long, thin nose, receding dark hair and deep-set eyes. He was not interested in women; people said he was a homosexual, though that opinion was not quite so openly expressed in the 1960s. He had a Svengali effect on Terry. Terry had tea with him most days – occasionally I was invited, too. They were on the phone to each other all the time, Terry slagging him off and playfully insulting him. This seemed to be the role that Woolf enjoyed. Terry no doubt tantalized Jimmy with his good looks in the same way that he tantalized me, but he never made a career move without Woolf's advice. There were those who felt that Woolf seemed to be more concerned with keeping his lunch and teatime companion than advancing Terry's career.

Woolf's closest friend was said to be Laurence Harvey, the actor who was then married to Margaret Leighton. She was an elegant and brittle actress who was a great deal older than him. Much later Harvey was to marry our old friend Paulene Stone, having previously married Joan Cohn, another older woman who was the enormously wealthy and influential widow of the head of Columbia Pictures.

Harvey lived mainly in Los Angeles, though his greatest success had been in the British film *Room at the Top*. He seemed to fill the same role in Woolf's life in the United States as Terry did in London. I thought it was all very odd, and of course I was right. It *was* odd. We met Harvey only once, when we went to a party at Simone Signoret's in Los Angeles. It seemed to me that Woolf carefully kept Terry and Harvey apart. His name was always cropping up in the conversation, but he never appeared.

We were only at the Grosvenor House for a week or two. I was miserable there and felt uncomfortable – it wasn't a normal life-style at all. Woolf was always pleasant to me, but there was something Machiavellian about him. Living like this was all very peculiar, but I had nowhere else to go so I put up

111

with it. Because I was famous I could not move with any ease. With the possible exception of Katie Merrigan, who lived next door in Primrose Hill, I had no friends. Katie certainly looked after Bailey when we split up, which was a relief to me. She had always liked him a lot.

Having always done what the men in my life wanted to do, I had failed to cultivate girlfriends, but can only blame myself for that. I am not good at friendships.

I felt isolated with Terry and Woolf as well. Not only was I a fish out of of water, but powerless. Woolf, who was always with us, seemed to be controlling our lives. Then, to my intense relief, Terry rented a flat from Vidal Sassoon – just for a short time while Vidal was in Los Angeles on business. Another of the East End escapees, Vidal was becoming as famous as any of them – and richer. His flat was in Curzon Street, Mayfair; it was furnished in modern style and there was a lot of black leather about. I was so happy that Terry and I were on our own again, yet I had an uncomfortable feeling that I was not particularly welcome. This sense of being in the way was unpleasant and I did not understand it. If Terry was supposed to be in love with me, which he said he was, why was I unwelcome in his home? Our relationship, which had been so happy while we were abroad, was already subtly changing. He seemed more restrained; there was no light-heartedness about him. Working on *The Collector* must have had rather a strange psychological effect, and there had been a lot of stress. I was learning that he had a clear mental picture, almost a fantasy, of how his life should be and he was constantly working to that end. Such a fixed idea left no room for any spontaneity. Life with him was in deep contrast to life with Bailey.

As besottedly in love with Terry as I was, I could see he was not a passionate person in any way. For him lovemaking was never a great priority. During those first few days together I thought he was being delicate because of Bailey. But it proved to be more complex than that, and as time went by the fact that he so rarely seemed to need me physically brought back all my buried feelings of rejection.

Nevertheless I wanted to be with him, so I hung on in at Vidal's flat. The unspoken situation came to a head when I rang the caretaker to ask if he would give Terry a message that I would be late home from work. I also asked if he could ask Terry to leave the keys for me if by any chance he was going out. I was having a problem getting in and out, since I was not allowed to have my own set of keys to the flat. Stamp said there was only one set, which was probably true, but in the three years we were together I was never given a key to any of his apartments.

The keys were waiting for me when I got back. Terry was out. All I found was a rude and offensive note on the lines of 'Don't bloody well leave messages like that with the caretaker giving people the idea you're living here. . . .' I was furious, as well as being deeply hurt. I went to bed in another room to keep out of his way. He came in later and never came near me. It was so unpleasant that the next morning I packed my bags and left without speaking to him. Fortunately I did have some work that morning. I was modelling for Caroline Combes, the fashion editor of one of the national newspapers. I cried on her shoulder, and she very sweetly said she had a flat in Battersea that I could rent for a fortnight; she was going away that afternoon. I decided to take her up on the offer and gave her two weeks' rent.

Later in the week I calmed down and decided to go back to Michael Caine's. My guess was that Terry would realize I would eventually go there and come looking for me, and that was what I wanted. We still had some possessions in the house, and the plan had been to move back temporarily when Vidal came home until Terry found a place of his own. I arrived to find Edina Ronay in. I said I was fed up. Terry and I had been together no more than two months and it was already going wrong. Edina made soothing noises about the instability of men.

I hung about, and sure enough Terry turned up. He looked pleased to see me, and I was extremely pleased to see him.

'Where have you been?' he asked with an air of injured

innocence. 'What's the matter?'

'You know perfectly well what's the matter,' I said stiffly.

He stood looking at me, chin tucked in, expression thoughtful. 'Were you upset about the note?'

I didn't reply.

'I'm sorry. I didn't mean it like that. It's just that I'm not sure if Vidal would like me having someone else there. I hadn't mentioned you, you see.'

In the face of those beguiling eyes I was beginning to feel that perhaps I had overreacted. It was difficult for me to deal with this because of the way Bailey and I had always been together. I was having to accept that that was not how Stamp saw his relationship with me at all – that he had a different view of a woman's place in *his* life. In retrospect I realize I was wrong to expect to automatically move in and live with him. He had every right to his freedom.

We made it up. Terry, however, realized that he had gone too far with his unpleasant note and he made a big effort to make up for it.

'I thought we might go to the South of France,' he said. 'Peter Glenville has invited us to his place on Cap Ferrat. Can you book yourself out for three or four days?'

I had never been to Cap Ferrat, that small piece of land awash with sunlight which pushes olive green and brilliant purple into the blue of the Mediterranean, and where only millionaires can afford to live. We had an idyllic four days. Theatre and film director Peter Glenville had a beautiful home overlooking the sea, where I sunbathed all day by his pool and spared myself the trouble of making conversation.

We were on what I called the social stay. I had observed that very wealthy, social people always stay with each other. They move from country to country, and there is always someone conveniently at the other end of the journey who will give them free room and board for a few days. Terry seemed to have been put on some mystery list where we were among those invited to join this wealthy circuit. I could never think why they asked us. I never uttered a word. I suppose I was there as decoration. I just used to thank God

114

there was something to eat!

While we were staying with Peter Glenville, David Niven asked us for drinks at his beautiful house nearby. That was fun. I was thrilled to meet him and he talked to me and I chatted back.

I remember him telling me never to take actors seriously. 'We're all children,' he said cheerfully, 'dressing up and painting our faces to entertain the grown-ups.'

Terry was so loving while we were away that I became certain that I had overreacted to his need to be alone when we were in London. But the minute we returned home, the situation was as before. We did not stay long at Vidal's. Terry had found a small apartment with a sitting room and one tiny bedroom in Mount Street, also in Mayfair. It was not particularly attractive, and I still did not get the key to the door. In the early days of the relationship Terry was more accommodating and I spent a lot of nights with him, but he did not like me to be in his flat on my own without him. He certainly never let me stay there while he was away. He was beginning to make noises about me finding somewhere of my own to live. It became clear that we were not going to live together, and the feelings of rejection were troubling me again.

'You don't *want* us to live together,' I accused him outright one day.

He came up with some lofty explanation about living in one's own space, which boiled down to the fact that he did not want us to live together. Perhaps I was presuming too much, but my outburst gave him the opportunity to urge me to find a place of my own. It was obvious that he wanted to be Jack the Lad and leave his options open. But where was I to go on the nights he had something better to do?

I enquired about hotels, but they were so expensive. I only knew big hotels like the Dorchester and I was appalled at the prices. I decided I could not possibly pay that much a week. I was not earning enough – I was not doing enough work.

On one occasion when Terry was out on business I went to a party. An old friend from my Bailey days, Geoffrey Bennison, was there. He was an antique dealer and a designer with elegant premises in Pimlico. On Jimmy Woolf's recommendation Terry had commissioned him to do up the Mount Street apartment. Bennison was to become like my second mum. He was very important in my life and he supported me through all the bad times with Terry.

Geoffrey was unashamedly camp. He used to call himself Big C because he believed he looked like Carol Channing, and he always wore the most terribly obvious wig. There were bits of something pink that kept it stuck on. I longed to ask why he wore it, but never dared. Word was that he had had TB and gone bald quite young.

I had been telling my problems to the party hostess (I seemed to be telling my problems to everyone at that point) and she reminded me that Geoffrey owned the Rushmore Hotel in Earl's Court.

'Why don't you talk to him about staying there?' she said. 'It can't be all that expensive.'

I pushed my way through the guests to find Geoffrey and told him the problem.

'Darling girl, you'll be welcome,' he assured me. 'Come and see me at the shop tomorrow and we'll talk about it.'

Geoffrey's hotel proved to be a typical bed and breakfast place with a lot of orange and beige paint and a musty smell. He himself lived in a grand apartment hidden away at the back. Rather like Nicky Haslam, Geoffrey chose to live in crumbling old buildings and create fantastic interiors inside for himself. I moved in the next day and was given a room down in the basement. Unfortunately the Rushmore was a terribly depressing place to be. The clientele were transients: no one stayed more than a night or two. The only crumb of comfort was that the staff always brought me in my breakfast in the morning and were unfailingly sweet to me.

After a few nights there – spent looking at the beige walls when Terry was otherwise engaged – I was really low. I went back to Primrose Hill to see Katie Merrigan and ask if she knew of anyone who wanted a flatmate. She told me that a friend of hers, Penny Bird, had a room to rent. It was a lifeline and I grabbed it. The ridiculous aspect of all this in retrospect is that I could have bought myself a house or a flat. I had just about enough money, but doing such a grown-up thing never crossed my mind. Older, settled people bought property; not me. In any case I had no idea of how much money I had – it did not interest me. Actually, there was not a great deal; less than people would have imagined. I had only done editorial work, modelling for magazine and newspaper features which was not well paid in those days.

Katie gave me Penny Bird's telephone number. I rang and she asked me to come round. I liked her the minute she opened the door of 20 Eton Villas in Belsize Park. She was an attractive blonde girl with a strong personality, slightly older than me. I also liked the flat. She had a sense of style, and here was a real home – she had created what I felt was a human and welcoming atmosphere after the stiffness of life with Stamp and the dreariness of the hotel. She had even upholstered all the chairs herself.

My semi-basement room in Penny's flat was very small, about eleven feet by six. There was a single bed behind the door which used up the width of the room. But the flat itself had a nice garden, mostly lawn but with lots of roses. The living room was pretty and the kitchen functional. She charged me hardly anything, and it was here that I kept my clothes and bits and pieces and where I stayed on the occasions when Terry made it clear I was not welcome at his place. Because he was not keen to see me, predictably I was desperate to see him.

Penny became the girlfriend I needed. She lived with a painter and had what seemed to me to be a settled domestic life. She was talented, was a good cook and was willing to let me share her comfortable home. There were nice people living upstairs and the atmosphere of the house was pleasant. Penny had once run round with the wild Irish actor Richard Harris, and she threw lunch parties which people like Michael Caine would attend. Terry would never come. Funnily enough we are both now running hotels. Hers is in St Lucia in the Caribbean – a rather more exotic location than Penzance.

Apart from the problems of where to lay my head, this new life with Terry seemed quite glamorous and sophisticated at first. No more driving down to Chang's in the East End for chicken chow mein; night after night we went to the White Elephant Club in Curzon Street or the Caprice in Arlington Place just down the road from the Ritz. In these watering-holes for the rich and famous we sat in pink satin and red plush surroundings while the waiters fussed over us. Everyone watched us as we sat at our usual table eating off fine china set on pink linen tablecloths and, equally curious, we watched back. The clientele was mostly celebrities – people like Richard Attenborough and his wife, John Mills and his wife, and Elizabeth Taylor when she was in town. In those days film people lived grander lives than they do today. We made our appearances in these obligatory restaurants with clockwork regularity. Terry and I were the young glamorous couple around town, on display each night with whoever he had invited to join us. There were mostly men around our table. If there were any women they were merely ornamental. The men did all the talking. Far too often Jimmy Woolf made up the party, leaving me uncertain which of us was the gooseberry.

We never talked about anything that mattered. In fact I barely spoke, but with Stamp I did not take my knitting; I would not have dared. I am a quiet person, but in the normal way I am not frightened of anyone or anything. I was, nevertheless, slightly frightened of Terry. I sensed a dangerous area in him that it was better not to explore or question. Indeed, Terry hated being questioned.

He was fine as long as everything went the way he wanted, but at times he could be difficult for no reason that I could fathom. It is possible that career problems were worrying him, but he never discussed his problems with me, only with Woolf or his agent, Jimmy Fraser. The reticence with which he guarded his life meant that I never knew what was troubling him, and I did not like to ask.

Our routine was set. On Sunday evenings we went to the Lotus House in the Edgware Road. This huge, dimly lit Chinese restaurant was owned by Johnnie Koon, a charming Jewish Chinese who had a gift for attracting celebrities to his

118

place. We used to go there on Sunday evenings with Francis Wyndham, a *Sunday Times* writer who wrote the words for Bailey's book *Box of Pinups*. One night the waiter put a bowl of boiled rice in front of me. 'You be careful,' he warned. 'Is diamond in rice.'

I stared at the bowl, astonished.

'He says there's a diamond in my rice,' I told Terry. Terry took no notice. I took a chopstick and began parting the thick, white grains, and there sure enough was something. I fished it out. It did not look like a diamond – more like a piece of glass. Terry and Wyndham were deep in conversation, disinterested. I called the waiter back and asked where this piece of glass, winking innocuously on the white tablecloth, had come from.

'The man gone,' said the waiter. And handed me a card.

A Bevel J. Rudd had left the card, with his business telephone number as well as the diamond. He was a diamond merchant.

The following Sunday the same thing happened again, except that this time I also received two little black velvet bags in which to house my uncut diamonds. Again Bevel J. Rudd had left the restaurant, and I never did get to set eyes on him. I still do not know whether I was supposed to get in touch with him and say 'thank you', but I did not. It never occurred to me that Bevel J. Rudd might have been trying to pick me up. I never thought anyone wanted to pick me up. Stamp showed no interest in either incident. He was too certain of my feelings for him to worry himself about strange men giving me diamonds in boiled rice.

— 6 —

Under Geoffrey's tender, loving care the flat in Mount Street was becoming beautiful. But nothing had changed. Stamp still did not want evidence of me in his home. I did not feel comfortable about leaving anything of myself about. I was aware of unspoken criticism, and felt guilty if I so much as left my mascara on the dressing table. I was only allowed to put two or three items of clothes into his wardrobes. It felt to me as if the flat always had to look as if I was not there.

Heaven knows for whose benefit all this subterfuge was intended. His own, I presume, since he was not having me living with him under any circumstances.

Once I fully grasped that I was a part-time girlfriend and not expected to live in, a fissure appeared in the relationship. We had been together for six months and our lives were already beginning to go in different directions. If I was not working I would either chat to Geoffrey in his shop or stay at Penny's flat and ring Terry to see if we were meeting or not. And I was beginning to wonder if that old spider Jimmy Woolf was masterminding the situation.

The flat had huge windows overlooking the Connaught Hotel. Terry had this high-backed swivel chair, and one day as I arrived he swung the chair round so he was facing out of the window with his back to me. He would not turn round and talk or even look at me. It seemed that the view of the Connaught had him enthralled. I suppose I had done something that did not please him and he was playing some role I certainly did not understand. But I was deeply upset. By this time my confidence was severely dented. He had an uncanny power over me which to this day I still do not understand. I should have turned and walked out. I did not. Perhaps he felt he would keep me if he was unpleasant to me and there was logic to that. I was stupid enough to think that because he did not want me, I wanted him. I am not a masochist but the fear of rejection does ring rather a loud bell.

The best times we had together were at the weekends when he occasionally came out to the farm with me on Saturdays. On Sundays we went to his home in Plaistow for lunch – his mother cooked the most wonderful roast potatoes. It was another of those East End houses where daily life is lived in the kitchen and the scullery. I am not sure if there was a bathroom, as I never went upstairs, but the lavatory was still outside the back door.

Terry was always drawn back to his mother, Ethel, and his home roots, and I appreciated why. She was a nice woman and a caring mother. I got on with her very well. She was different from Bailey's mother. Glad was stern, but that was just Glad's way. She had thought I was a bit hoitytoity, but before Bailey and I split she had become used to me. Ethel, on the other hand, seemed really to like me. I sometimes thought she was also nervous of Stamp and that we shared the same unspoken knowledge about her beautiful son. It was not that he ever did anything, but when he was angry there was something that made me hold my breath. It was easy to upset him.

We usually went home to Plaistow with his brother Chris who was into rock and roll. Chris, who managed The Who with Kit Lambert, was attractive and much less complicated than his older brother, and he and I were good friends. They were a big family – four boys and one girl – and all of them were enormously proud of Terry. He in turn was truly fond of them. He saw his whole family as special, and cared about them a great deal.

Terry liked to mastermind all of our lives and was exceptionally generous with his support, his money and his advice. There was a reforming zeal about him. Later he bought his parents a house, but he also tried to make them eat what he thought of as proper food. He persuaded his father, a tugboat man, to move on to a health-food regime; he also stopped him drinking beer and tried to interest him in wine. Everything he did was well intentioned, but it seemed to me that his family must be slightly in awe of him to go along with all this.

I myself went along with it. Because my hair was falling out he sent me to his trichologist – a man whose own hair was hardly an advert for his profession. He sent me to his doctor and his dentist – all fashionable ones with the very best of reputations, of course. I never stayed long with any of them.

All of Stamp's medical advisers were very smooth-talking, and I didn't like them a lot. His dentist sometimes put his patients out with sodium pentathol even for a simple little filling. A filling was all I needed. I sat in his waiting room surrounded by his glossy reading matter and his glossy clients, feeling rather embarrassed because my face was staring at me from the covers of several of the magazines. I went in for my filling and they put me out with a general anaesthetic. I remember nothing until I woke up in this little tiny cubicle, soaking wet. Humiliatingly, I had wet my knickers. It was a damp reminder of my first days at school, but all I could think of were those magazine covers outside and me in there with wet knickers.

I went home suicidally depressed from the effects of the drug. I had not been indoors and in bed long before the dentist rang up.

'Are you feeling all right?' he asked rather anxiously. I was not, and I burst into tears. He sent round some pills, which eased the depression but did not help the humiliation at all.

Stamp was forever trying to send me to these people. It was his way of taking care of me, just as he was trying to take care of his parents. He believed it showed I was important to him. Not unnaturally, he presumed that what was good for him was good for me.

Like many people whose appearance is important in their work he had bought the whole health-food culture as he bought the drug culture later on. But I never took to the wheatgerm, the yogurt, the carrots and his machine whizzing all the time making those digusting drinks.

'I am not going to drink that muck,' I would say, but it never stopped him trying to convert me. Then he became obsessed with Canadian Air Force exercises, trying to build up his body and attempting to persuade me to do the same. If there is anything I hate it is conscious exercise.

'I do not exercise,' I told him. 'I never have. I do not do these things. Nor am I going to eat your bloody yogurt.'

He believed obsessively in the rightness of all this and there was me, this peculiar person who did not. The trouble was that I was too ordinary and too sensible.

We met for one of our ritual dinners one evening in the autumn of 1964 and Terry was in an exceptionally good mood. That day he had been meeting at his flat with the playwright Bill Naughton, who wrote *Alfie*. Terry was excited.

'It looks as if I'll be doing *Alfie* on Broadway,' he said.

'Gosh.' I was impressed.

'It's the most wonderful part,' he told me. 'Hell to learn. The character is on stage all the way through.'

He had not worked for some time, and this opportunity was important to him. As, unusually for him, he chattered on about the role, I was apprehensive for him. I could appreciate that it was an enormous undertaking and would take a great deal of courage – Terry was a film star basically, not a stage actor.

'I want you to come to New York with me,' he said. He was being warmer and more open with me than he had been in a long time. Perhaps that was all that had been wrong, I told myself – his career problems.

A week or so before we were due to leave for the States my New York agent, Eileen Ford, rang me and said that she had work for me. Richard Avedon wanted to use me. It was my turn to be excited. To be photographed by Avedon was a long-held ambition of mine, and there was a bonus. The work I had been offered included a session for American *Vogue* with Steve McQueen. Avedon was to take the photographs in Los Angeles. The offer was irresistible.

'Do you mind if I go to New York ahead of you?' I asked Terry, certain that he would not object. He was engrossed in learning the enormously long part of Alfie, walking around the flat, the streets, everywhere with the script in his hand, and I was hardly seeing him. My evenings were spent mostly at Penny's. He was happy for me to go and seemed pleased that I was to work with Avedon. Things were going well for both of us.

I rang Eileen and said I would fly over. She found me a model girl's flat to rent and I began to get in touch with old friends. Nicky Haslam was about and still on the party scene. He took me around with him, and I found that I was becoming so well known that people were really quite pleased when he brought me along. He introduced me to David McEwen, a lovely, melancholy, aristocratic Scot with a predilection for hard alcohol. David became a great friend. He would amble round to my flat, pick me up and take me out for dinner. He would then drop me home at about ten. It was with him that I started to drink a little. We got through a great many rather lethal cocktails of coffee liqueur and vodka. I liked the mixture because it was so sweet.

Then Stamp arrived. I was waiting for him in the one-room flat I had rented. He was staying in New York only for a short while – the play was to be on the road for some weeks, trying out at different towns. He explained that he would rather I didn't travel with him. As it happened, I was not keen to do so: I would only have been an appendage. However, he was still in New York when the date for my Steve McQueen session drew near. I was already feeling slightly redundant because Terry was naturally so absorbed in *Alfie*. I had nothing to contribute to his stage career, and this assignment of my own was something worthwhile.

I rarely make announcements. Stamp looked surprised when I did.

'I have to go to California on Tuesday for that session with Steve McQueen,' I told him.

'Haven't you done that yet?' He sounded slightly piqued.

'Not yet.'

124

'I thought it would be over by now.'

'No, it's happening on Tuesday.'

He looked downcast, and I debated whether I should cancel the job and stay with him. Then I thought: What the hell! Why shouldn't I go ahead? McQueen was not only a bigger star than Stamp but one of the most attractive men in the world, and I was young enough to be impressed by the idea that I was going to be photographed with him. Maybe the thought of McQueen with me in the intimacy of a studio would even make Stamp jealous, and that would be no bad thing.

I flew to Los Angeles with Avedon, where *Vogue* had rented a studio, but when McQueen arrived for the session his wife Neil, a dark, pretty woman, came along too. I had the distinct impression that she did not let him out of her sight a lot – and who could blame her!

It was a jewellery shot. We were both in profile and I was wearing an earring and a bracelet. I had to hold McQueen's ear between my thumb and forefinger. Avedon had placed us very close together and was directing operations. It was slightly embarrassing being so close. He was in his early thirties then, and I noticed that his eyes were deep blue and his skin was brown – slightly leathery from too much sun. His features were a little displaced, as if he had been in the occasional fight.

Avedon is very theatrical when he shoots. Disco music was pounding, and his instructions to me were to gaze very lovingly at this man. I knew what he wanted: he wanted me to come on strong.

Steve McQueen was not entirely comfortable, probably because acting and modelling have nothing in common: they are two entirely different skills. Avedon began to shoot, and while he clicked off his first twelve exposures I sat even closer to McQueen and held his ear gently between my thumb and forefinger. I did what was required – I came on strong looking lovingly into the bright blue eyes just a breath away.

Avedon was urging: 'Fine, beautiful, hold it. That's it! Still now. G-r-e-a-t . . .'.

Models learn to count the clicks of the camera without knowing they are doing it. As soon as I was aware that the twelve exposures had been taken I let all my muscles go loose and relaxed into lethargy until Avedon was ready to shoot again. I think McQueen suspected I really was coming on strong with him. I wasn't: that's how models work. I was not turning on my sexuality for any reason to do with him; I was simply doing my job. It was an automatic reflex: turn on, stop, sit back, wait, and then turn on again until the photographer was happy. All good models have the ability to do that. And even if I had found him attractive (which admittedly I did) I would never have let it show while the camera was not on us – particularly as his wife was there.

These sudden switches of mood surprised McQueen. He said with a sort of academic interest: 'You just turn it on and off.'

I shrugged. 'It's my job.'

When Avedon was happy with the pictures he had taken lunch was brought in. One of the studio assistants went out and got me a hamburger in a brown paper bag. McQueen's lunch had been specially prepared, and into the studio was wheeled a trolley laden with grape juice and health food. I looked at it in all its fresh green and brown-bread purity as I enjoyed my juicy hamburger and thought: 'Oh God! It's Stamp all over again!'

I went back to New York to find that Terry had booked us into the Brevoort Hotel, a much smarter resting place than the flat I had found and about four times as expensive. Even though I should have anticipated that Terry would find a bedsitter too small, I still felt put down and as if I could get nothing right. It seemed an unnecessary move, as he was about to leave New York for the out-of-town tour and would not be back until the New York opening night. When he did return I hardly saw him on the big day, and David McEwen took me to the theatre that evening. We were in front-row seats, and I felt as jittery as he must have been as we waited for the curtain to go up.

Terry came on stage looking wonderful. It was the first time I had seen his performance – indeed, the first time I had seen him on stage. I was tense. I had no way of judging him as I find it difficult to watch someone I know acting, but I quickly realized it was not going well. People were fidgeting. The audience did not understand the Cockney rhyming slang; in fact they did not understand the play at all. Terry was dynamic enough, but this near-monologue from him in an East End accent was baffling the audience. It seemed to me it was not going to work, and it didn't. The applause at the end was polite, and the critics delivered the *coup de grâce* the next morning. The play was a flop. It ran for a month and closed.

For Terry it was a disaster. It was the first real setback in his entire career, and he was bitterly disappointed. The worst of it was that he had to go on playing Alfie until the show closed. He stuck it out for the month, even playing on Christmas Day. We moved out of the Brevoort – it was too expensive now that Stamp was not going to be a big Broadway star. I found us an apartment owned by the actress Elizabeth Ashley, who was married to George Peppard.

That Christmas was pretty miserable. Terry was doing his best to look as if he did not care about the panning *Alfie* had received, and he was right not to care. The play was wonderful, and so was his performance. The problem was that the USA was not ready for the nefarious Alfie. Alfie was 100 per cent sixties British and the Americans, for once, were way behind us. Terry was offered the film role later and turned it down, saying he'd done that, thanks. A pity. Michael Caine accepted, and today the film is a classic.

We went to a friend of Bill Naughton's for lunch on Christmas Day. It was not a lot of fun, and no one was very cheerful. We were served rather nasty beef in Guinness – no turkey or Christmas pudding. Terry had let his guard down. He was fed up and, most unusually for him, he drank too much. He did not want to go on stage that night, and I had to manoeuvre him to the theatre. But he pulled himself together, and miraculously there was nothing wrong with his performance.

Immediately after Christmas he was off the hook, spared having to perform every night in a dying play. He had been very brave and had stuck it out. There can be nothing worse than playing to small audiences in a failed Broadway production.

When it was all over he suddenly said: 'I need to go away to get over this.'

'Where shall we go?' I asked, immediately mentally reorganizing my work.

He shook his head. 'Not us, me. I think it's better if I'm on my own. I'm not going to be very good company at the moment.'

I was bitterly hurt. I thought I had done my best to be supportive through the rotten time he was going through, and now I was to be left alone in New York in the middle of winter. A wave of misery swept over me, but I did not argue. I did not say anything. I was under a spell, and the only person who could break the spell was me.

'I think I'll go to the Bahamas for a while,' he went on. 'Anyway, you really ought to do some work, and if you're not going to work here you ought to go back to England.'

I knew perfectly well that he was not going to the Bahamas on his own – that was not his style. His companion in Nassau was almost certainly going to be some other lady. I was just not sure who. He really did not want me at all at this stage, and I was probably clinging on.

So he flew off and I was left behind, not knowing what he was up to. My suspicions were that he was meeting Candice Bergen. I had a gut feeling that there was something going on there, which was hardly surprising as she was the most stunning-looking woman. I had no real reason to think this except that he had met her in Los Angeles with Jimmy Woolf and he was talking about her just a little too much. Maybe I was wrong. Terry always accused me of imagining things.

The mental picture of him with some other girl not unnaturally made me feel low. Fortunately David McEwen wandered back into my life once Terry had disappeared and started taking me out again. I would have preferred to go straight back to London, but I had a problem. Because I had thought that Terry and I would be in New York for at least a year while *Alfie* ran on Broadway I had given up my room with Penny Bird, who had rented it to someone else. I knew there was no way I would be permitted to stay in Terry's flat. Once again I was homeless.

I explained my anxiety to David.

'That's no problem,' he said. 'You can stay at my sister's house. It's just off the Fulham Road.'

I jumped at the offer, and David promised to fix it for me.

New Year's Eve arrived without any word from Terry. That really depressed me. David refused to let me sit and mope. He insisted on taking me to a New Year's Eve party given by Emil De Antonio, a rather wild political film-maker. One of the guests was Marguerite Littman, a wealthy Southerner who was married to Mark Littman, an American lawyer based in London. She was a remarkable woman who knew everyone who had even the remotest claim to fame. She wore dark glasses all the time – if you went to her room to say goodnight she would be sitting up reading, dark glasses on her nose. And they were certainly in evidence first thing in the morning.

She was to become a good friend, and it was she who at midnight decided that she, David and I would fly to Palm Beach the next morning. I had never been there. It was, David explained, the smartest place on the Florida coast, inhabited mainly by the mega-rich and elderly – a sort of Bournemouth with palms and a good deal more sunshine. Imperiously she gave us our instructions. We were to be at the airport on time and we were not to bring too much luggage. I agreed to go, but never thought it would happen. Sure enough, the next morning David was banging on my apartment door, saying 'Come on, we're going.' I crawled out of bed and got myself together. I did not take long – packing was a problem I solved by never taking anything anywhere. I just grabbed one change of underwear and my toilet bag and stuffed them in a plastic bag. David, who had difficulty sleeping, had brought a lot of books. Bleary-eyed, we arrived at the airport as ordered to find Marguerite already there, sunglasses in place. We bought our tickets, boarded a plane and on New Year's Day flew to Palm Beach, where Marguerite had booked us into an hotel.

The moment we were settled she was on the phone looking for the action. She contacted Mary Sanford, the Queen of Palm Beach society, to see if anything was going on. There was. We were all invited to a party. I didn't know a soul, but all the guests had one thing in common – wealth. I was not prepared for a party. All I had was what I was wearing – a little smock dress which another model had given me. It proved to be the most elegant party, and the English contingent stood out by their sheer scruffiness. But it didn't matter, because by this time the Beatles had burst upon the world. The guests were happy to think that David McEwen was Ringo Starr and I was just an eccentric English model, which I suppose I was. Palm Beach took my mind off my loneliness. It was a rather enjoyable drifting experience. We stayed a couple of days and then jetted back to New York.

David McEwen and Marguerite continued to keep an eye on me. David was forever taking me to these grand parties where the women had to retire after dinner, which I thought was pretty stupid. He took me to have tea with Bobby Kennedy just after his book *To Seek a Newer World* had come out. Kennedy was waiting for us in his extremely grand apartment and his first words to me were: 'Have you read my book?'

'No,' I said.

And that was the end of that. Once he found I hadn't read his book he completely lost interest in me. He obviously had another appointment as he stayed only about five minutes, having hurriedly swallowed his tea. He chatted to David briefly, then excused himself. When he was later assassinated, in 1968, by chance I was again in America. Now I sometimes think I dreamed that I sat next to him at tea that day.

As 1965 rolled in, Terry was still somewhere in the Bahamas without a forwarding address. I had no idea exactly where he was, and he was not sending me any postcards. I went back home to London on my own. Low and homesick, I was relieved that David had kept his word and arranged for me to stay at his sister's house, where I had a room at the top of a big, four-storey house full of handsome young upper-class men who took not the slightest notice of me. Penny had said she would have me back as soon as she possibly could, and I was longing to return to what was familiar and comfortable.

It was a bad time, waiting in this new room with no idea of when Terry was coming back. I lay in bed most of the time wondering where he was and what he was doing. I would turn over and over in the bed, reluctant to get up because I could not face the day. I was not eating properly. I would go downstairs and cook myself some sausages and then go back to bed and eat them, often with my fingers. I did nothing. I had no interest in anything. I saw hardly anyone. I went home to see my mum, but I never told her much about what was going on. I suppose I was heading for a nervous breakdown. I had no interest in anything whatsoever.

Terry eventually reappeared in London. Nothing was said. I asked no questions, and it seemed to me that he was down-hearted. I think the failure of *Alfie* was still hitting him badly. But better things were beginning to happen for me. I was at the top of my career. I did not see myself as having any competition, because the handful of girls like Marisa Berenson, Verushka and myself who were at the top did not see each other as competitors. We all had different qualities, and I can honestly say I do not remember any bitchiness from other girls.

It was at this time that New York *Harper's* asked if I would do the spring collections with Avedon in Paris, staying at the St Regis Hotel near the Champs-Elysées (and there aren't many pleasanter places to stay in Paris). I was delighted. I was dying to work for Avedon again. He is a small, complex man, with dark brown, lively eyes and a great deal of energy. He had John French's gift of making women look fantastic, but in a more modern way, and he knew exactly how to get a model to give her best. He made us all feel he was totally in love with us right up until the moment when the last superb picture was taken. He had that gift in greater strength than any other photographer I ever worked with.

All photographers have their quirks: Avedon was ruthless in the quest for the perfect picture. All the models who worked for him knew perfectly well he would give them a different body if their own was not up to his exacting standards. I have seen my head on someone else's body – he had doctored a photograph of me he took for Revlon, the cosmetic house. He had photographed me with a teddy bear, but when I saw the advertisement the hands holding the teddy were not mine. They were much better hands, with longer nails. It did not worry me. It was still a privilege working for him.

So I went off to Paris for ten exhausting days. Doing the couture collections is nonstop work and the hours are long. But model girls do not complain. To be chosen for the collections by American *Vogue* or *Harper's*, working with Penn or Avedon, is a career pinnacle. A magazine will usually choose about four girls and they may come from all over the world. The day's work does not start early – generally about 11 a.m. – but it is rare to finish much before three the next morning. There was one occasion when we worked through until after 4 a.m. Satisfied at last, Avedon told me to relax. I was already relaxed and had been for some time. I was asleep, eyes wide open and staring. (The pictures were fine).

The main problem with the collections was getting the garments to photograph. If the fashion editor and her assistant had been lucky, the clothes they had chosen from the couturiers were waiting to be photographed by 11 a.m. But not always. The couturiers seem to have a deliberate policy of making everyone's life difficult. I have known fashion editors literally on their knees to the fierce women who permit the clothes to leave their premises. In fairness, the couture houses have their problems. They need their collection to be complete for each showing and they are also afraid of their clothes being copied. Sometimes a combination of pernickety photographer and overworked fashion editor keeps the garments in the studio for too long. Then frantic, threatening phone calls are received from the couture house, demanding: Bring them back . . . or else!

A great deal of waiting went on in the studio while the magazine girls scuttled around Paris, snatching what garments they could. We model girls would be sitting around smoking in the unlit, dead studio, having our hair done by the top Parisian hairdressers (not a patch on the British ones) and waiting, waiting, waiting. There was always a lot of food around. (The French do keep you well fuelled, thank God.) Then the door would burst open. Girls carrying armfuls of horrendously expensive clothes would arrive, generally out of breath. Their appearance initiated instant lights, music and a sudden flurry of activity. There was an urgent excitement that defeated exhaustion.

It was after I came back from Paris, half-dead and wanting only to sleep for a day and a night, that I convinced myself that Terry was involved with Candice Bergen. My suspicions were confirmed when Geoffrey was going to Mount Street to do some work on the flat. He had a set of keys and asked if I would like to go with him. It was an odd feeling being there and knowing that Stamp might not approve. I felt a little as if I were trespassing. As I sat waiting for Geoffrey to finish doing whatever it was he had come to do, the phone rang.

I picked it up. In those pre-direct dialling days it was the international operator on the line, who said: 'We have Mr Stamp's call to the United States.'

On impulse I asked: 'Is it for Miss Candice Bergen?'

It was.

I explained that Mr Stamp was not available, and put down the phone with exaggerated gentleness. The incident caused me pain, but it still did not break the hold that Terry had over me. And, of course, I never said a word. It would have meant confessing that I had been in his flat without him.

When we were first together I went along with much of what he wanted me to do, but I never felt secure. He was curiously elusive. He never told me what he was thinking or feeling, and he never told me anything about his work. We had planned to go to the Cannes Film Festival for the showing of *The Collector* in May 1965. He and Samantha Eggar had won the awards for best actor and actress. But

133

we missed the plane and Terry went on afterwards without me. I was disappointed. Our trip to Cap Ferrat had been such a success, and I was beginning to see that Terry was a more loving, better companion and a generally happier person when we were away from London.

To compensate for the disappointment of the Film Festival he took me to the South of France that June. We stayed slightly inland in the hill village of St Paul de Vence at La Colombe d'Or, a wonderful old hotel on the edge of the quaint village with its pretty, narrow, cobbled streets and spectacular views. It was a wonderfully romantic place. The hotel had a vast terrace overlooking a wide, scented valley, dotted with the dark fingers of cypress trees. We ate there, sitting in the shade of ancient fig trees grown so vast that their branches rested on wooden props. We ate like kings from great bowls of fresh, raw vegetables and wooden platters laden with sausages of every kind. That was just the hors d'oeuvres. The food was more than ample – old-fashioned French cooking – and the management positively encouraged greediness. The hotel sparked in me an interest in French food, and also in modern painting. In the Colombe d'Or's early days the proprietor had been host to struggling modern painters. When they could not pay, they settled their bills with a painting. The walls are now hung with a priceless collection of works by Picasso, Matisse, Léger and others. Terry and I lazed beside the swimming pool and dozed in the afternoons in our shady, sun-striped bedroom. It was a blissful time.

Times like this confirmed my realization that Terry and I were really only happy together when we were abroad and on holiday. In London, my life with him was empty: I was bored, and we must have been exceedingly boring to others. I found life trivial then, and looking back I do not understand why I stuck with it. We were so vain that we continued to dress ourselves up and go out to be looked at. Terry always looked amazing, and I had to look good to match. I was so insecure that I was always fiddling in the bathroom or running to the Ladies' to check my appearance. It was pathetic! Here I was, at the height of my fame, behaving like this. I was just an accessory to this beautiful star, and it was his beauty that I was in love with and that kept me with him – not the man himself. I was under a spell, but had no energy left to break it.

In his autobiography *Double Feature*, Terry stresses constantly how much in love with me he was. I find that hard to believe. Perhaps it was true, but since he never communicated with me how could I have known? I suppose that since I never complained, as far as he was concerned everything was all right. Actors and pop stars were encouraged to have adoring women fans and to be seen with glamorous girls, but it was considered death to their image to become seriously involved or to marry too young. Perhaps this was the reason for Terry's cavalier behaviour towards me. Or did he see me as his collected butterfly? I don't know. But I do know he made me bloody miserable.

He himself became more cheerful when he signed up to star as the Cockney heavy Willie Garvin in the film *Modesty Blaise*. It was to be filmed later in the year and he would be playing opposite the brooding and charismatic Italian actress Monica Vitti. The news did little to cheer *me*, but part of the action was to be filmed in Sicily and he did invite me to join him there for a week.

It was at this time that he achieved his ambition to take a set of rooms in the most exclusive gentlemen's chambers – Albany, off Piccadilly, just along from Burlington House. It is probably the smartest address in London that a young bachelor could have. He was thrilled that he had managed to lease one of these marvellous old suites of rooms, and Geoffrey Bennison was decorating them for him. For the meantime Terry was still living in Mount Street, and he was beginning to become aware that things were not well with me. I was withdrawn, more silent than usual. I couldn't be bothered to make myself up, I never washed my hair unless I was working, and I had become very thin.

'You ought to be working more,' Terry would say, but I was beginning to think I did not want to model. I did not want to do anything much.

'I'm tired of modelling,' I said. 'I'm bored with it.'

'Then become a personality,' he suggested.

He introduced me to John Heyman, a chunkily built agent who, irritatingly, was always scratching. Heyman was also masterminding Elizabeth Taylor and Richard Burton. He was thrusting, youngish, an ex-film publicity man with energy and ambition who had managed to get his own agency together. His burning ambition was to be a film producer – which, indeed, he has become.

John Heyman agreed with Terence Stamp that Jean Shrimpton could become a commodity and I was directed to go to see one of Heyman's employees, a woman called Felice Gordon whom he had elected to look after me. I went to their offices in Brook Street, just off Grosvenor Square. I was twenty-two years old and I wore a smock and socks – the same smock that I had worn for the New Year's Eve party in Palm Beach – and, Felice told me later, I looked about twelve. She also told me later that she had little enthusiasm for either the meeting or the prospect of turning me into a celebrity.

'I thought that looking after some stupid model was going to be a bloody bore,' she subsequently confessed. As it happened, we liked each other on sight. She was Jewish, warm and loving, practical and shrewd – a fierce little woman. She saw at a glance of her black and beady eye that I was in a state and set about sorting me out. She realized I was misplaced, with no friends, no home and no anchor. I had never thought of burdening my mother with my troubles, so I had nowhere to turn. I was floundering until Felice seized hold of me. It was a very, very bleak period, and slowly she pulled me through it and out of it. She pushed me to work again. Whether it was good work or not did not matter to her. All she was determined to do was to get me out of bed, fill my day and get me away from the looming, silent telephone.

Realizing that Terry was bad news as far as I was concerned, with quiet determination she set about moving me away from him. She dragged me off to her home and introduced me to her sister, Marion Massey, who had discovered and then managed Lulu and Mickey Most. Both sisters were dark and small – a pair of half-pint dynamos.

Almost immediately Felice arranged some television commercials for me in Italy, and as I was beyond looking after myself she travelled with me to make sure that everything went smoothly. She was amazingly loyal, bursting with energy and did not let anyone get away with anything. Because the Italians were such terrible payers she would not let me set foot on the set until they had coughed up my fee. I sat in the car for a whole day while she argued with them. She was absolutely right, because it became obvious that the Italians did not want to pay if they could avoid it.

This all took place in the days when moving money between different countries was frowned upon, so Felice used to carry all the money I had earned back to Britain stuffed in her knickers. This would make her skirt around two inches shorter. She was fantastic. She fought for me and she was fun. I was beginning to laugh again and get out of bed in the mornings. There was no way she was going to let me lie there listening for the telephone. The phone would ring and I would grab at it, hoping it would be Stamp, but it was usually her.

'Come on, get up, out of bed,' she would order. 'We're going out to lunch' or 'to see Marion' or 'to the pictures', or 'you have an appointment'. There was always some alternative to staying in bed. She not only got me working again, she brought me back to life. And I owe her the most enormous debt of gratitude.

Eventually Stamp sent for me to join him in Sicily. I was in better health, thanks to Felice, and he was in a good mood and pleased to have my company. The rather solemn director Joe Losey and the other star, Dirk Bogarde, were close, conferring all the time. Monica Vitti, the female star, was proving difficult to work with. I think Terry felt a little isolated, and it was a help to have someone there who was on his side. Sicily was beautiful and we had a happy time together. I made myself scarce when he was working; he preferred not to be distracted, which I can understand. But when he was free we enjoyed ourselves. Again, we were so much closer when he was away from London and – could it have been? – away from Jimmy Woolf. Not that Woolf was ever unpleasant to me – he was always perfectly courteous and civil.

When Terry eventually returned to England the pattern persisted. Abroad he was fine; in London, nothing had changed. Besotted as ever, I still waited for the command to his presence. Sometimes my routine was to park outside his flat once I thought he would be home and then go to the call box round the corner to ring to check what was happening. If he wasn't there I would go back and sit in the car and keep running back to the phone box until I got an answer.

That was how I lost one of my uncut diamonds. I left my purse with the diamond in it in the call box. Terry was either not in or not answering the call. Back in the car I realized I had forgotten my purse and went rushing back. Too late. It and the diamond had gone. It was not such a terrible loss. Years later when I was hard up I sold the second one to a friend who made jewellery. She gave me £40 for it.

I had two ways of killing time. I might go to John Heyman's offices which were round the corner, and have a chat with Felice and ring Terry from there; or, looking for company, I would spend my afternoons in Geoffrey Bennison's soothing shop, drinking endless cups of tea, having a gossip and eventually making my phone call from there.

Geoffrey was well aware that Terry treated me badly and he thought I was stupid to put up with it. 'It's all rotten, darling,' he would say. 'He gives you a rotten time.' But he never advised me to pack him in. He and his little troop of friends, all called by girls' names like Carlotta and Babs, looked after me. They told me I was 'a mad girl', 'a daft girl'. They would patiently listen to my troubles for a while and then say: 'Oh, do shut up, darling. You're boring.'

Dear Geoffrey Bennison! Original, bitchy, funny, enormously shrewd and highly talented; also a wonderful decorator. He could be grand on occasions and had been educated at Oxford. Geoffrey came from quite an ordinary family in Wales and he adored his mother, who was deaf. She wore a rather large hearing aid, and I remember when we were having dinner in the Savoy one night and she was twiddling the hearing aid, trying to get the sound right. Suddenly she said in loud, ringing tones, stopping the restaurant dead: 'It's like a bleeding thunderstorm in here, Geoffrey.'

He was very camp and used all that weird gay backslang of the fifties mixed up with rhyming slang. Hair was always riah, polone was a woman, bona was good. 'Clock the ecaf, dear!' they would say (look at the face). 'Polari', they called this curious language. I sat in his shop and watched him operate with the rich people who came in during those afternoons when I sat waiting for Terry. Geoffrey was so funny with the women that it distracted me from my own depression.

'Oh, dear,' he would say, rolling his eyes. 'You're going to have to open your handbag wide today, dear. Mind the cobwebs on the chequebook.' Then, as a loud aside in my direction, 'God, she's tight!' He could be so rude and funny and still get away with it. During the Terry period he and Felice were my lifelines.

Geoffrey did not do too much decorating at that time. It is such hard work, and clients could be tiresome, but before his death he restored many grand apartments most superbly. He had style and he knew a lot about pictures. With him I bought a quarter of a picture by James Seymour, an eighteenth-century painter. It had been sawn in half at some time and Geoffrey saw the two pieces in the saleroom and recognized that they belonged to each other. He needed backing to buy them. I put in £4000 and he restored the picture, rejoining the horses at the bottom to the landscape at the top – and sold the result for £40,000. The picture cost a lot to restore, but we still made a handsome profit. I loved going to sales with him. He was so funny because he never wanted to be seen bidding as too many people knew how knowledgeable he was. Bidding is always very subtle, but subtlety was not his strong point, so he made

139

a big thing of peeping out in a coy way from behind his catalogue.

I loved him and worried about him. He and his friends led such dangerous lives, picking up the most peculiar people. He and his friends did not want to know their own kind. The little group he employed to run the shop all had the same preferences. They were all gay, arranging his dinner parties, answering the phone and running his home, but they hankered after normal men. They would dress up in drag with balloons in their brassieres and go down Charing Cross Road, trolling. Not unnaturally the pickings were lean, so they used to go to Morocco for their sex.

Sometimes, as a woman, I found it all got a bit heavy and this smother of gays became somewhat claustrophobic. But Geoffrey was charismatic. I never saw him in drag, and I never wanted to. I felt there came a point when it was better not to know too much. Other people's sexual habits are their own business, and as a friend it is better not to have too much knowledge.

It was because of Geoffrey that I started looking at antiques and pictures. He didn't teach me – he was not interested in doing that and I was not interested in taking lessons. Anyway, he thought I had dreadful taste, which I suppose I did, but just being there in the shop all those afternoons began to rub off.

Then Felice phoned me up one day, highly pleased with herself. She had landed me a job in Australia in November, away from the British winter.

'All you have to do is go to the Melbourne races wearing clothes made of Orlon and present the prizes for the Melbourne Cup,' she explained. 'The money is good as well. A thousand pounds a week for two weeks of appearances and all expenses paid.'

It sounded all right to me, and even Terry thought it was a good deal. Amazingly, he said he would come with me.

'Australia's a long way away,' he said. 'Let's both go. We'll come back by way of San Francisco.'

140

It all sounded wonderful. The company employing me paid his expenses – not because he was Terence Stamp, but because he was escorting me. I was always allowed to take someone with me on this kind of engagement.

Unfortunately, through ignorance, it was all to go disastrously wrong. I was very unprofessional. Orlon were paying me all this money, but they never bothered to choreograph me. I was not given any proper briefing and I never bothered to ask any questions. They merely sent me some inexpensive dress and suit lengths of synthetic fibres which did not impress me a great deal. My modelling work for *Vogue* had accustomed me to something rather better.

I was supposed to have some smart, race-going outfits made up from these lengths, and it was left to me to design what I wanted and arrange for them to be made. Someone told me about a dressmaker called Colin Rolfe and he did the job. That was boring enough, having to go for fittings and to be pinned. Also, there was not quite sufficient fabric. Colin Rolfe was anxious about this, but I said cheerfully: 'Oh, it doesn't matter. Make them a bit shorter – no one's going to notice.'

So he did. And that was how the mini was born.

I had settled for very simple shapes for all four outfits, and all were above the knee. It didn't seem to matter. I wore my clothes on the short side anyway and, in Britain, hemlines were beginning to creep up.

Apart from being four inches above the knee, the outfits seemed all right – though, to be truthful, rather dull. I put a large piece of costume jewellery in the middle of the little white shift dress that was to cause all the trouble – just to cheer it up.

Things began to go wrong the minute Terry and I arrived in Melbourne. We had travelled out alone, and the people who were promoting the appearance met us at the airport and took us by limo to a modern Melbourne hotel. The first panic was that our luggage – holding the Orlon dresses – had disappeared. It turned up a day late. The organizers should have been pleased at having Terry thrown

141

in, but they didn't seem to know who he was – which, not surprisingly, didn't exactly please him. As far as they were concerned, boyfriends meant trouble. He was wearing a flowery shirt, and to their untutored eyes he looked like one of the Beatles. His hair was Beatle-length and he wasn't conventional enough for them. They did not recognize that the Beatles were Carnaby Street while Terry was Savile Row. Then, when we got to the hotel, I found they had put us in separate rooms.

'We don't need two rooms,' I said politely. 'One will be fine.'

'But you can't share a room,' one of the organizers said, and with typical Australian bluntness added: 'You and Mr Stamp are not married.'

I wasn't having that. I have never been one for hypocrisy – and besides, I was positive there was one man there in the Orlon group who was sharing with a woman who wasn't his wife. I didn't know this for sure, but my intuition told me. So I pointed an accusing finger and said: 'But he's sharing a room with a woman he isn't married to. Why do you expect me not to share?'

My intuition was spot on. After some embarrassed umm-ing and ah-ing they reluctantly agreed that we could have a double room, but the atmosphere was not good. It proved to be hardly worth the argument.

The day of the races was a hot one, so I didn't bother to wear any stockings. My legs were still brown from the summer, and as the dress was short it was hardly formal. I had no hat or gloves with me, for the very good reason that I owned neither. I went downstairs cheerfully from my hotel room, all regardless of what was to come.

The organizers were waiting in the hall.

'Where is your hat? Where are your gloves?' one of the women asked, looking pointedly at my bare legs.

'Haven't got any,' I said. No one moved. I couldn't think why everyone looked so cross. 'Isn't it time to go?' I asked as they hovered, staring at me.

In the limo that the promoters had hired to take me to

the racecourse, I thought the men from the fibre company who were escorting me continued to look cross. Terry, smart in his dark needlecord suit, didn't say anything. He was used to the way I dressed. But when we arrived at the racecourse it didn't take long to realize I had committed the most terrible faux pas. The Melbourne women, in stockings, hats and long white gloves, were pointing at me and glaring. The men, as usual, didn't take too much notice.

What I had not appreciated was that the Melbourne Cup was the smartest event of the Australian year. The conservative Melbourne matrons in their somewhat out-of-date best were terribly shocked: my appearance was described as insulting and disgraceful. Opinion was that I had been rude and not bothered about an occasion that was important to my hosts and to Australian society generally. They were affronted.

I suppose it was discourteous of me, but any rudeness was unintended. I discovered too late that the sponsors expected me to go all dolled up with hat and gloves, looking like a fashion plate. I was under the delusion that they had hired Jean Shrimpton, the girl next door, the gawky waif – not a clothes horse.

I was very much mistaken – and what a target for the press photographers I was, trapped in this short skirt four inches above the knee. I was surrounded by cameramen, all on their knees like proposing Victorian swains, shooting upwards to make my skirt look even shorter. I had no idea this was going to happen – this was publicity that I certainly had not planned. Unfortunately it was not quite the sort of publicity that Orlon had in mind.

I became a *cause célèbre*. Australia was miles behind Europe in those days: the sixties as experienced in Britain had not yet arrived there. A certain section of Australian society was aghast that I had apparently thumbed my nose at all the stuffy old conservative Sheilas. Younger people, particularly those who couldn't afford to go to the races, were on my side. The newspapers got so heated that they actually said I had split Australia in two. It was ludicrous; I couldn't believe it. My picture was all over the front pages –

worldwide! – and fashion editors argued for and against this rather boring little short white shift.

I was so fed up that I was on the verge of leaving, but Orlon were aware that at least they were getting a lot of publicity. They gently talked me into staying, and tried to persuade me to dress rather more suitably the next day.

I am afraid I became rather pompous. 'I will wear what I want where I want – and nobody's opinion will change me,' I declared. 'I rose to the top of my profession being what I am. And I shall continue to be just that.'

Fighting talk. But the next day I capitulated. I went to their wretched race meeting to present the prizes dressed in a slightly longer suit and wearing a hat that the sponsors had rushed out and bought me, plus gloves and stockings. I publicly complained that I did not feel comfortable with all these extras, adding defiantly that I had worn them only because the sponsors had asked me to.

It did not stop the publicity. The criticism over my appearance on the first day had not died down, yet on this second day I was described as looking 'exquisite'. That was just as much over the top as the criticisms had been the day before.

I seemed to ride out the publicity, but Terry found the sense of disapproval coming from every direction uncomfortable. That, coupled with the fact that I was getting all the attention, caused him to take off for San Francisco on the third day.

Under the rules of the contract, I had to go to the races four times. On the last day I wore a flecked off-white coat, still well above the knee, and stockings, and carried a handbag. But I did not wear gloves and I tied my hair back with a big bow. It was my last little gesture of defiance. I then fled to Sydney. Asked for a statement by the rather less conservative Sydney press I said, rather crossly: 'The trouble is they should never have asked me to come here in the first place. They wanted a mannequin, not a photographic model. I'm not interested in clothes and I hate people staring at me. I certainly didn't think I was going

144

to cause all this trouble, and I'm sorry for the people who brought me out here.'

I suppose the people who brought me out there could have said I was not exactly dragged there, screaming. I had agreed to go. But at twenty-three, you don't think as logically as that.

The end result was that all over Australia young girls started shortening their skirts. The pictures which the British newspapers used had the same results back home. Suddenly the mini, which had had a half-hearted start in Paris, became fashionable.

Mary Quant rode in on the back of it, immediately making shorter skirts. Many people gave her the credit for the new craze, but the truth was that the mini took off because Orlon had been stingy with their fabric.

As I had another couple of jobs to do I stayed in Australia for ten days more. I was miserable and kept ringing up Felice. Some long-forgotten guy took me out and showed me round, which was nice of him. I got by, but I was wondering all the time what Terry was up to and I was not happy until I caught up with him in San Francisco. He met me off the plane, and we drove to LA, where we booked into a log cabin-type hotel near Carmel that was a sort of glorified health farm.

'There are sulphur baths,' Terry explained. 'They're wonderfully good for the skin.'

He was feeling guilty. He knew he should not have left me to cope alone in Australia and was trying to make it up to me by treating me kindly. So we went and had a sulphur bath together in the dark in the middle of the night. It was meant to be romantic, but I think it was more romantic for him than for me: the smell of the sulphur was hardly erotic. I was exhausted, jet-lagged and on a time change. Australia had been one hell of a strain, and I just wanted to go to bed and get some sleep.

Wherever we were, Terry was always into all these experiences that were meant to be good for us – health food, exercise, massage. Massage I hated the most; I can't bear being fiddled with. I was fiddled with plenty when I was modelling – quite enough to last me for a lifetime.

Looking back, it seems to me that Terry and I were always on a different footing. We did not see what was going on in the same way. The fact that we never talked was not helpful, nor did we do anything much except float around and let ourselves be looked at. That seemed to be enough for him, but it left us with no shared experience. It was not surprising that I was beginning to be dissatisfied with the emptiness of my life. It had no quality. And all this attention to my appearance was beginning to become a burden. I longed for some degree of normal behaviour.

We came back to London to find the Albany apartment nearly ready, and there was great excitement when Stamp eventually moved in. Geoffrey had done a wonderful job; it was decorated in the grand manner. Terry loved the boulle tables, the paintings of half-naked men and the wonderful figures of blackamoors that Geoffrey had found for him. As I was more into plain pine and country things I found it somewhat gloomy, rather like living in a museum. Albany was not a home, and again there was no place for me. I hated tramping that open central corridor to his flat. The porter was nice, but everyone who lived there could see you coming and going. I am a private person by nature, and I felt that this lack of privacy would make things even more difficult for me with Stamp. The only thing that made Albany bearable was dear Janet, the little old cleaning lady who cooked for him for years. She used to make lovely things like stuffed hearts and pernickity as she called it (she meant pan haggerty, a kind of sausage pie). But that soon stopped when he got into macrobiotic foods.

I was still in love with him, but I was beginning more and more to question what it was all about. He did not make me happy. He did not open my eyes to anything. Stamp wanted to live the film star life of grand restaurants, grand clothes, grand furniture and Being Seen. I wanted something more down to earth like a nice quiet evening together in front of the television.

In the summer of 1966 Jimmy Woolf told us he was going on one of his trips to California. He wanted Terry to go with him, and as Terry was not working, he was free to go.

There was no conversation between us about it. Terry just informed me he was off and off he went, leaving me in London. I assumed he was going to chat up – or worse! – Candy Bergen. Not unnaturally this threw me into a fit of the blues.

Unexpectedly, after having been away for only about three days, Terry returned. Obviously something had not gone according to plan, and when we met up he was in a most peculiar mood. I did not ask any questions. I had learned never to ask any questions.

The next day Terry phoned to ask me to come round to Albany. He wanted to see me urgently as he had just had some bad news. Once we were inside the door he said baldly: 'Jimmy died last night.'

I stared at him, thunderstruck. 'But how?' I asked.

'Drug overdose. Too many sleeping pills.'

It was the most terrible shock, and I was deeply worried about how this would affect Terry.

He had great courage. As usual, he had himself under complete control. He hid all signs of grief, but I was aware that he was deeply distressed. We went out to dinner that night as we always did, and I tried to keep his mind off the subject and comfort him as much as I could.

For Terry, it must have been the end of an era; he had relied so much on Jimmy Woolf for professional advice. I knew he could not fail to miss this friend who had taken such a close interest in his career.

Perhaps a little selfishly, I did wonder if perhaps now there would be a touch more room for me in his life. But nothing was to change . . .

Now that I was back in London, after a few weeks at David McEwen's sister's flat in Gilston Road, Penny Bird rang me – to my great relief – to say that my old room was free once more, and I went back to her cosy little house.

It was about this time, in the early summer of 1966, that Felice approached me about making a film called *Privilege*. This was a package being put together by John Heyman and Peter Watkins, one of Heyman's clients, who was to be the director. Paul Jones, the heart-throb pop star turned actor, was playing the male lead and there had been talk of Sarah Miles as his co-star. Sarah Miles seemed to me to be a hard act to follow.

'But I can't act,' I said to Felice.

'Anyone can act if they're directed properly,' Felice said briskly. 'You have to do something.'

We argued it back and forth. There were aspects of the idea that appealed to me. It was going to be a serious film, and in those days I wanted to be serious. I was always anxious not to appear frivolous. Peter Watkins, on the other hand, was a serious film director. He had never made a big, expensive movie, but his work on *The War* and *Culloden*, both low-budget films, had received strong critical acclaim. I felt that he had a credible reputation.

It was arranged for Peter Watkins and me to meet. I was aware that he really wanted Sarah Miles for the part. He already had one untried actor in Paul Jones, so it was not surprising that he was uncertain about coping with two of us. As it happened, I think Watkins rather fell for me in a quiet way, because surprisingly he gave in and said he would make the film with me.

I was not entirely sure that this was a good idea, and Stamp had no doubts at all that it was a bad one. He did not want me to do the film.

'You're an amateur,' he said flatly, 'and I'm dead against amateurs being used when professionals are available. And anyway, you won't be any good.'

Before we had even started work on *Privilege*, Felice was back with yet another film proposition. She was doing her best to push me in the direction of movies. Michael Cacoyannis, the director of *Zorba the Greek*, was making a film called *The Day of the Fish* and it seemed he wanted me in it. She had fixed up for me to go for a screen test in Greece.

148

'If you get it,' she said, 'we'll have to decide which of the two films is best for you.'

'Terry won't approve,' I said, though I had already made up my mind that I was going to take the screen test.

'It's stupid to let that man ruin your life,' she said angrily.

'I'm not going to. I'll go to Greece,' I said.

'And how are you going to explain where you've been?'

'We'll say it was an advertising job,' I suggested.

'He'll know it wasn't.'

'How could he possibly know if you back me up?'

'Because he sees the books, of course,' she said flatly.

I couldn't think what she was talking about. 'What books?'

'The company accounts.' She sounded impatient. 'He knows exactly what you earn.'

I was bewildered. 'But why should he see the books? Why does he know what I earn?'

'Because he gets 10 per cent of your earnings.'

I thought I must have misheard. I couldn't believe it. 'What did you say?'

'He gets 10 per cent of your earnings.'

I felt winded as I took in the implications of this unwelcome information. I was not only upset but really angry.

'You didn't know?' she asked.

I could see she was dismayed. 'No, I didn't know.'

There was a long silence. 'I'd better tell John,' she said.

'That's all right,' I said. 'I need a minute on my own to think.'

Looking worried, she hurried out of her office.

I sat there thinking about it. I paid John Heyman 25 per cent of my earnings, but why should Stamp secretly be getting a slice of it? It seemed dreadful to me, and I couldn't believe how angry I was. If, of course, it were really true. I picked up Felice's phone and rang Geoffrey.

'Geoffrey,' I said tearfully. 'I can't believe what I've just heard. Terry gets 10 per cent of my earnings. Did you know?'

Geoffrey had not known, but he commiserated with me and let me unleash some of my fury down the telephone. I was still sitting there fuming when Felice came back.

'There's nothing sinister about it, Jean,' she said. 'It's just that Terry brought you into the agency and so we gave him a share of the commission you pay us. He didn't ask for it.'

'But why didn't he tell me?' I asked.

Felice looked unhappy. 'I have no idea,' she said. 'I suppose he was saving it up as a surprise.'

I did not ring Stamp to ask if I were persona grata as his evening companion. I went straight home to bed at Penny's.

As luck would have it, I was booked for a job with Bailey the next day. I was to be photographed with Cecil Beaton at his home somewhere in Yorkshire. I never said a word to Bailey about what I had found out, but he remarked I was looking tired. I just said I had not slept well because Terry and I had had a row and Bailey accepted that as one of life's norms. Funnily, on this second meeting Beaton was quite sweet. The job was a couple of fashion shots for *Vogue*, and the house distracted me from my troubles for a time. It was full of exotic things, including wonderful pictures of people like Garbo, and there was a superb conservatory filled with lush green plants.

It was fortunate that the job was with Bailey who, by that time, had become like a brother. I am so fond of him, and we have a very good relationship. I know I can rely on him, and he has always helped me out at times in my life when I have needed to earn money.

After the session he drove me back to Penny's place, where again I went early to bed. The next day, having calmed down a little, I sat sunbathing in the garden with Penny, discussing the situation. I was still feeling very shaky and she, too, was shocked. I had done nothing about Stamp.

I was in turmoil and I could tell that my feelings for him were changing. I made no phone calls. I did nothing except get more and more angry and upset. What had happened had caused me to rethink. I was outraged and disappointed, and above all baffled about why he should want to do such a thing. I would have given him any money I had if he had wanted it. At a time when my estimation of myself was low, this news made me feel as if my world was falling apart. I was torn by conflicting emotions.

Normally Stamp rarely came to Penny's house, but amazingly he turned up. Penny opened the door to find him on the doorstep.

'Is Jean in?' he asked.

'She's in the garden,' Penny told him. 'Go through.'

I was sitting on a blanket on the lawn, and I looked up to see him standing in front of me.

'Jean,' he said tentatively.

'Oh, hello.' I did not sound welcoming.

'What's the matter? Where have you been?' He seemed nervous, a touch shaky; all his confidence had gone and the bravado was not there.

'Ha!' I thought. 'Someone's tipped you off.' I squinted up at him through the sunlight. 'I've just found out about the 10 per cent you're taking,' I said coldly. The ball was in my court. I was the one with strength, and I felt I was seeing him straight for the first time.

He wasn't in control at all. 'Jean, I wasn't going to take it. I was putting it aside for a rainy day – for you. You know you never take care of your money. Someone has to look after you. I was only being responsible on your behalf.'

He sat down beside me and took my hands in his, but I was not convinced.

'Why didn't you tell me?'

'I was going to give you a surprise.'

He had certainly done that. As it happened there was very little money involved and he swore that he had never received any – no payments had been made. Today I am absolutely certain that was true, but at the time I was not

151

convinced. In retrospect I can see he was not remotely interested in the money. This was one of his power games, no doubt learned from Jimmy Woolf. I was so acquiescent and never stood up for myself, and this gave him more power over me. He had never stopped to think about the end result. By agreeing with John Heyman to take 10 per cent of me, he lost me altogether.

As always when he had gone too far, he wanted to make up. We went off to a favourite place of his at Sandwich Bay in Kent. We used my car and he drove – badly. My nerves were shot to pieces. I was in a funny mood, barely speaking and not doing anything to help our relationship. I am not sure if he noticed. He had always accepted my silence and my acquiescence as acceptance. It's called wishful thinking.

I would not say Sandwich Bay was a success. A freezing wind swept across a sullen sea and a vast featureless pebble beach where seabirds cried, but at least by the time we drove back we were both behaving more normally. Even so, without telling him I went to Greece for the screen test for *The Day of the Fish*. I didn't get the part; ironically, Candice Bergen did. I then told Terry that I was definitely doing *Privilege*. I had nothing to lose. Once it was a *fait accompli* he did try to help me by sending me to see his voice coach, but I was too lazy to stick with the lessons.

I have to allow that he was right in his gloomy predictions about my acting abilities. I was terrible. Anyone could have seen I was going to be bad but, from Felice's point of view, bad or brilliant, at least I was not hiding in bed. Unfortunately the film was not the answer to my problems. The first day's work was on location, and I had not the faintest idea of what was going on around me. I was also about to discover that modelling is a bad preparation for acting. A good model is constantly aware of the camera; a good actor has to forget that it is there. Also, my voice was too small. Stamp had been right to send me to his coach.

'Speak up, dear,' the sound man kept saying, and finally in desperation to the director: 'Can't hear her.'

Basically everyone was tolerant and nice, but by the end of day one I wanted to break my contract.

'Felice, can I get out of it?' I begged.

'No way,' she said briskly.

There was no room for argument. I knew I had done something dreadful. I was going to make a fool of myself — and publicly. I was stuck with it.

I was so tense that I kept passing out. We went one Sunday with Terry Donovan to see his Aunt Doll and I felt very peculiar so they gave me a brandy. When we got home I just blacked out and keeled over. I was worn out.

Two weeks into the filming I was appalled to discover Stamp was saying that he felt I had cheated him by agreeing to do the film. 'You don't have to climb into bed with a man to be unfaithful,' he told one of the cheaper Sunday newspapers. That was bad enough, but he went on to say that for me to announce I was playing a lead in a film was like him announcing that he was going to perform complicated brain surgery the next morning.

'Crazy, man. I mean, that's it,' he said in the sixties' mode of speech he affected. 'That's the strength of it. For her to feel she can cope with a big part in a feature film must take a great deal of conceit or a genuine unawareness of the bloody pressures when you're making a film . . . it's like casting Mick Jagger to play Hamlet. A bloody stunt.'

None of this improved the film. I was playing a painter who was by no means a happy, smiling character. The film was futuristic – about a pop star who was being manipulated by both the government and the Church. I think even Felice was dismayed at the way it was going. In consolation she said to me: 'You should be a comedienne – you're quite a funny girl.' No doubt she too had realized by then that I would never make a serious actress. I just stuck at it, trying to do my best and telling myself more than that I could not do. Paul Jones was fine. For him, in fact, the film was to be the bridge between the pop world and the acting world. He took it all much more seriously than I did, but he was in general more serious – committed to CND and political causes. Also, he had his wife on the set with him all the time; she was his strength, and he depended on her. I was struggling along on my own, though both Penny, who was working as my stand-in, and Felice were as supportive as they could be. Happily, Paul Jones and I got along with each other well.

I did not enjoy making *Privilege*, but, as Felice said, it filled in time and got me away from Stamp. Slowly his influence was beginning to fade. I was starting to come alive again.

It was at this point that I decided to buy a house. Felice was nagging me to do something about how I lived.

'With all your money, living in a bedsit is stupid,' she said. 'You must do something sensible. For God's sake, buy yourself a house.'

I had no idea how much money I had. My wealth meant nothing to me. All I earned went into the bank, and I never gave it another thought. Felice made me go and see John Heyman's accountant, a man called Harry Pinsker. He was exactly like every accountant I had ever dealt with since the Lucie Clayton days. They all said the same things – I must spend *some* money. Where were my bills for hairdressing . . . clothes . . . make-up . . .? As I never spent any money, I never had any bills. 'But you must spend money,' they would persist. 'You must buy some clothes. You have to have bills for the tax man.'

Mr Pinsker said the same things, but he also confirmed that I had quite enough money to buy a house if that was what I wanted to do. He assured me that property was the best investment I could possibly make.

I was not looking for an investment – I simply wanted somewhere of my own: a home. I was quite ready to leave Penny's house in Eton Villas, which was becoming a little too casual. As my comings and goings there were so erratic and I was paying hardly any rent, it was understandable that some nights I would come home and find someone in my bed. Understandable, but still irritating when I just wanted to crash. One day when I went home and found Penny's mother installed and asleep I suddenly realized how truly ridiculous it was. At long last it dawned on me that it was absurd for a top model to be living like this – though in fairness to myself, life was more casual then, and I was still only twenty-three.

A couple of days later I spotted some pretty two-storey old cottages in Cheval Place, Knightsbridge, and I thought: 'What dear little houses.' The idea struck me that perhaps I could buy one like them. So I did. I bought almost the first house I saw, a bijou residence nearby at 1 Montpelier Place. It was a dear little early Victorian house that cost £13,000, and I paid cash. It was 1966, and at last I had become a property owner.

I was still battling my way through the film, forcing myself to go to the studio every day. To take my mind off the work, and with Geoffrey's help, I was getting my house ready. At least I was enjoying that – and in the fullness of time, thank God, the film was finished.

It was going to be months before *Privilege* would be released, so I put the whole thing out of my mind and tried to pretend that it had never happened. My horizons were beginning to widen. I had started having lunch out instead of staying in bed with a plate of sausages. I was even making friends. Life was going fast, but I was at least beginning to reconsider it.

I was very thin and worn out once the filming was finished, but Felice was still insisting on me taking jobs to keep myself moving. I was booked by Avedon for an American *Vogue* feature to be shot on a fantastic yacht owned by Niarchos, the Greek shipping millionaire. It was the most splendidly luxurious work I have ever done. Eight of us sailed the Greek islands for ten days with a Greek crew of thirty-five to look after us. They cooked for us by day and danced for us by night. It was idyllic, particularly as Jean Loup Sieff was on board, working with a different model. It was not like work at all.

When I came home, by another stroke of luck both David McEwen and Marguerite Littman were in town. Marguerite gave very social lunches with an impressive guest list of serious celebrities like Christopher Isherwood and David Hockney. David McEwen used to take me to them. As usual I did not say a great deal, but the conversation was worth listening to and never for a moment was I bored. Marguerite's homes, in both London and New York, were wonderfully stylish and I was beginning to notice details about them. My childhood home was ordinary: extremely comfortable, but functional. We lived in the room where we ate, and it was a house without books. I wanted something different. The first fabric I bought for my house was one Marguerite had used in her London home. She told me it came from Colefax and Fowler, the famous interior decorators, and I immediately took myself off there. I now had some real interests to occupy me, friends and my home. I was also more aware of antiques and paintings.

Tom Parr of Colefax and Fowler made me this wonderful bed topped by a corona with beautiful drapes hanging from it. When it arrived and I looked at it I thought: 'If they don't fancy me in that they won't fancy me in anything!' In an odd way I felt I wasn't good-looking enough for the bed. Waking up in the morning pale and washed out and not looking anywhere near as glamorous as the furniture seemed wrong. It made me wonder why people have such beautiful beds, only to let them down. I still have the bed today in one of our hotel rooms. I hope it doesn't have the same effect on the guests as it had on me.

Eventually and inevitably, *Privilege* caught up with me. It was to be shown in a small private cinema. Stamp was away somewhere filming, thank God, and his brother Chris volunteered to escort me. I squirmed lower in my seat every time I appeared on the screen. I was a spectacular failure: one critic said I should stick to getting on and off planes and wearing paper dresses. Alexander Walker, the London *Evening Standard* film critic, said I looked as if I had been directed by an anaesthetist. And that is exactly what I did look like. I was wooden, my embarrassment with the whole thing palpably obvious. The results of this disaster were hard to live with. I remember going to a restaurant and hearing people whisper: 'She's pretty, but she can't act.' It was

mortifying, and for a month I hardly went out. I certainly
did not go near the West End, the scene of my humiliation.

There was one bonus that came from making *Privilege*.
In the script the girl I played was originally meant to be a
journalist, but Peter Watkins decided that no way would I
ever be convincing as a newspaper-woman, so he changed
the character to a painter. That decision expanded the start
I had had at the Colombe d'Or in the South of France in
opening my eyes to modern art. Peter wanted me to take
painting lessons so that at least I held the brush correctly.
I wish now I had been more diligent about the lessons,
but I did learn something. The man who was teaching me
had a catalogue of Egon Schiele's work. I had never heard
of Egon Schiele, an incredible draughtsman who had died
when he was only twenty-eight. He and his wife both died
in the flu epidemic of 1918 – an epidemic that killed more
people than the First World War itself. I looked at these
reproductions of his paintings and felt the tug that something
of remarkable strength and beauty brings. I was enthralled.
They were pictures of emaciated people and objects, full of
power and strange eroticism. I found them unforgettable
and they were very much in my consciousness for days.
I was talking to Desmond Fitzgerald, the Knight of Glin,
who worked at Sotheby's, about the effect they had had
on me and he said: 'The Marlborough Gallery has some
of Schiele's work if you're that interested.' I went straight
there and bought two of his pictures. They were expensive,
but nothing compared with what they are worth now – not
that I have them any more. And from then on I began to
develop an interest in buying pictures.

I was so enjoying this domesticity that I could not
believe I had taken so long before buying a place of my
own. But after I had been settled in for a few months
something happened that spoiled the house – happily only
temporarily – for me.

I was having lunch in my dining room with Geoffrey's
manager, Terry Green. We were just drinking our coffee
when the phone rang.

I answered it and an American voice said: 'Hi, baby, how are you?'

My first thought was that someone was gee-ing me up.

'Who is it?' I said, and then it occurred to me that it must be Mark London, a young Canadian actor who had worked with me on *Privilege*. 'Is that you, Mark?' I asked.

'That's right, baby.'

It did not sound like Mark, but I did not know anyone else who sounded transatlantic so I decided it must be distortion from a bad line that was making him sound so different.

'How are you?' I asked.

'Fine, fine. Listen, baby, I've got some friends here and they'd really like to meet you.'

I groaned. 'Oh, Mark, you know I don't like meeting people. Anyway, I'm just finishing lunch.'

'Oh, come on, it won't hurt you to have a coffee with them. Do it as a favour to me.'

I am absolutely hopeless at saying a flat no, and I heard myself agreeing to meet his friends.

'Do you know where Montpelier Place is?' I asked.

The caller was not certain.

'All right, I'll tell you what,' I said. 'I'll meet you at the Aer Lingus building at the corner of Brompton Road where the Moyses Stevens flower shop is, and I'll bring you back here. Is that all right?'

As I put the phone down I felt uneasy, saying to Terry Green: 'I don't know, there's something funny about all that. Mark London wants me to meet some friends. . . . It's a bore.' But the nagging sense of something not being right persisted. 'Will you just come with me to meet them?' I asked.

'I'll drop you there,' he said, 'but then I'll have to get off. I should be back at work.'

Terry drove me the short distance to the Aer Lingus building. There was no sign of Mark and I got out of the car. There was nowhere for Terry to park.

'Don't worry,' I said. 'You'd better get back to work.'

He drove off, leaving me hovering on the pavement. After a minute I noticed a swarthy-looking guy in a Che Guevara beret just a few paces from me. There was another man, same colour, same beret, on the other side of the road. As I was looking round for Mark, the man on my side of the pavement came up to me.

'Hi,' he said. 'I'm a friend of Mark's. He couldn't make it, but we can have coffee, can't we?' And then he signalled to his counterpart on the other side of the road.

Alarm bells rang. He didn't look like anyone Mark would know, and I recognized the voice. It was the man who had been on the phone. The other man was trying to cross towards us, but fortunately at that point, just past the Victoria and Albert Museum, the road is very wide and the traffic was moving. I looked round for assistance should I need it.

'No,' I said. 'If Mark's not here I don't want to have coffee.'

I knew I couldn't just turn and walk home: they would follow me and find out where I lived. Happily, a cruising cab was just going by. I hailed it frantically, jumped in thankfully and directed the driver to Geoffrey's shop. Once in the cab I found I was trembling. I did not look back to see what had become of the two men.

What had that all been about? I asked myself. A kidnap attempt? It seemed one logical explanation, and I had helped them by mistaking the man's voice for Mark's. But how had they got my telephone number? More important, did they know whose phone they were ringing?

That night I didn't go back to Montpelier Place – I went home to Mum's.

'Something funny happened,' I told my father. Thoroughly alarmed by the story, he went out the next morning and bought me an Alsatian. I, too, was alarmed for weeks afterwards. There were funny messages coming through on my answering machine which I suspect were left by these same people. Before that had happened I had hardly bothered to lock a door – we all trusted everyone in the sixties. I was a hippie in mentality, but the incident made me much more careful. I was glad to have the dog, but he was young and proved to be too boisterous for a town house. When I went to the States to work again I gave him back to Mum. She didn't mind. It was no problem: we always had Alsatians at the farm for protection.

I eventually forgot the incident. Today I would be much more worried. But if it was a kidnap attempt I have often wondered how much they thought I was worth.

— 7 —

Terry was away in Dorset filming *Far From the Madding Crowd* with Julie Christie. If my whole attitude to him had not changed, that knowledge would have caused me severe anxiety; but I had reached the stage where I did not care whether I saw him or not.

I did not need him any more. The entire time he was filming I went neither to the studios nor to the locations. The nearest I came to the film was when he brought me home a flowered lavatory from the set. I was pleased with it, as I had been looking for one for my bathroom. Terry did give me a lot of presents – a Piaget watch which I still wear, and a Cartier one which instead of having Cartier on the face had Shrimpton written across it. I gave that away in later years. I didn't need reminding of my name.

I suppose Terry did love me – in the working-class way, in which the men love their women as long as the women aren't any trouble.

Felice kept me working and she had landed me a huge American contract with Yardley, the cosmetics firm. I refused to make commercials or appear on television in England and was only prepared to do this kind of work in America. I did not wish to be that recognizable at home, but this three-year contract was strictly for the States. I was to tour America twice a year for two weeks, making personal appearances and talking to teenagers about the company's hair products. The rest of the contract was taken up with television commercials and still photography for a magazine advertising campaign. They were paying me £70,000 for the package – a fortune in those days.

The American photographer Mel Sokolsky and his partner Jordan Kalfus (both of whom I had cast interested eyes upon when I was ready to leave Bailey) were appointed to do the commercial work. Jordan was no longer with Ali McGraw. She had left her job as Sokolsky's stylist, gone off to be a film star and was to make a great success in *Goodbye Columbus*. I was not surprised – I had always thought that she was beautiful. She had the confidence never to wear make-up and she was not as thin at that time as she became later. She looked wonderful when she was more rounded. Many times when she was dressing me for a session I had thought: 'Crumbs, this girl looks better than I do!'

It was her job to get the clothes together and she was very good at decorating the sets. Anything she did, she did well. She was shrewd and stylish. She had always wanted to act and went off to dancing classes after a full day's work. Jordan was very smooth and dark and they had made a lovely-looking couple, but by the time he and Sokolsky came to London to make the first of the Yardley commercials the relationship had finished. Jordan was around the studio while Sokolsky was shooting, keeping the client – Yardley's advertising agency – happy, making sure the money was available and doing all those businesslike things that a producer does. And I noticed him again.

He was hard to miss. Sophisticated and tanned, he had broad shoulders and a narrow waist and looked good in Mafia-style suits with dark shirts for which he paid a great deal of money. His hair was as silky and glossy as a blackbird's wing. He had good teeth and a wonderful smile.

When the work in London was finished, his last words to me were: 'Give me a call when you get to New York.'

I had no illusions that there was any hidden meaning involved in the invitation; he was just being casually polite. I was not his type – not if Ali was anything to go by.

Nevertheless, I knew I would ring him when I got to New York.

Terry was going to Los Angeles to make a Western called *Blue*, and he was excited about it. When we met he kept talking about how good he would look as a cowboy, and I had to agree. He was preoccupied with his film and I had my Yardley contract to think about. We both had business in the States and he suggested that we went there together. I said something cautious like: 'Why not?' The emphasis between us had changed. He was the one making some effort to make our relationship work, but I knew I was slipping away from him.

Now I had my own home he had taken to coming and staying the night there with me. I did not like this new development a great deal. Montpelier Place was my territory. There was nothing of him there, just as there had never been anything of me in his homes.

Terry was at Montpelier Place with me one evening when I broke the news that I was going to the States ahead of him. Yardley were giving the awards for the Young British Designer Fashion Show in New York and I was to be one of the judges. It was almost a replay of the scenario with Bailey three years before.

'You're going ahead of me?' He sounded indignant.

'I have to,' I said, which was true.

'Well, I suppose I can stop over there on my way to LA.'

I nodded.

'And you *will* join me in LA when you're through in New York, won't you?'

'Sure,' I said, without making any promises.

The balance had shifted. *He* was anxious that I joined him in Los Angeles. *He* was the eager one now.

In New York Yardley had booked me in at the Drake Hotel with my friend Valerie Wade, a fashion journalist who worked on *Vanity Fair*. She had been Terry Donovan's girlfriend for ages. We were cosy, all girls together and having a pleasant time. When Stamp eventually arrived I was not particularly pleased to see him. The atmosphere

163

was awkward. Valerie and I had been sharing a suite, and I had to move out to be with him. I went reluctantly, and he may have been aware of my lack of enthusiasm. I could sense that he felt an intruder. He was not calling the tune and he no longer fitted in. He had no role in this particular scenario and nothing went right. Oddly, Donovan was being a bit funny with Valerie at this time too. He kept making querulous phone calls to her from England. Men don't like the girls being out on their own.

Eventually Terry went off to Los Angeles, and the minute he had gone I did what I had been itching to do – I called Jordan. I had a good excuse to do so: we were starting work on photographing the Yardley commercials in the next few days. I had already set my sights on him, and the realization that I was attracted to him was helping me cope with the problem of Terry. I was weak: I needed something to prise me away from a relationship, and I did not want to be alone. It is difficult to be alone at the best of times, and even more so when you are famous.

Jordan did not sound unhappy to hear from me when I phoned, and he asked politely: 'Would you like to go out to dinner?'

'Yes, I would,' I said without a moment's hesitation.

That evening when he came to pick me up at the Drake I looked at him and liked what I saw. He was eleven years older than me, a pleasant Jewish man of Romanian descent. He was divorced, and there were a couple of children from the marriage who lived with their mother. With Ali McGraw gone from his life, he was unencumbered. I knew I was going to leave Stamp, and I knew he was going to be the one I left Stamp for.

I had been with Terry for three years, and most of that time – even when I had been so besotted with him – subconsciously I had been slowly trying to work my life out. It is hard for me now to remember how terribly stupid I was in my humble, compliant attitude towards him. I must have been very lost. Realigning my life with Jordan was the best thing I could have done. He was older. He was kind. I could

164

talk to him and he listened to me. He also had a domestic quality. He was rooted in reality.

He took me to a Jewish restaurant down near the Bowery where there was sawdust on the floor and the speciality was steak. I was due to fly out to California to join Terry a couple of days later and there, on my first date with Jordan – blow me! – the first person I saw was Chris Stamp. And with him in this unlikely place was a friend of Terry's, a guy called Pete. I was well and truly caught in the act. It was ironic. Jordan had asked me where I wanted to go, and I had tactfully suggested that it might be as well to pick somewhere not too public. And that, of course, was what aroused suspicions. We would have looked a lot less obvious at the Four Seasons, where everybody went. Chris kept quiet, but Pete passed on the news to Terry that he had seen me with another man.

The next morning Jordan sent me white lilac. I was impressed. He had hit on exactly the right flower. I don't care for anything as obvious as red roses. The lilac could have been a publicity gesture from the producer to the model, but I did not think it was. I felt myself begin to smile as I breathed in the scent of the blossom.

Jordan offered to drive me to the airport. He had no way of knowing how reluctant I was to leave. I did not want to go to Los Angeles; I wanted to stay in New York and get to know Jordan better. On the stop-and-start drive through the clogged freeway to Kennedy he was polite and charming but said nothing of any significance. He just gave me a light kiss on the cheek when we said goodbye.

'See you next time you're in New York,' he said, unaware of how soon that would be.

I did not enjoy the journey. I sat there asking myself how I was going to tell Terry that I was leaving him. I could not even doze for worrying, and I was in no hurry for the plane to land. Telling Stamp that I was off was a daunting prospect, particularly as I was still a little frightened of him.

The plane was on time, and Terry was waiting for me at the airport. He kissed me as if he meant it, grabbed my bags and led me out to where he had parked the car. He made it obvious that he was pleased to see me – but it was all too late.

'I've rented Margaret Leighton's house,' he said. 'You'll love it. It's just off Sunset Strip, convenient for everywhere.'

'Oh, yes,' I said. Margaret Leighton, who had been married to Laurence Harvey, brought back memories of Jimmy Woolf.

'Chris is staying, and Pete, so you'll have company.'

'Great,' I said, thinking I didn't need Pete for company.

We didn't speak much for the rest of the journey. I was already fed up. I did not want to be there. I wanted to get back to Jordan, who kept invading my thoughts.

As far as I remember, Margaret Leighton's house was pretty – but I never took it in because I was desperately nervous about saying goodbye to Terry. I could not find the courage to break the news, and there was a lot of tension about the place. I was silent most of the time, and relieved that Chris was staying there – he acted as a buffer.

By the end of the second day I was in a state; I still could not think how I was going to break the news. I was afraid to broach the subject and I wanted to talk to Jordan, but I could hardly ring him from Terry's home. Stamp was jumpy, too. The atmosphere was terrible. He knew something was wrong.

I got up late the third morning and we shared a silent breakfast in the sunshine on the terrace outside the bedroom by the pool. Then I took a swim and came back to the table. He started to roll himself a joint rather clumsily. He had just got into pot, and the house stank of the stuff.

'Why don't you have one?' he suggested. 'It'll relax you.'

I had never been interested in drugs and wasn't then, but it seemed like something to do. He went through the ritual of rolling the tobacco and the spindly brown whiskers of the hash together and blending them inside a cigarette paper. Then he handed me the thin white tube.

'You have to draw the smoke right in and get it into your lungs along with some air,' he explained.

I took it cautiously and puffed. The taste was harsh and made me cough a lot.

'Try again,' he said.

I did, and coughed some more, but after a while I did begin to feel different. I felt brave – almost insolently carefree. And I sat staring at him as if he were someone I didn't know.

'Are you all right?' he asked.

I didn't answer.

'Something's wrong?'

I took a deep breath. 'That's right,' I said. 'Something's wrong.'

'Aren't you happy with me any more?'

'Not really.'

There were many things I could have said, but there seemed to be no point in recriminations now. I did not want a row; I just wanted to get out. The less said the better in these circumstances. He sat with his head bowed as I told him in as few words as possible, and with amazing calm, that I wanted to end it. That it was over. He had gone white under the carefully nurtured tan. Funny, I thought – now it had come to the point he was not so frightening after all. Perhaps I had seen him as being more frightening than he really was.

Finally he said, rather pathetically: 'But I was going to marry you.'

I believed him, but it was too late. This late in the day when he was losing me, he thought he loved me.

I didn't reply.

'Don't you want to marry me?'

'No, I don't,' I said flatly, and burst into tears. I was suddenly conscious of what I had done. I had thrown myself into the unknown, leaving another failure behind me. Dejected and miserable, I cried but said no more.

He stood staring at me. There was no expression on his face, but I knew he was uncertain what to do next. He made no attempt to touch me.

Then he said: 'I have to go.' He sounded distracted. 'I must.' He was backing away from the table, as desperate to break away from this painful scene as I was. 'What are you going to do?' he asked.

I had not thought that far. 'I don't know yet. But I'll leave here. Go back to New York. Go and see Felice. . . .' I wanted to get out of the house as quickly as possible.

'Are you sure about all this?' He sounded humble, just as I once used to sound humble. I found no pleasure in it.

I nodded.

'Will you ring me in a week?'

'In case I change my mind?'

'In case you change your mind.'

'OK,' I said wearily, knowing that I would not.

He went. I heard the front door slam and his car rev up. I sat there in the sunshine, still tearful, but gradually feeling the liberating relief that comes after a difficult decision is made. It occurred to me that he had never asked me if there was another man. But of course not. All that enormous masculine ego and pride would not let him do that.

When the last muffled sound of his car had faded I went into the house and rang Felice. She was now living in California while her husband tried to get into films. Fortunately she was at home and answered the phone.

'Felice, it's Jean,' I said. 'I'm at Terry's, here in Los Angeles. I've just told him it's over. I need to get away. Can I come to you?'

'You've done what?' Felice sounded astonished.

'Told Terry it's over.'

A brief silence.

'About time, too,' she said in her normal brisk manner. 'Come on over and tell me all about it.'

Still tear-stained, I got myself to Felice's in a taxi and at the sight of her burst into tears again.

She offered me coffee, sympathy and common sense. She even said that to make absolutely sure I was not making a mistake I should see Terry again and talk it over sensibly.

I listened and said I would do that, but Jordan was on my mind. As soon as I could decently suggest it, I asked if I could use her phone to call New York. I needed to talk to him, and

With Federico Fellini and Marcello Mastroianni for American *Vogue*
(David Bailey. Courtesy Vogue © *1963 by The Condé Nast Publications Inc)*

In Taormina, Sicily with
Terence Stamp *(Rex Features)*

The famous mini I wore for the
Melbourne Gold Cup in 1965
(Topham)

Richard Avedon's photograph of me
with Steve McQueen for *Harper's Bazaar*

(© 1964 by Richard Avedon. All rights reserved)

Above: In a scene from *Privilege*
with Paul Jones
(Terry O'Neill. Reproduced from Vogue©
1966 The Condé Nast Publications Ltd)

Right: Heathcote Williams *(© BBC)*

Left: On location in Rome in 1966
(Rex Features)

On location for British *Vogue* in Egypt in 1972 *(David Bailey)*

The *bikini life in Hawaii*

The Shrimp out of water, left warms up in a fluffy white knitted tunic that closes briefly at the bosom, opens to show a stretch of midriff and tiny bikini panties... on the paradisiac beach of Kauai—an island that's all garden. Tunic sweater by Econ-Picone, of angora lambs wool, and nylon; $25. At Best & Co. Patchwork print bikini, right, to enliven the placid sands of Kauai. Adding another blaze of colour—a beaded medallion strung from a chain. Bikini by Florence Eiseman, of Helanca stretch nylon; about $26. At Bonwit Teller. Medallion, The Phoenix.

The picture of me in Hawaii that appeared in American *Vogue*

(David Bailey. Courtesy Vogue *© 1970 by The Condé Nast Publications Inc)*

Above: With Michael
at the Abbey Hotel
(David Steen)

With Thaddeus in
1981 *(David Steen)*

yet when he answered the phone I was in a state of shock and he sounded so surprised I could not think what to say.

'I can remember an awful lot about you,' I said, improvising wildly, 'but I can't remember your feet.' (Not that I had ever noticed his feet.)

'My feet?' He sounded astonished.

'That's right,' I said. 'Your feet.'

He was silent, digesting this curious, mind-boggling conversation.

'OK,' he finally said. 'I've only got a big toe on my right foot.'

'No little toes?'

'No little toes.'

I laughed. I thought he was joking. But later I discovered it was true. He had lost his toes when his foot was crushed between two boats when he was in the Marines. This extraordinary conversation ended with me telling Jordan that I would ring him again when I got back to New York.

'Great,' he said. 'I look forward to it.'

I stayed with Felice for three days, calming down; and as she had suggested, I had dinner with Terry. It was ghastly. He never mentioned marriage again, thank God, and I forced myself to tell him that there was another man whom I wanted to get to know better. He asked no questions. He just sat there with his face set, the blue eyes staring at me, as beautiful as ever. But the magic had gone.

'You'll ring in a week's time?' he said when we parted.

'I'll ring,' I promised.

Back in New York I booked into a rather expensive hotel. The minute I had put my bags down I rang Jordan again. I think he was rather startled. This was not exactly surprising, as he was being catapulted into a situation he had not even considered. I realized that he had been hurt by Ali McGraw and was in no great hurry to get involved with another woman. I was the one making the running. I stayed at the hotel for a while and, very sweetly, Jordan paid for it. I did not ask him to, but it was his nature to do the gallant thing. I had not completely severed relations with

Stamp, and I still had not slept with Jordan when I made the promised phone call a week later.

The conversation was brief.

'It's me,' I said.

'Jean. Is everything OK?'

I took a deep breath. 'I'm not coming back, Terry.'

There was a long silence. Then he did break down – the only time I remember that happening. His voice faltered. 'Are you sure?' he asked, and I knew he was near to tears.

'I'm certain,' I said.

He said no more. He just hung up.

I was ringing from Jordan's flat. Being there had given me the courage to make the call. I put down the phone gently and took another deep breath to cancel threatening tears. I felt a kind of sweet sadness. It was over. I had once been so besotted, so enamoured of him, and now everything I had once felt had drained away. I could get on with my own life again.

I decided to stay in New York. My official reason was that there was more work for me in the United States and that the Yardley tour was coming up. My personal reasons were that I had made up my mind to move into Jordan's big three-bedroomed apartment on East 35th Street. He was not quite ready for me to move in on his life, and he did not exactly ask me. But I was not going to let him get away. I waited for the right moment. It was curious that I was so forward, because it would not be true to say that I was in love with him. I did come to care for him a lot later, when I discovered what an extremely nice person he was, but at the start it was sheer physical attraction. There is no doubt that I was the keen one. He liked me well enough, but he was not looking for a new relationship.

Then, a day or two after my final call to Stamp, he half-suggested that it would make more sense if I moved in with him. I didn't mess about. I immediately booked out of the hotel and arrived at his apartment with my bits and pieces of baggage. As usual I was travelling light.

And that night I found out that he hadn't been joking about his right foot.

Only one toe.

I luxuriated in living in a proper home with a proper partner again, and I enjoyed finding out about this new culture I had manoeuvred myself into. I did not know New York that well, and living with a New Yorker showed me the city in a whole different light. We went to different places – Italian restaurants in Little Italy, and to the famous P.J. Clarke's bar round the corner from the apartment. P.J. Clarke's was meant to look like a pub and failed miserably. I loved going to Elaine's, which in those days was the Langan's of New York. It was always full of celebrities and was presided over by Elaine herself – an outsized lady with an equally outsized personality to match. People like Norman Mailer and Woody Allen went there. The atmosphere and the Italian food were wonderful.

Jordan's outlook on life was different from mine. He was not insecure, nor was he impressed with me – which came as a relief. In his eyes I was not that famous or that beautiful, since his work had accustomed him to fame and beauty. I might have fallen for him with a bump, but his feelings for me grew slowly. And that was good.

The smallest, strangest things can sometimes cement a relationship. I made him a pair of needlepoint slippers and, because he liked the sun, moon and stars, I thought I would put them on his feet so he would not have to look up to see them. I cut out the shape of his feet and then drew the design. The slippers themselves were navy blue embroidered in bright orange, red and yellow. The finished result was un-chic and unprofessional, but somehow they looked good and he was really touched by all the trouble I had taken with them. I think the slippers were one of the things that helped him to fall in love with me. I know he came to love me in the end.

I liked his apartment and I was happy living there. Again it was different from anything I had been used to. It had wooden floors and a lot of art nouveau decoration, there were books and music, and the effect was aesthetically pleasing and spacious. Ali McGraw had decorated it, and being a stylist she knew where to buy lovely, unusual fabrics. It never bothered me that she had been responsible for the decor of the apartment since I always saw it as Jordan's home, though I admit I did get irritated when I came across pressed flowers and romantic mementoes in his dictionary. Pressed flowers in such a functional book seemed odd to me.

I started reading more and I talked to Jordan a lot. I found I could talk to him and he would discuss things with me. This was something new in my life. We used to go out to the movies all the time – about three or four times a week. It was all such a change from Stamp, and I was happier than I had been in a long, long time.

Jordan was good for me – very comforting, a mature man who taught me a lot. I was always wanting to learn and he was older and could teach me. I remember him saying to me, 'Where's your imagination? You haven't got any.' I had been insular for so long, and this change of pace was good for me. With his encouragement I began going to museums and art galleries. I wanted to 'culturize' myself and think about what I was going to do with my life. It was occurring to me that perhaps I could do something in the art world. I was now completely bored with modelling. In London Geoffrey had given me a passing acquaintance with antiques, *Privilege* had reawakened my interest in paintings, and now in New York it was being stimulated again.

I had not been in New York long when that wretched film caught up with me. I thought I had left it behind in England, but now here it was showing downtown. I did not mind so much as in Britain, because I always felt much more anonymous in America. I begged Jordan not to go to see it, but he sneaked off without telling me when I was on a Yardley tour. He was polite about it – justly, since it was a well-intentioned film. But I have to admit he was noncommittal about my performance!

Apparently Warren Beatty also went to see *Privilege* when it arrived in the States. My agent said that Beatty was in New York and he wanted to talk to me about a film part. At that time I had not completely given up the idea of being an actress – there was always a chance that next time I would be better – so I agreed to go to see him. Beatty was what they call 'hot' in the film business. He had just made *Bonnie*

172

and Clyde, and everyone wanted to star with him. Intrigued, I took myself off to the hotel on Park Avenue where he was staying. A porter escorted me up to his room where he was waiting for me, looking all blue-eyed, beautiful and beguiling – but I had been through all that with Terry.

He sat me down on the sofa and settled himself next to me. Then the phone rang. He picked it up, stretched himself out with his head on my lap and just stayed there. I was amazed, sitting there with his dark head in my lap, waiting for the phone call to end. But one call followed another, and even when the phone remained silent he stayed exactly where he was, looking soulfully up into my face while we talked. He was obviously not afraid to come on strong. I acted as if his behaviour was normal. I wasn't going to give him any satisfaction. I sat there stifling laughter so as not to wound his Casanova ego and thinking to myself that no doubt most of the time these tactics worked with women. He was good-looking to the point of prettiness. 'You are being silly, you know,' I said eventually, but he took no notice. We then had a brief, pointless conversation about films which made it clear that Warren had only summoned me to his presence out of curiosity (and probably as another notch on the bedpost). Since I was not responding, he suddenly jumped to his feet.

'Hey,' he said. 'I have to get down to Columbia Pictures. Like to come?'

Slightly flattered to be asked, I said OK, but as we went out of the room he made one last play. He got hold of my arm and tried to pull me into the bedroom.

'You must be joking,' I said and this time I did laugh. He gave me a quick sharp look, realized there was nothing doing, and had the grace to laugh himself before giving me a friendly pat. He was not in the least rebuffed or offended. Obviously attempted conquest was a game he did not care if he won or lost – since according to a string of Hollywood ladies' memoirs he usually won. Whether I had said yes or no, it was all the same to him. So, instead of a bed, we shared a pleasant, chatty walk to Columbia Pictures on a sunny New

York afternoon. I never did make a film with him, though he came into my life again much later.

Jordan, like most New Yorkers, liked to get away at the weekend so we rented houses in the summer. There was one in Newhope, Pennsylvania, and another in Woodstock in upstate New York. Bob Dylan lived there, and there the hippie culture flourished. Perhaps it was because I had little imagination or because I had been brought up on a farm that I could never understand all the fuss these sophisticated New Yorkers made about the country. The first thing they did on arrival was to get stoned on pot, and then they sat around saying how beautiful it all was. As I was not into drugs it all seemed a bit excessive to me.

Eventually we bought a house near New Milford in Connecticut. I put up £6000 towards it – which Jordan gave me back when we parted. I also bought a lot of furniture, including a Queen Anne rolltop desk, shipped over from Geoffrey Bennison. The house was white clapboard and had a pleasant swimming pool. If I was not modelling I would drive out and stay there while Jordan was working.

We used to have his kids at the weekends. Lisa was ten, and Ali was eight. Lisa was quite beautiful with long black hair and topaz eyes. She was also very spoilt. They lived in Greenwich Village with their mother and they were bright, zappy kids. I enjoyed having them with us – it was a challenge. What was odd was that I was jealous of Lisa and she was jealous of me, but we still had a good relationship. In some curious way we were drawn to each other. She was very close to Jordan and openly affectionate. This was the first time that I had encountered Jewish sensuality. Jordan was a very sensual person: even his fingertips were sensual when he touched me, however lightly, and there he was living with me, this inhibited English woman who was not a 'toucher' at all. Jordan would hug and kiss his kids, and they would hug and kiss me. We would go to the cinema and Lisa would sit on my lap and wiggle her little bum and put her arms up round my neck. They were such sensual people, and I felt out of it because his friends all used to hug each other. I used to envy the way they talked and hugged and quarrelled and carried on. I was not, and am not, like that, and there was no way I could pretend to be.

They called me Jordan's goy girl. I went to bar mitzvahs and Jewish weddings with him, and everyone was kissing everyone else. And they were all so little. His mother was barely five feet tall. They would kiss me all the time, and because I was so much taller than all of them I was for ever bending down for the obligatory peck on the cheek. All the woman had false eyelashes and hair backcombed sky-high and they were constantly arguing and bitching at each other.

Such a strange culture! It was quite a shock. Sometimes it jarred, and sometimes I liked it. In turn they did at times resent the fact that I was not Jewish. 'Why aren't you marrying a nice Jewish girl?' his mother would say to him. His first wife had been Jewish, but as I wasn't thinking of marrying Jordan they didn't have a problem.

I had been with Jordan for only a couple of weeks when the time came to earn all this money from Yardley that Felice had arranged for me. The first of the two tours was scheduled for the autumn of 1967, visiting big towns in different states. Yardley had cleverly latched on to swinging London – the town (close run by Liverpool) where every Beatlemaniac kid in the States yearned to be. In the States at that time anything British was best. There was little more traditionally British on the market than Yardley's Old English Lavender, but the company were aiming for a more modern image and attempting to sell their products to American teenagers.

Felice had negotiated for me to have a friend with me all the time, so Valerie Wade and I travelled together, all expenses paid. In addition Yardley were providing someone employed by them to look after me.

I woke up the morning we were leaving for the first stop – Philadelphia – feeling absolutely dreadful. I could hardly lift my head from the pillow it was pounding so much. I ached from head to foot and I could not stop sneezing.

'I think I've got the flu,' I croaked to Valerie.

'Oh, my God!' she said, and got on the phone to Yardley's.

They were not exactly sympathetic as they had the plane booked, the press waiting in Philadelphia, interviews lined up and hundreds of kids coming to meet me that evening.

'There's no question of not going,' they told me. I was going to have to stagger through it. At least they did send round a doctor who gave me a vitamin B injection before saying that was the best he could do for me.

We landed at Philadelphia and I left the plane on wobbly legs. The first thing I saw through my streaming eyes was this girl coming towards me. She wore a brilliant raspberry pink trouser suit which hurt my aching head. The trouser legs were much too short and ended halfway up her ankles. She had these wonderful bosoms, of which she was justifiably proud, advancing ahead of her (I discovered later she was a size 42). The ensemble was finished off by big dangly earrings. I watched her walking towards me. 'Golly!' I whispered to Valerie. 'Is this the American idea of swinging London?'

Her name was Anne Toye, and she took one look at me and spotted that all was not well. She hustled me into a car, straight to the hotel and to my room, where she got me an aspirin.

'Now there must be someone you want to talk to,' she said. 'Can't I get your boyfriend on the phone?'

I felt too poorly to talk to anyone and said so, but Anne turned out to be fantastic. She was an English girl regarded by the Americans as possessing the perfect British image. Perhaps she did. She did not care what people thought of her or how she dressed. She was comfortable in her own skin; a terrific, gutsy, energetic girl and very protective of me, just as Felice was. In those days I had a quality that seemed to make other women want to protect me. Once I learned how to look after myself, those relationships melted away. It was as if those who protected me had needed me as much as I needed them.

I did not particularly enjoy the Yardley tour. I had to appear nightly on stage in a theatre following on the heels of a half-hour slide show about swinging London. I was announced with a fanfare before making my entrance. Anne Toye sat on the stage with me and we did a bit of banter. Then members of the audience (several hundred teenagers) asked questions. Anne was brilliant at keeping it all going. There was usually an actor travelling with us. As well as the swinging London slides, Yardley put on a show with films of the Monkees or other pop groups to keep the teenagers happy.

The absurdity of the situation – trying to sell these youngsters the idea of using Yardley hair products – was that my own hair had started falling out when I was filming *Privilege* and was continuing to get thinner and thinner. It had gone from being very thick to so horribly thin that I had to hang my head upside down to blow dry it and brush out what little there was in an attempt to make it look more generous. I kept hoping the sponsors would not notice. I think maybe the problem was caused by stress, or perhaps it had something to do with the Pill.

It made me fairly neurotic, but Anne, Valerie and I managed to get a bit of a laugh out of the situation. We never saw anything of the towns we visited, but stayed in the hotel most of the time, creating our own little home from home and sending down for club sandwiches with French fries and endless pots of tea. Most of the time we did not even know which town we were in. They all blended into a comfortable blur. But I do remember we went to see *Gone with the Wind* in Denver, and the three of us just sat there and cried our eyes out. It was lovely!

Anne was much more popular with the American males than I. Indeed, on one occasion when we got off the plane and they saw her magnificent bosom they were convinced she was what they had been waiting for. They immediately started photographing her.

'Stop it! I'm not Jean Shrimpton,' she told them, pointing vigorously in my direction.

'Aw! You're kidding,' they said, and went on taking photographs.

Sometimes they didn't recognize us at all. When we left the plane at some stop in Texas there was a little group waiting for us, all lined up on the tarmac with a huge bouquet of shrimp-coloured roses. They missed us completely. We walked past them and left them gawping at the plane steps. When there was no one left to get off the plane and the cleaners were getting on we found them scurrying behind us, trying to catch up. I'm afraid we were giggling.

Off duty, I never looked like a model. Valerie, who is dark and exotic and stylish, could have passed, but both of us were going through a hippie period. I wore flared suede trousers below one of those Mongolian lamb jackets with the terrible stitching that were all the rage. Heaven knows why. The Mongolians never got the hang of curing the skins, and how they stank! Under this smelly layer I wore a satin shirt à la Ossie Clark. The Americans were so old-fashioned then that they did not understand the way we dressed at all. American model girls would have put on a hat and presented themselves. Val and I travelled looking like hippies – pretty hippies admittedly, though Anne was vaguely more conventional in a flash kind of way.

Those tours were relentless and exhausting. I would do as many as nine interviews in one day as well as a couple of television slots, some radio interviews and then a full-scale press conference for the local newspapers. I hated being interviewed, because I do not like talking about myself. It was exceedingly tedious having to say the same thing over and over again, particularly as I did not believe what I was spouting – I disliked endorsing something I did not believe in. I was used to modelling clothes for editorial features but I never personally endorsed any garment I wore. The picture was pretty, the price was printed and the reader could take it or leave it. Pushing a product was different. I was selling things to little girls who probably did not need them, and I did not feel right about it. I did everything I was paid for most diligently but without much enthusiasm. If I had needed confirmation that it was time to get out of this life, I had found it.

I used to enrage the Yardley people by saying to the kids: 'You have nice young skin (or pretty hair). Just leave it alone.' Not surprisingly, I was in deep trouble. I was supposed to be selling Yardley hair products, not putting the paying customers off. Twiggy, whose career as a personality was well on its way, was advertising their cosmetics. I might have been more enthusiastic about the eye products since the only make-up I ever used was mascara and eyeshadow, but Yardley had turned me down for those – because of my bags. Twiggy and I never met on these tours, but she was much more famous than me in New York and the Americans practically mobbed her on the streets. But our careers had little in common.

The Yardley reps did try to control me. One, a tall lanky American in the James Stewart mould, was called Marty and there was a woman called Jackie. Valerie and I did not like them much, and they did not have much control over us. It is not really surprising that I never did the third-year tour. Two were enough for Yardley, who were fed up with me by then.

Back in New York, modelling came as a relief. I was doing something I was good at, comfortable and competent in my own world. I worked most of the time with Avedon and Penn, and nearly always for *Vogue*. New York was becoming home, except for the occasional bout of home-sickness when I wanted my mother, the farm, London and my English friends. But I was having a good time. In the modelling world we were always being invited to parties through the various photographers' studios. Model girls would check with each other where the action was that evening, and no formal invitation was required. Under a sort of 'rent-a-model' system we could be at a party every night if we chose, though I do not doubt that we were invited simply as decoration.

The invitation that I received to Teddy Kennedy's birthday party was rather more formal. It was addressed to me personally and came through my old friend David McEwen. I took Jordan as my partner for what was a sit-down dinner party at the big Park Avenue house belonging to Jean Shriver, Teddy's sister and wife of Sergeant Shriver. As usual I did not have much in the way of clothes, and I wore an Ossie Clark hippie-style outfit. It consisted of a low-cut satin jacket in red, black and white over black flared

crêpe trousers. The other women were much more formally
dressed.

The guest list was impressive and catholic: the econo-
mist John Kenneth Galbraith, Lauren Bacall, Peter Glenville,
Lee Bouvier (Jackie Onassis's sister), the odd fashion editor,
the Kennedy family *en masse*, plus Jordan and myself and many
others. The guests were on three big separate tables. I found
that I had been placed next to Teddy Kennedy while another
model called Anne Turkel (who was once married to Richard
Harris) was on his other side. Neither of us knew him and he
certainly did not know us. I sat quietly and watched. Teddy
Kennedy did most of the talking with Anne Turkel, who was
much more his type than I.

Halfway through the evening Teddy's wife Joan left the
party. She had an alcohol problem, and as I watched her
leave I thought that I, too, might have taken to the bottle if
my husband on his birthday was sitting next to two strange
women who had been asked merely because they looked
good. I felt terribly sorry for her. Teddy Kennedy professed
not to notice her departure while he chatted up Anne, but
perhaps he had his problems living with the reality of being
Jack Kennedy's brother. Often fame is not much fun.

I did get some spectacular invitations at the height of
my own fame, but I could never think why anyone asked me.
Disliking both crowds and strangers, I was not scintil-
lating company. I usually accepted the more exotic-
sounding invitations just for the hell of it. Sometimes
the results were farcical. I was given two tickets to
Rio de Janeiro – one for Jordan – hotel accommodation for
us both, all expenses paid, plus $1000 thrown in, just for
attending a socialite party. It sounded too good to turn
down, so we went. The joke was that, though we dutifully
appeared at the party, no one had the faintest idea who I
was – probably because I was wearing my one and only
simple evening dress. People never understood that the many
images I presented in glossy magazines bore no resemblance
to how I looked in the flesh. Therefore I was rarely
recognized.

Jordan and I did not stay long either at the party or in Rio itself. The fellow guests might not have known who I was, but the local press did. They were climbing up the hotel walls to peer in through our bedroom window.

By this time I had a new agent. With Felice in Los Angeles, my arrangement with John Heyman had drifted away. Anne Toye had introduced me to Mark McCormack, the American agent and entrepreneur. He had taken me on his books, and these well-paid personal appearances were coming through his office. Mark himself and the black actor/comedian Bill Cosby were judges with me at a Bunny Girl contest at the Playboy headquarters in Chicago. I did buy myself a new dress for that – a very tight Biba metallic tube which made me look as if I had bosoms. Even so, no way could I compete with the Bunnies. I remember I chose a black girl, and so did Bill Cosby. She won. I have to say I found him attractive, but he was not remotely interested in me. He was much more taken with my dark and exotic friend Valerie. Anyway, I had a terrible cold that night and was feeling so ill that all I wanted was to crawl into bed with a long, hot drink.

The 1969 Yardley tours encouraged me to make a conscious decision to give up modelling. I was tired, and it was a strain having to look good all the time. I had wanted to get to the top and I had done it. Avedon was the top in my estimation, and I worked for him continually. It was coming up to the start of a new decade. I was twenty-six and had been modelling for eight years; I had had a wonderful time, seeing the world, wearing beautiful clothes, meeting fascinating people and getting paid for it. I did not want to be second-best, and though no one was hovering in the wings to take my place it seemed more sensible to get out before the competition was baying at my heels. I think I was shrewd to pull back. I did not want to fight to stay on top. I had had a good run, and it was the right time to get out.

If I was going to quit modelling I felt I should change direction for something really worthwhile – something quite different from the one-dimensional life I was living. I was fed up with the excesses of success and a life where everyone was pigeonholed, wearing the same clothes, the same perfume and holding the same opinions.

But what was I going to do? I had lived with Jordan for two years, from 1967 to 1969, and it was getting to be decision time as far as he was concerned, too. The cultural differences between us did cause the relationship to suffer. I enjoyed Jewish New York for a while, but when we came to England together I felt uncomfortable.

Unfortunately Jordan sensed this. He was saddened by my inability to accept him in my own country, and he saw it as a great failure on my part – which it was. I knew I could never live in England with him, and equally I could never live indefinitely in New York. The relationship was doomed.

My feelings for him were beginning to change. I liked him as much as ever, but I was ripe to fall into the arms of another man of a totally different kind. I felt in an anarchistic mood, and an anarchist is exactly what I found.

— 8 —

While I was in this uncertain frame of mind, and when Jordan and I were in London, Francis Wyndham asked Valerie Wade and us out to dinner at my favourite restaurant, L'Etoile in Charlotte Street. We were already seated and studying the menu when Francis told us that he had invited another person.

'He's a writer called Heathcote Williams.'

Eventually Heathcote arrived. He was small and slight with the extremely curly hair of a satyr, restless brown eyes and an aggressive manner. He wore old trousers and a shirt with no tie, and he did not look too clean. He seemed to be held together with safety pins.

This intense-looking young man sat next to me. He established who I was and immediately launched into a diatribe which became a monologue before the evening was out. He had a surprisingly quiet but resonant voice, and he was relentlessly provocative to the point of rudeness. Yet somehow I was not offended. His conversation was fascinating. He attacked me throughout the entire meal. 'Fame is the first disgrace,' he informed me, adding that the thought was not his own but a Chinese proverb. He accused me of being a capitalist. He accused me of many things, all to do with fame, success, money and the triviality of the life I led. It was plain that he did not approve of the modelling world and yet most of what he was saying somehow struck a chord in me. I understood his polemics and was amused and enjoying myself. Little did he know that I agreed with him on most points, but I was not going to tell him so. At moments he was funny. 'All great men are dead or in the madhouse,' he announced. 'Oscar Wilde is dead. Omar Khayyám is dead. And I'm not feeling very well myself.' What was alarming was that I found him very attractive, and in spite of the flying insults I could tell that the attraction was mutual.

When we met it was early in 1970 and Heathcote was unknown except in the curious world of underground publishing. He was part of that late sixties' group of intellectual writers who saw it as their bounden duty to shock the world out of its complacency, using obscenity, blasphemy and antisocial behaviour as their weapons. It is ironic that, all these years later, Heathcote is finding the fame that he so deplored creeping up on him with his poetry about elephants and whales and dolphins. By identifying himself with threatened species he has happened upon causes which move people and do not offend as did so much of his work – particularly his attacks on Christ and religion – back in the early seventies.

I went back to New York with Jordan, but I did not forget Heathcote Williams.

I returned to London on my own about three months later on one of my regular trips to see my mother. I had borrowed a friend's flat since my house in Knightsbridge was rented out to André Previn and his then wife, Mia Farrow.

I had been in town a couple of days when Geoffrey Bennison rang to say he was throwing a party at his flat in Soho and would I come. I was not much of a one for parties, but I liked them when I came back to England – I was on my own, and they gave me the chance to see friends.

'It'll be lovely, darling,' he told me on the phone. 'All the most interesting people are coming.'

'Interesting people' rang a loud bell. 'Geoffrey,' I said, 'would you ask Francis Wyndham to ask Heathcote Williams to come?'

'All right, dear, if you want me to.'

I put down the phone and brooded about the dangerous thing I had just done.

He came, and I knew for sure he was interested in me. The note that gave him away was that his hair smelt newly shampooed. He was definitely cleaner than he had been the previous time we met. He was still holding his shirt together with safety pins, but at least the shirt was not the same one.

It was a big party and I circulated and so did he, but we were never far from each other. We kept drifting into the same groups. I had a sense of anticipation. Something was going to happen. I was sure he would not leave without me, and no more did he. At about one in the morning he came over to me.

'I'm leaving,' he said. 'I'm going to the Arts Lab. Do you want to come?'

'What's that?'

'A sort of club. A place we put on plays.'

'OK,' I said.

We left the smoke and noise of the party and walked through Golden Square, where Geoffrey then lived, and into Soho proper. The lights of Raymond's Revue Bar still flashed, and night people drifted in the streets. Little was said as we walked. We were both rather shy and not very comfortable together – we were such an unlikely couple.

The Arts Lab was deserted when we got there.

'Everyone must have gone home,' he said, sounding disappointed.

It was an artistic commune, typical of the underground places that proliferated in London at the beginning of the seventies. It was completely outside my experience and I was interested. There were a series of dark and dingy rooms for poetry readings, and a small, primitive theatre where playwrights could try out their work. Heathcote explained that anyone was welcome to doss on the floor in a sleeping bag if they had nowhere else to go. I had the feeling that he might well have done this himself at some time. The place most certainly did not suffer from the excesses of success.

Since nothing was happening at the Arts Lab we drifted off into Soho. Heathcote said he wanted something to eat, and at about five o'clock in the morning he ate a horrible hard-boiled egg at a café. I had my usual cup of tea. He was in no hurry to go home since he had no home to go to. Heathcote didn't live anywhere. He sort of squatted ('Squat now while stocks last' was one of the maxims he painted on walls). His most regular resting-place was in the offices of *Transatlantic Review* – one of the era's magazines – for which he worked. It seemed there was a bedroom there which the owner was quite happy for him to use. He was very unconventional. He appealed to me because he had nothing and wanted nothing, and I had stumbled upon him when I was aware that everyone I knew, including myself, had too much. Jordan and I both lived lucrative lives. Every time Jordan put on a shirt it was clean, and the idea of him holding his clothing together with safety pins was unthinkable.

Heathcote's total rejection of things material was very attractive to me. He seemed to be anti-everything – Church, police, family, money, monarchy. Name it and he did not approve. He was an espouser of way-out causes and out of step with most of the rest of the world. He talked enthusiastically, telling me his dreams. Dawn was tingeing the sky when we parted. As I climbed exhausted into a taxi, he called: 'I'll be on the Mall on Saturday. The Queen is going down. We're going to throw a lot of money about so everyone's bums will be in the air when she goes by. Want to come?'

That, I thought, sounded pretty stupid. I was not going to become a petty irritation to the Queen, but heard myself saying that I would try to be there. Though I had no serious intention of going, I felt I might as well leave my options open.

I spent the weekend thinking about him and resisting the urge to go to the Mall. On the Monday morning I phoned the *Transatlantic Review* office. I was due back in America in a couple of days, so it was now or never.

'I just rang to say I'm sorry I didn't make the Mall,' I told him, 'and that I'm going back to New York in a couple of days. . . .'

He chipped in immediately. 'Can we meet?'

I felt ridiculously pleased. 'Why don't we have lunch?' I suggested.

'If you like,' he said.

I went round to the offices of *Transatlantic Review*. He was sitting on the windowsill, watching, waiting for me to come. He jumped up the minute I came into his view and hurried to meet me, wild hair on end as if fired by electricity.

He paid for an ordinary, hurried lunch at a café he patronized round the corner. We both knew we had better things to do than eat. Then, without any discussion, we returned to my borrowed flat and went to bed.

I told myself that all this unseemly haste was because I needed to know if there was anything going for us. Unfortunately there was. The moment he touched me I knew I was in trouble. What there was between Heathcote and me was very physical.

But it was all there was between us. I found I had scant sympathy for his more extreme views and he despised my way of life, but we were battling with a mutual physical attraction. We spent the next two days either wandering the streets together or in the bedroom of the flat. And then I went back to New York where Jordan was waiting for me.

I wanted to try to forget what had happened, knowing that any relationship between Heathcote and me could only be disastrous. My intention was to try to purge it from my memory, but I could not: Heathcote was lodged firmly in my mind. I found myself thinking about him constantly. It was a bad time. I knew that I had done something stupid and disloyal; it was hard to live with the knowledge that I had been unfaithful to Jordan. My betrayal coloured my relationship with him: I found it impossible to be normal, and he was aware that something was wrong. I really tried to make it work, but the effort seemed beyond me. I could not shed this fierce infatuation for a totally unsuitable man.

Heathcote wrote me a long letter in which, to give him his due, he warned me that our relationship would be terribly painful. 'I cannot bear domestic situations,' he wrote. 'I have no need of friends or family. I can't bear any ties. I don't want relationships.'

I suppose I did not entirely believe what he was saying. The physical attraction was so strong that I believed he would want to be with me. But it was beyond him to commit himself, and I had to learn the truth of that for myself.

Three months later Jordan had some work in Paris and we travelled back to Europe together. I opted to stay in England, saying that I wanted to see my parents; I also had a bad abscess on a tooth which needed treatment from my own dentist. I was going to be in London for a week and then join Jordan in Paris.

The minute I was on my own I rang Heathcote.

Again I went to the *Transatlantic Review* offices to meet him and again he was sitting on the windowsill waiting for me to arrive. He was truly pleased to see me. He had feelings for me, but what he felt did not sit easily with his extreme views. Also, he was confused because I was not what he expected. I did not lead a pampered life buying clothes and visiting the hairdresser's, which surprised him. As his aggression disappeared I perceived a childlike quality in him. Our relationship became gentle and simple and there was an innocence about it – but only at the beginning.

We spent the week together, and then I flew to join Jordan in Paris at L'Hotel. I knew I could not continue this double life any longer, and I had to tell Jordan that my feelings had changed. The trouble was that I was too much of a coward to tell him about Heathcote. It was the Stamp scene all over again. I knew he would never understand – and in any case, since I had no idea whether Heathcote and I were going to be together, there was nothing positive to tell. Except, of course, that I had been unfaithful, but I was not going to tell him that.

In the splendid room at L'Hotel I broached the subject. We had been out to dinner and I was dreading the moment when we would have to share a bed. I had tried to be sensible, but I could not be sensible any longer.

'Jordan,' I said abruptly. 'Look. I'm sorry. But it's not working, is it?'

'It doesn't appear to be.' His voice was cold, and he stood looking at me, his tie in his hand, clean, tidy, glossy and elegant – so different from Heathcote – waiting for me to elaborate.

'It's nothing to do with you,' I said. 'It's the homesickness. I can't bear it. I don't want to live in New York any longer. I don't want to go back there.'

'And what else is pulling you back to England?' he asked.

I shook my head. 'Nothing else,' I lied, and took refuge in silence.

He was beginning to be angry. 'It's about time you grew up,' he said. 'You're pathetic – acting like an immature, stupid young girl.'

'I know,' I muttered, and whimpered that I couldn't help it.

Jordan thought I could help it, and he told me so. 'Why can't you work at a relationship instead of clearing off when things get difficult?' His voice was rising. 'I love you. I'm prepared to work at it. Why can't you? We've been happy enough together up until recently. What is the matter?'

'I need my freedom.'

He snorted. 'Freedom! You do exactly what you like. You go back to England whenever you want. Do I ask what you do with your time in New York? Do I ever restrict you? It's ridiculous. A woman of your age breaking up a good relationship over homesickness. You're not a child any more. There has to be more to it than that.'

We had a terrible night. The more pathetic I became, the angrier he was. I suppose he knew I was not telling the whole truth, and I could not bring myself to do that. What was true was that I did not want to go back to New York. I wanted to stay in England where Heathcote was.

I would never have stayed permanently with Jordan, but he was right. I was being ridiculous, and I deserved every harsh word he directed at me. I had hurt him, and I knew that I was hurting myself a great deal more, and that did not make it any better.

Jordan discovered, as Bailey and Stamp had, that I cannot be swayed once my mind is made up. I left L'Hotel first thing in the morning and got myself to the airport and on to the first plane back to London. I was terribly upset. I cried when I said goodbye to a grim-faced Jordan, I cried in the taxi, and I cried all the way over in the plane.

I was still crying at London Airport when some man came and asked for my autograph. He stood there in front of me, the autograph book in his hand. With tears streaming down my face I said: 'Go away.' He didn't. He stood there looking at me until I snatched his pen and signed.

I got back to the flat I had borrowed in a terrible state. Heathcote was there but he was writing, deeply engrossed in his work. He took absolutely no notice of either my arrival or my tear-stained face. He barely said 'Hello', but just kept on writing. He acknowledged the fact I was back only when he was good and ready. I was certain I was in deep trouble then. Not for the first time I asked myself: What have I done?

What I had done was walk out on a nice dependable man. And for what kind of man?

Since I could not move back into my own home until André Previn's lease ran out, I rented a place in Camberwell from Geoffrey's manager, Terry Green. Heathcote and I went there for a month. Jordan took it badly; he called me and wrote to me. He was sad. He had grown to love me, and once he was over his anger he tried to persuade me to come back. Eventually I confessed that I was having an affair with the strange person he had met at dinner that night. I told him I knew it was crazy but that it was beyond my control. I said I would pick up my few bits of personal pieces when I was next in New York.

Of course, I was starting to swing from one side of the pendulum to the other. I already felt immensely guilty at the amount of money I was able to earn. I also felt lucky, which was strange because I was not really happy. I felt I had too much. I was quite good-looking and I was reasonably intelligent, and people seemed to like me. I was forever dismayed that life is so unfair to so many people. Therefore I was an easy target for Heathcote's total, all-embracing kind of anarchy. It is important to say that I was never party to any of the more extreme things he did; I always drew back. He had a life that was quite separate from me; we rarely, if ever, went out together.

I never really *believed* in any of what he preached. The peace-and-love society struck no chords in me, nor did the rejection of old-fashioned values. Where they could and did get at me was through my guilt about my money. I shared my money until it had gone. I do not regret it, even though I realize that all that cash could have gone to much more worthy causes.

Before I had left New York American *Vogue* had booked me for a job in Hawaii with Bailey. The other model was Penelope Tree, an American girl who was living with Bailey at the time. This did not bother me. Rivers of water had gone under quite a few bridges by then and I had recently worked with Bailey a lot. He knew Stamp and Jordan, and he had been married to Catherine Deneuve. We were comfortable with each other and there was no embarrassment. And Penelope Tree was far too sophisticated to be concerned about an old girlfriend appearing on the same assignment.

I did not want to leave Heathcote, but I had to work. I flew from London with a stopover in Los Angeles, and the journey was horrendous. Yet in a way the endlessness of the flights was almost a blessing: this was the break I needed from all the dramas. I arrived shattered, to find Bailey and Penelope already there. *Vogue* suggested that I have a day off to recover from jetlag and get some suntan as well. It was October and, though my skin was pale, it was only a question of topping up. We were photographing summer beach clothes – lots of jungle prints which matched the scenery and looked better with a tan. One of the problems of being a model is that clients don't want a suntan for cosmetic work or magazine covers, but they expect instant bronze for shots of summer clothing.

I lay in the sun and thought about Heathcote, and accepted that I had done the only thing possible. The infatuation was too strong to ignore. And having forgiven myself for what I had done, I let myself enjoy Hawaii. Eating always creates enjoyment and pleasure for me, and here the food was wonderful. The hotel where we stayed presented huge tables full of fresh fruit and cooling drinks that were served all day. I kept trotting back for more pineapple and mango.

Back in London I resumed my strange relationship with Heathcote. The trouble was that, for someone practical and sensible like me, his beliefs were difficult to swallow. For example he believed, as some primitive peoples do, that madness is the highest form of intelligence.

'Madness means that the gods have taken possession of the person's mind,' he would say, 'and a man or woman must have a great mind when the gods have need of it. . . .' He was fascinated by the topic. 'If you go around London talking to yourself everyone says you are mad,' he would say. 'If you go around London talking to your wife and she's not listening, they say you are normal.' This statement had a certain indisputable logic about it.

While we were together Heathcote became obsessed by the story of a man who had crucified himself in Hampstead. He sought out the man and spent a lot of time talking to him. He wanted to write about the man's experience and eventually wrote a play called *The Local Stigmatic*. When he was young he had written a book on the speakers of Hyde Park and had lived rough with them in order to get the material. This was after he had been asked to leave Eton, which he said was the best thing that ever happened to him. He seemed to believe that living with the speakers had completed his education in a way that the most famous public school in the world could never have achieved. He had a rough ride at Eton. He had hated that great theatre of the upper classes and, being rebellious by nature, had gone completely the other way and become an anarchist.

His father was a QC and Heathcote had rebelled against everything he tried to do for him. It was an unresolved relationship as his father died before he could see his son's success. That, coupled with the Eton experience, had produced enormous aggression and anger in him.

He and I never really lived together. He was forever moving in and out as the mood struck him, but the offices of *Transatlantic Review* were fairly near and he stayed there most of the time. He did not spend much time with other people and only flitted in and out of the causes he espoused. In many ways he was much more of an observer than a true participant. He liked to watch how people reacted under pressure, and it was all stored away as material for his writing.

Our relationship was happy at times, mainly because it was so simple and did not go through any conventional patterns. He slept when he was tired and he ate when food appeared before him (he was never hungry), and did not care at all what it was he was eating. He did not actually raid rubbish bins but his eating habits were not that far removed. Very little troubled Heathcote. He had little money, but we did not indulge ourselves in a lifestyle that required a great deal. For me the attraction was his disinterest in material things.

At the time we were together he finished writing a play called *AC/DC* that was put on at the Royal Court Theatre. The theatre management did admit that it was the weirdest play they had ever staged. Heathcote was attacking the media and the culture of fame, using psychedelic language and the hallucinations of madness. His intention was to attack what he called psychic capitalism. *AC/DC* was very hard to read, mad and cryptic. Many people found it difficult to understand – including the judges of the *Evening Standard* award for the most promising new playwright. Though baffled, they said that his was a genuine voice of the future and awarded him the prize.

I had one of his plays printed and gave some money to the Soho Poly Theatre which was performing his works. It was a time when everyone was meant to share everything. The difficulty was that I was the only one who had anything to share. Heathcote did make a small wage and was friendly with wealthy people from his schooldays. Lord Peregrine Eliot (now the Earl of St Germans) was a particular friend and we often went to stay at Port Eliot, his estate in Cornwall.

193

Heathcote could always get a bed simply because he was unusual and entertaining. He was a very good conjuror and there was always someone who would put him up in return for his obscure but brilliant conversation and the childish pleasure of watching him perform conjuring tricks.

His attitudes did cause some problems. Occasionally he would bring home the odd tramp. He picked up a down-and-out on Paddington Station on one occasion when we were meeting Francis Wyndham to go to a private showing of the film *Kes*. Heathcote turned up with this middle-aged man in a rather greasy old raincoat who sat with us through the showing. Afterwards we all went on to Mr Chow's extremely smart Chinese restaurant in Knightsbridge for dinner as Francis's guests, and Heathcote insisted that his new-found friend came too. Happily Francis was highly amused. Heathcote also suggested we take him home for the night, but there I drew the line.

Along with 150,000 other people we went to Shepton Mallet for the Glastonbury Pop Festival in 1970, and it was definitely the wrong place for me – quite a few people were walking about with no clothes on and I reckon that, generally speaking, people look a lot better with their clothes on. Heathcote and I shared a tent, but half the time he was not there. There were thousands of people littering the countryside, sleeping in tents or caravans or just on the springy ground in sleeping bags, staring up at the wide and starry sky. They were looking for UFOs and insisted that they had seen them.

I was twenty-seven and felt I was too old to be sleeping in a tent surrounded by half-naked people. I felt totally out of place. Heathcote (fully clothed, thank God) was wandering about gathering material while I mooched around on my own. Fortunately the weather was beautiful, which made it less squalid. All day we were surrounded by the sounds of pop music. It was a hippie experience of which I never felt part. I couldn't relate to this love and peace which were the *raison d'être* of the festival. Perhaps that was a pity. The people who went to Glastonbury went in a spirit of goodwill; they were having a peaceful time. There was the odd drug freak-out, but people were getting on with each other and for many it must have been an unforgettable experience. My problem was my incurable dislike of crowds, and Glastonbury was very crowded indeed.

I stayed a couple of days and then decided to make my departure. Heathcote said nothing when I told him I was off. He was perfectly content to be on his own.

Some light relief – and a fresh injection of funds – came into my life when Bailey rang me to say that *Vogue* wanted the two of us for a job in Egypt. I accepted with alacrity. It was for ten days, sailing up the Nile. I was the only model, but Bailey was taking Penelope Tree along with him for the trip. Polly Hamilton, the *Vogue* fashion editor, was also with us.

We had a marvellous time. We flew to Cairo, where we boarded a Nile boat. There were no other passengers aboard but there was a highly efficient crew. I found it wonderfully relaxing. Most of the photography went on ashore at places like Luxor, where we photographed at the Temple of Karnak and the tomb of Rameses, but once the work was done we did nothing but drift peacefully along the river watching biblical scenery unfold. In this primitive culture men fished and farmed along the banks much as they had done for thousands of years.

The highlight for me was visiting the Pyramids. Bailey photographed me on a camel – a most odd feeling, since it rolled like a drunken sailor. I was then given the opportunity to ride an Arab stallion. It was the first time I had been on a horse for many years; this one was powerful and fast, yet a joy to ride. I galloped at breathtaking speed into the great expanse of desert ahead. When I wheeled to return, pounding towards the ancient structures of the Pyramids, the sun was setting ahead, leaving a dramatic pattern of black triangles on rose-coloured sand. It was one of the finest moments of my life.

Back in London I bought a new house. I sold Montpelier Place for £25,000 and purchased a larger house in Darnley Terrace in Holland Park, an area that Heathcote liked. It cost £22,000, which left me with a little cash remaining. But the extra cash was not entirely my reason for moving – money was still plentiful at that stage. The new house had a study, and I believed that if Heathcote had somewhere to write he might stay around a little more. He had been complaining that he could not stand living in such a domestic way. In fact, buying the house made no difference to our lives, except it was dawning on me that the more I tried to accommodate Heathcote, the more threatened he felt and the more he shied away from me.

Shortly after I bought Darnley Terrace he took a room of his own in Lancaster Road in North Kensington. At that time this area was the home of hippies, inhabited by those who sincerely believed that the world was about to be transformed. There were poets and playwrights galore congregating in the pubs and new wine bars. As the swinging sixties faced up to the seventies, new music, new drugs, new fashions and a great deal of new thinking appeared. The spirit of irreverence was abroad. Heathcote was to create a commune in Notting Hill which he called the Albion Free State. And he declared UDI (not that anyone took a blind bit of notice). He was becoming more outrageous all the time. I saw less and less of him and had little idea of what was going on in his life. Not long after this he ran a 'squat' estate agency, giving out addresses of unused houses and offering to jemmy doors open should breaking in prove difficult. Some of his closest friends were alarmed to find their homes on his books. Heathcote never showed favouritism.

In a way his moving out was a relief. People were coming and going at Darnley Terrace all the time when he was there. There were usually two or three people at the place: he did not exactly encourage open house, but he did not discourage it either. When he was working with people on underground magazine projects they would all stay – but they did not contribute to the household expenses, not even towards the telephone calls they made. I suppose they couldn't. I was the only one who had any money. I did not take too much notice at first, but when the money began to run out and I was forced to look for work I began to think differently.

Looking back, it was a hurtful period. I was paying for everything, but the people who sponged off me had no regard for me at all – it was not a healthy situation. It was such a cushy number for them to stay with me. The house was not grand, but everything they needed was there: food, wine, a bed and the all-important telephone. I felt like a leper. I had no rapport with any of these people, who were a different, alienating species, full of theories of how the world should be run without the slightest intention of paying their way through it. Not that they were after my money. They had no regard for money as long as someone else supplied it. In the end I became sadly disillusioned.

I had picked wrongly again. I just kept picking the wrong men, and yet I stayed with Heathcote for a couple of years before his flits became permanent. By this time he did not want to be with me and I did not particularly want to be with him. My tolerance for his way of life and the infatuation I suffered had both gone. I had begun to ask myself what I had originally seen in him, and I came to the conclusion that he aroused some sort of maternal instinct in me. There was something in his face that could occasionally remind me of someone from my own family, though I was never quite sure who. And at certain rare times there was a still-lingering innocence in his face and demeanour. I sensed something troubled that needed protection, and it stirred my maternal instinct. I could see in him the lost and confused child that he must once have been.

But those feelings had faded, and it seemed to me that he was becoming alarmingly crazy. My suspicions were confirmed when he turned up at the house unexpectedly. He was pretty hyped up, though not from drugs – with Heathcote his own craziness was enough. I had been trying to listen to music when Heathcote appeared on the doorstep looking manic. I was not in the mood for him, but there was no way of getting rid of him if he had decided to stay. My welcome was chilly. He took no notice but barged into the house.

'I'm practising fire-eating,' he said, 'do you want to see?'

197

'No,' I said. 'I want to listen to some music.' I went over to the record player and began to put on some Mozart.

'Oh, come on. Don't you want to see?' he persisted, jigging up and down on the spot.

'I'm not interested in seeing any fire-eating.'

He ignored what I had said. 'Have you got any meths or paraffin?' he asked.

'No,' I said flatly.

He thought for a minute. 'You've got a can of petrol in the car,' he said, triumphantly. 'That'll do.'

He went rushing out of the front door and I put on my record and sat down again, wondering how I was going to get rid of him. It was to prove dramatically simple.

He took the can of petrol from the car and started to practise fire-eating. Unfortunately the wind was in the wrong direction and he caught on fire. I was horrified when he rushed back into the house, his satyr hair like a fiery halo, his clothes burning. He very sensibly threw himself on the sofa while I, like a fool, ran to the kitchen for water – which, I realized later, was not at all the right thing to do. When I came back he was rolling around on the sofa, where the cushions had put out most of the fire. The water I threw over him put out what few flames were left. Trembling, I then rang 999 for an ambulance. Happily it came quickly, since I had no idea of how to begin to deal with such burns. He made little fuss. Even in the hospital he was chatting up nurses and being ridiculous. He was quite high because of the stuff they gave him to kill the pain.

After he was safe in the hands of the hospital and I had been assured that the burns would heal, I sat down and thought seriously about what I should do next. The affair with Heathcote was burned out, in more ways than one. It was time to start again. I could not go on living on this knife edge any longer. But as I sat there, finally listening to the Mozart, a thought struck me. There was one thing one could say for Heathcote – he might have made me miserable and confused, but at least he was not boring.

198

— 9 —

Once I rediscovered anger and was able to bring my affair with Heathcote to an end I certainly did not miss him, but I was lonely and concerned about my life. The sense of confusion returned. It seemed to me that I had been marking time for the past two years. I needed something to do, some kind of break in the disaster area that my life seemed to be. Fortuitously, the Mark McCormack office rang and asked if I would go to New York for a week to make a commercial. I had no hesitation in accepting.

It was about two days before I was due to leave for the States when one of Heathcote's friends called at the house. I opened the front door to find a tall, thin young man with blue eyes and a hesitant manner standing on the doorstep.

'Hello, I'm Malcolm. Is Heathcote in?' he asked politely.

I shook my head. 'He doesn't live here any more. You should find him round at Lancaster Road.'

'Where's that?' he asked. 'Is it far?'

'No,' I said and explained how to get there.

'Thank you,' he said, and I noted that his smile was surprisingly sweet.

He went off to find Heathcote, but some time later he was back on the doorstep looking dejected. 'He's not there,' he said. 'You don't know where else he might be?'

I had no idea, but said he had better come in while I phoned around to see if I could find out. This young man seemed pleasant enough. He explained that he had just travelled up from Cornwall, and he looked tired and vulnerable. I sat him down and gave him a cup of tea and started phoning friends. The difficulty was that Heathcote was not only an adept conjuror – he was also brilliant at performing vanishing tricks. He could disappear from his known haunts for weeks at a time without telling anyone where he was. My phone calls unearthed no trace of him.

'Haven't you anywhere to stay?' I asked the young man.

'No,' he said. 'I thought . . .' he hesitated.

'You thought you'd stay with Heathcote.'

'Well, he usually finds me a bed.' He was embarrassed.

'Don't you have any money?'

He shook his head. 'No, but if you could just take a message for him . . .'

'Of course,' I said.

Another one of them without a penny! But this one had good manners, a pleasant speaking voice and considerable charm. I gave him another cup of tea. He was in a highly nervous state and seemed rather broken, as if something vital had snapped somewhere inside. He explained that he and Heathcote were friends and that he was a contributor to the *Transatlantic Review*. I listened to him, thinking that he was easy to talk to and rather gentle in his manner. I let him sit and talk. He was company, and I was lonely in the house on my own.

He was telling me how he had once worked as a male nurse in a mental hospital and how at present he was working for a Jungian analyst called John Layard. I found him interesting and on impulse heard myself saying: 'You can stay here if you like.'

His face lit up. 'Could I?'

'Why not? Heathcote's friends generally do,' I said ruefully.

He was a good house guest. His presence was unobtrusive and my impression of him had been right. He was quiet. I didn't mind having him about the place. I was a touch uneasy about how Heathcote would react to my having his friend in the house now he had gone – though heaven knew, it was none of his business any more.

Heathcote had not reappeared when I had to go off to New York, and I left Malcolm as a house sitter. I thoroughly enjoyed the trip. This was a rather unusual type of commercial that I had been booked for: with Richard Avedon photographing, it was shot like a small playlet. I had to arrive in Avedon's studio looking my normal windswept, waifish, ungroomed self and appear to be breathless. My one line was: 'Sorry, Dick, I'm late', at which point a team of hairdressers, dressers and make-up artists, using the advertiser's products, transformed me into a glamorous creature. Avedon himself was part of the cast, and the session was a lot of fun. I liked the fact that I was able to appear as myself for once. There were a series of these commercials, all of them on the transformation theme and each using a different top model of the day. Lauren Hutton was photographed in the dressing room while Ira Gallant did her hair. Anjelica Huston starred in another. Avedon himself appeared in them all. As far as I was concerned, apart from being pleased with the money it was a job which came at just the right moment.

After I had been gone about five days I rang home to make sure everything was all right. Malcolm answered, sounding distressed.

'Heathcote's been round,' he said. 'He came to collect some books and he found me in his work room. He's gone crazy. I am sorry, Jean. Should I go?'

'Of course not,' I said, savouring the irony of it. In Heathcote's book everything had to be shared, but he was not very good at sharing anything that invaded his working territory. It was not even his territory. He had made it clear he was not living in my house any more, therefore Malcolm had as much (or as little) right to be in the small study as anyone. Yet apparently Heathcote was incandescent with rage.

When I came back from New York Malcolm was still installed and I did not have the heart to turn him out. He was easy company, and as usual I could not face being on my own.

He was sweet and gentle, and when he crept into my bed I did not send him away from there either. His presence was cosy and comforting. After two years of a man with a wirewool personality I was in need of someone softer. I was not in love with Malcolm, but this rather precipitous arrangement seemed to suit us both.

I had only been back a few days when Heathcote reappeared. This creator of situations demanded that I choose between him and Malcolm. At that point there was nothing much to choose between either of them. I liked Malcolm a lot, but it was dawning on me that he himself was not entirely rational. The infatuation I had felt for Heathcote had gone and I knew that he was being manipulative: all he wanted was to see what would happen if I let him back in the house while Malcolm was there.

The three of us sat around the kitchen table discussing the bizarre situation Heathcote had created, although, since he had never been able to manipulate me, all the talking was basically done by the two men – I could have been the proverbial fly on the wall for all the notice they took of me. Their crazy dialogue went on for hours. Periodically they both descended into wild rages and then briefly became rational again. I felt I was shut up with a couple of lunatics.

When an overexcited Heathcote again demanded I choose between them for the sake of peace and quiet, I decided to settle for Malcolm. Then I said, with what was amazing firmness for me, 'I'd like you to go, Heathcote. You don't want to be here. You've taken a room somewhere else. Your whole life is tied up with doing other things and with your work. You don't really want to be with me, so would you please go away.'

He refused point-blank to leave the house. Observing how people behaved under pressure was just the kind of drama he liked. Finally in desperation I said to Malcolm: 'OK. If he won't go, we will.'

I gathered up a shaken Malcolm and we left Heathcote in total possession of No. 2 Darnley Terrace.

'Where now?' Malcolm asked nervously as we got into my car. Having won the day, he looked as if he was not sure it was worth the battle.

'Verity's. She'll put us up,' I said, slamming the gears in my irritation with the whole situation. I was trembling with both anger and anxiety.

'Who's Verity?'

'She runs the Soho Theatre.'

Verity Bargate, whose theatre had been one of my beneficiaries, was happy to put us up for the night. She was another sixties person, talented, sometimes mixed-up, who was a good friend. Sadly, she was to die young of cancer. But that night she gave Malcolm and I a roof and discussed the problem of how to get Heathcote out of my house. Desperate, I rang Peregrine Eliot and begged him to go to Darnley Terrace and take Heathcote away. I was pretty sure that this time Heathcote had really flipped and needed help. Peregrine agreed to have a go and I went gratefully to bed.

When Perry arrived at the house and found Heathcote still in possession, he came to the same conclusion as me and rushed him off to Springfield Mental Hospital at Tooting. Whether or not he had really flipped is hard to say, since he was always quite at home in psychiatric clinics. He wrote extensively about mental instability. I often thought that he really preferred the company of the irrational to that of people of sound mind. He roamed the streets chatting to disturbed people. He liked them.

Even though I was in a shaky state myself I decided I had better go and see him. But when I went into the street outside Verity's house I found that my car had been towed away. It was the last straw.

Malcolm came with me to the hospital, where Heathcote seemed calmer and insisted he was all right. There wasn't much more I could do. I rang Peregrine again, who told me that Heathcote might have seemed normal but he was in fact quite disturbed and in a threatening frame of mind. I did not ask what he was threatening – I did not want to know. But

Perry suggested I went away for a while. He sounded worried and, though I did not want to take all this drama too seriously, getting away did seem like a good idea. My life was again out of control. I did not want to go back to Darnley Terrace. In the end, we retrieved the car, drove back to the house, locked it up and left, leaving behind expensive paintings, furniture – everything.

I did not feel up to driving any distance, so we decided not to take the car with us. The woman who lived next door worked for my agent Mark McCormack and was learning to drive. I told her she could borrow the car for a few days while I was away. Then Malcolm and I caught the train to Hampshire, where we stayed with Anne Toye. She and her husband were worried about me. She had always been very protective, and she could see at a glance that Malcolm was not wholly stable. She thought I was leaping out of the frying pan into the fire.

Being in such normal surroundings calmed me down and I decided we might as well collect the car. Back in London we were met by my distraught neighbour. The car had vanished. Her stepbrother, who was obviously a trial to the family, had taken it from outside the house. It turned up – happily within a very short time – near their family home at Sidmouth, Devon. Malcolm and I took the train to pick it up. All this took us halfway to Cornwall, where Malcolm, coincidentally, wanted to be. He had studied at Falmouth Art School and had worked in the town in an antique shop. He had a lot of connections in the area, including a Cornish wife from whom he had been separated for some time. There was also a girl who had had his baby before parting from him.

On the run as we were from Heathcote, Cornwall seemed to me to be as good a place as any. We began by driving aimlessly round, staying in hotels. I had hardly any clothes with me and bought what I needed as we went along. There had been no time to pack luggage. Luggage requires thought. All I had taken from Darnley Terrace was my eye make-up. The situation was bizarre. We had to settle somewhere, and finally a friend of Malcolm's, an antique dealer called Di Cottrell, put us up for a while. She was an attractive woman in her late thirties and was to become another of the strong ladies in my life. Di was Cornish, hard-working and energetic, but above all lively. She had that Celtic quality of intuition in good measure, and she ran an antique shop that was always full of eccentric people. It was not unlike being back with Geoffrey Bennison, though on a much simpler scale. I liked the oddballs of the antique trade. Di had an aunt who was a clairvoyant. I never actually met this woman, but she did once catch a glimpse of me going up a flight of stairs at Di's home. She left a long letter for me. 'Your life is like a revolving door,' it said, 'and there are two men in it. I have to tell you that one day you will be free of both of them.'

She was right. Heathcote soon disappeared without trace, but it was to be nearly seven years before Malcolm went from my life.

I rented a granite cottage in Zennor, a village about seven miles from Penzance. It belonged to Patrick Heron, a painter who lives and works in Cornwall. Zennor is a tiny but powerful place set in the middle of wild moorland. In winter it is about as bleak and threatening a spot as you can find. The sea mists swirl in over the granite cliffs, and the whole area seems shrouded in ancient mystery. Ruins of long-abandoned tin mines litter the landscape, grubby brick fingers left pointing at the sky. I liked it. There was something about the starkness of the land and the lack of compromise that appealed to me. We settled down happily until new trouble loomed. Malcolm's ex-girlfriend had heard that he was with me and showed signs of wanting to come back into his life. The last thing I needed was more trouble with yet another ex, so we decided to move on again. We packed our few belongings and, like a pair of gypsies, drove aimlessly across moors and mountains for a few weeks until we found ourselves in Wales, in Breconshire.

I had been there before, but Wales was new to Malcolm. We were both drawn to Celtic areas and he was instantly attracted by the power and beauty of the mountains. They so pleased him that I said: 'Why don't we find somewhere to rent here?' I myself was ready to stop roaming, and all this running away from people was becoming farcical.

He, too, felt that it was a good idea. 'I think I could write here,' he said. 'It is beautiful.'

Malcolm suffered from depression and I knew that Anne Toye was right: I had gone from the frying pan into the fire, and he was not stable. I could see it in his face. Not that this troubled me – I was used to instability and he was basically a good person; a gentle man who found much of the modern world intolerable. He was plagued by unpredictable rages, and when the tension was building and one of his rages came on he would get out of the house as fast as he could since he was inclined to smash things up. His failure to complete the simplest task left him enraged with both himself and the recalcitrant object. His rages were terribly distressing to him, and after they had died away he looked awful, drained, wiped out. I was sorry that anyone had to go through such mental anguish.

He also had a fear of social situations and could not always cope with company – if we had to go anywhere and meet people, there were times when it was impossible for him to remain in the room. He had to get out. The rages and his fear were both easily triggered and yet I was never frightened by him – he was never violent with people.

While I liked him a lot, I was never in love with Malcolm. When I took up with him I had nothing else to do and no one else to be with. The problem was I had not learned to be on my own. So I threw in my lot with him, and there we were, a pair of runaways on a freezing February day in 1971 in the middle of Wales, looking in an estate agent's window in Builth Wells for somewhere to find shelter and set up home.

The estate agent was a little puzzled by this bedraggled pair who eventually went into his office. It was hardly the time of year for country lets.

'We do have a property that the owners have been thinking of letting,' he said. 'It's called the Golf House. It used to be a hotel, but it's dilapidated and the water is turned off. I don't know if the owner will want to go to the trouble of

206

getting it ready for a let. They were really thinking of selling it.'

'Why don't we have a look?' I said. 'We might buy it.'

He gave me a doubtful look, but rang the owner, who agreed to show us round. The first view as we came up the lane which led to the house was not encouraging. The house was certainly not beautiful – in fact rather shacklike – but I liked it. It was odd and different; part wood-boarding with a corrugated-iron roof, and completely isolated. The owner let us in; inside it was quite spooky and absolutely freezing cold. Downstairs was a grim, narrow corridor with six rooms off – three on one side, two on the other plus the former boiler room. The atmosphere was horrible, but the top two floors were lovely, with lots of light. Unusually for Wales, the house had big windows giving on to wonderful views, and fortunately these floors had a much pleasanter atmosphere than the ground floor.

We wandered around, and it was the views plus the fact that we desperately needed somewhere to stay that persuaded me to buy it. Malcolm was unhappy in London, and I did not want to be anywhere near Heathcote. Cornwall was spoilt for us now that his girlfriend was pursuing him.

'How much?' I asked.

The man looked startled.

'Seven thousand?' he suggested tentatively.

'OK, we'll buy it.'

His mouth fell open. He had not expected such an easy sale.

It was a strange house, supposed to be on ley lines – invisible lines that date back to 4000 BC and are believed to be threads of energy that join up ancient monuments and the sites of pagan rituals. Ley lines were all the rage in the late sixties and early seventies. The house certainly had a powerful atmosphere, but then the Welsh mountains and all Celtic areas are naturally atmospheric. These places are definitely not cosy, and I love them for it. At night all we could see from the windows were a few lights dotted here and there.

We acquired some rather depressing, spartan furniture along with the house, and I gradually replaced it as I found other pieces that pleased me. We lived on the top two floors. Because it had been a hotel the place was all little rooms, so we knocked down walls to make larger ones. We painted the outside bright yellow.

We were surrounded by trees, which at night would knock on the corrugated-iron roof as if demanding admittance. The noise was not a reassuring one, and could be alarming when I was there on my own. But much of it I loved. Whenever we left the house for a few days the squirrels would get inside and fill our wellington boots with nuts. They didn't mind the cold; but we did. There was no heating, and when we did get the water running it was so cold that it froze in the lavatories. We used to go to bed with our clothes on and stay there. Finally we had some night storage heaters installed, but we were never really warm.

It did not matter. I loved the mountains, and visually I loved it all. Malcolm was gently nuts and kept meditating, but I was content with him. He was deeply involved in psychoanalysis and alchemy – subjects I found interesting, and which at that period were highly fashionable. Our only real problem was money.

So it was sheer financial desperation that made me accept a 'catwalk' job for a fashion house in Turkey. By this time I was hardly doing any photographic work at all, and I had never done any floor modelling. I was strictly a photographic model, which is a very different kettle of fish. I had never felt confident enough to parade up and down a catwalk showing clothes, but the money was good and I was to be the star. I only had to wear four outfits, while the other girls were wearing many more. The fact that the location was Turkey appealed to me. I was inclined to take jobs abroad where I could be reasonably anonymous. Even so, I was nervous because I cannot walk in time to music – I have no sense of rhythm. I was convinced I would make a mess of it.

I flew out after the other girls, and fortunately found myself travelling with a charming girl called Carina who had also left London later than the others. She was both a photographic and a floor model and she was kind enough to try and reassure me that all would be well. We eventually caught up with the other models in Istanbul. Floor models are a rather different breed from photographic models. They are much more 'girly'. They travel and work together, and they get to know each other so well that they become rather like an extended family. Photographic models rarely work in groups. This particular group were sweet girls, and it was all rather embarrassing as they had to work so much harder than I did. I disliked being the star and being given the more expensive hotel rooms; it seemed to set me apart from the rest of them, but having made friends with Carina helped. She and I got on very well.

We went to three different towns in Turkey, where we were put up in good hotels. The shows themselves were a bit primitive, and we all did our own hair and make-up. When the time came for the first of my four appearances I was so nervous that I was shaking. The other girls, who were perfectly at home, were highly amused because I could not walk in time to the music, but this inability endeared me to them and helped me become part of the group. I had my camera with me and took photographs of everyone, and whenever we could we lay round the hotel swimming pool. One of the girls, who looked rather like Marilyn Monroe, was a topless model, and she had to keep sunbathing all the time – it was essential for her job to keep her suntan topped up. She could not wear a bikini like the rest of us, because of the white marks it would leave. But Turkey was not the best place to sunbathe topless, for Turkish men are lecherous. There was a party one night when a Turk climbed up on to the table with a bottle stuffed down his trousers. Then he launched into a rather obscene dance, trying to jerk the liquid up to his mouth. We had all had a few drinks and thought it quite funny. For me, the whole week was more like a holiday than a job, and much more amusing than my life in Wales.

I came back to London £1000 richer and went to see my new friend, Carina, at her flat in Fulham. A copy of *Country*

Life was on the coffee table, open at a picture of a superb stately home.

'That's Carlton, our family home,' Carina said casually.

My mouth fell open. 'My God!' I said. 'You must be grand. Who are you exactly?'

She was Carina Fitz-Alan Howard, daughter of the Duke of Norfolk. Later, she married the TV personality David Frost. And Carlton was only one of her family homes.

I went back to Wales and, though Malcolm was difficult and his rages were tiresome, I was reasonably content to stay with him. There did not seem to be anything else to do. He was writing diligently but not selling anything, and I decided to concentrate on photography. I had begun taking pictures when I needed something to occupy me during the time I was with Heathcote. One day I had met Terry Donovan by chance in the street and he took me to buy my cameras. The meeting sparked a new friendship. He gave me tips and showed me how to set up a darkroom. He would often wander round the antique markets with me on Saturday afternoons.

Now I decided to put what he had taught me into practice. I set up a darkroom in one of the sinister, icy little rooms on the ground floor, and found myself looking nervously over my shoulder whenever I was developing my pictures. I started to take pictures of farmers with their sheep. I photographed what appealed to me, which meant I was not photographing the right things to succeed commercially. Anyone who might buy my pictures wanted me to photograph glamorous things connected with my modelling life. I went round photographing dead crows because I was in a pretty dismal state of mind. Not surprisingly, I never made a penny out of my photography.

Gradually we were making friends and becoming part of the community. One of our most amusing friends was the local policeman, who roared up to the house on his motorbike one day in a shower of mud.

'Oh, God!' I said as I saw him out of the window. 'We haven't paid those parking fines.'

The man banged on the door, I let him in and he politely took off his crash helmet. Underneath was a leather flying helmet. He left that in place to frame a strong, primitive face with black eyes and jet-black hair.

He had not come about the parking fines; he had come to make our acquaintance. He introduced himself as Charlie and sat chatting for a while. We had begun to realize that he was odd when suddenly he patted his flying helmet and boomed: 'We're all homosexual inside. I like a bit of leather myself.'

We both roared with laughter and relaxed. This was not your typical policeman.

Charlie used to come and visit us all the time. He had the most lovely wife and hordes of children. He came from a gypsy family, and he and his brother had managed to join the local police force. Not surprisingly he was an unorthodox policeman and managed things in his own unorthodox manner. When the local lads got into trouble his method was to throw the offenders in the river, fish them out and then give them a good talking to. He was over the top, loved opera and was full of Welsh rhetoric.

He spent a lot of time with us and told us spooky stories, always at night when we were surrounded by blackness. His favourite was about a strange ragged woman who seemed to have no permanent abode and crept around the town carrying an envelope full of photographs of leaping cats. Charlie's brother had followed her to the local graveyard one dark and stormy night and she had frightened the hell out of him by turning into a cat (according to Charlie) and leaping out at him from behind a gravestone.

Whether he made his stories up we never knew, but you found yourself believing him when he told them. He could grip us with his tales of mystery and imagination, and by the time he left we could hardly move from terror and every creak in the house petrified us. Having frightened us silly he would go out of the house, throw his arms into the air and shout enigmatically, 'God, can't you feel the po-wer!'

He was eventually moved away to another Welsh village. Charlie was delightfully and gently potty, but I liked him and I am in touch with him and his wife to this day.

211

Our one problem remained money. Despite the Turkish trip, what I had was shrinking fast. I was not earning, and there were Malcolm's wife, girlfriend and two children to consider. He never contributed very much to them – indeed he was not then capable of doing so, so I helped them both out a little. It seemed quite a normal thing to do as we were still in the prevailing climate of 'whoever had the money paid'.

We stayed in Wales for a couple of years, occasionally going back to London, but not often. Malcolm could not really cope with cities, but I liked to return from time to time for some light relief. Living in Wales we were so thrown back on ourselves: there was little social life, and not many people to get to know. Friends and family visited us – the house was big and we had plenty of room. My mother liked Malcolm; he was nice to her and she often came with her friends. I loved living there, but there was nothing to do and I was always worried about money.

Eventually I decided we would have to go back to London. I needed breathing space and more stimulation than Wales offered, and it seemed silly to keep the big London house shut up and unused. Having made the decision, I promptly put Darnley Terrace on the market. It was an inconvenient narrow house with small rooms on four floors and we were forever running up and down the stairs. I felt I wanted something lower and more spacious. The girl next door had said that if I ever sold she would be interested – she wanted to knock the two houses into one – so I already had a buyer. I had the house valued. I had paid £22,000 for it and it sold for £55,000, which at least gave us some financial respite. I wanted to keep something in London and so I bought a maisonette in St Mark's Road near Ladbroke Grove tube station. It was a much bigger property, but being in a less fashionable neighbourhood was cheaper. Soon afterwards I had to sell this and move downmarket yet again for financial reasons, to a small flat in Blenheim Crescent.

Malcolm managed to get some work with John Layard, the distinguished Oxford psychoanalyst with whom he had worked before. For some months he travelled to Oxford every day and Layard paid him a minimal amount of money; he was also getting a sort of unofficial training in psychiatry. While Malcolm was working, I just did the house up. I was beginning to enjoy doing houses up.

I met the actor Jack Nicholson again at this time. We had met in New York sometime previously as fellow guests at a dinner party. He drove me home, invited himself in, but I said I was tired and sent him on his way. Now he rang up again and I invited him to come over.

'I'll be late,' he warned me.

'That's all right,' I said, not knowing how late he meant. He did not arrive until two in the morning, by which time I was exhausted. He was not in the least interested in me at that point – he was very cut up about his girlfriend, the actress Anjelica Huston, who had just run off with someone else. As I sat there listening to him I realized he was a night bird and he wanted to make it through until morning talking about her. I assured him she would come back – and, of course, she did. He flirted gently with me, but only because he felt it was expected of him. Famous men feel impelled to try to pull famous women.

But Malcolm was insecure enough without Jack Nicholson ringing me up (though his insecurity was not caused by me) and he was also homesick for Cornwall.

'I don't think I can stand being in London much longer,' he said one day after we had been back for a few months. 'Can't we go back to Cornwall?'

It did not matter to me where I was. I liked Cornwall, so he rang Di Cottrell and asked if we could stay for a time while we looked for somewhere to live. She said she would be happy to have us, so we locked up the house again and drove west.

If we were going to find another house in Cornwall the chances were that it would cost more than we would realize on the Golf House; therefore I was going to need some money. I rang my agent and asked if there was any work going.

They came up with something almost immediately – a job in the Algarve in southern Portugal. It was three days of straight-forward photographic work with one of the new top models – a stunning Dutch girl called Willie who looked exactly like a young Marlene Dietrich.

It was this job that made me very much aware that I was becoming a has-been in the modelling world. When I was at the top, if there were two of us on a session I was the one whose pictures filled more pages in the magazine. I was always given the best clothes to model and was usually booked for one day more than the other girl. I no longer had that importance. In Portugal, working with Willie, it became obvious that I was Number Two – and rightly and fairly so. Willie was younger and fresher and was given the best clothes and more shots. I felt I had no power. I had been superseded – a realization nobody welcomes. I did not feel it mattered to me at the time, but the cold fact that I was about to be passé probably concerned me more than I allowed myself to admit. I am not insecure, but my ego is not as strong as it should be and being at the top had a vibrance and importance for me. In Portugal I missed it for the first time. Even today I am not totally free of the sense of being a has-been, though in truth I do not have much regard for the feeling and I am not going to let it trouble me.

On the plane back to London I sat next to a harassed-looking middle-aged man. We started one of those casual conversations that seem unavoidable on planes.

'You're Jean Shrimpton, aren't you?' he asked.

Inwardly I sighed, but agreed that, 'Yes, I'm Jean Shrimpton.'

He needed someone to talk to. His wife had died a few months previously from cancer, and he had taken his two children on holiday to the Algarve. The children were sweet, a boy and a girl, and it was a sad situation. He seemed a pleasant enough fellow who was trying to come to terms with his grief, and I felt sorry for him. I let him talk to me for most of the journey, and when we arrived at Heathrow I said a normal, friendly goodbye and moved away quickly so as not to become any more involved.

I was to regret having been so sympathetic, for he developed a total obsession about me. Thank heavens he did not know where I lived, but he did not have much trouble tracking down my parents. He turned up at Rose Hill Farm, bought a pony from my father and then wanted to stable the animal there. This was ridiculous, as he came from the north of England. He tried to get close to me through anyone who had come into contact with me. He wrote me a letter saying that he would like to get to know me better. I did not want to see him and ignored it. Then he tracked me to Wales – which was another reason I was not sorry that we were going to Cornwall.

I was at the Golf House one day just before we were about to sell up. I had gone there to collect things we wanted to take to Cornwall with us. Malcolm was not with me. For company I had my two dogs, a mongrel called Harpo and a sheepdog we called Gravity – so called because Malcolm had an obsession about gravity. He was always trying to kick the gravity habit and float off. While I was at the Golf House I discovered that this man had visited the people I had bought the house from and had cultivated them to find out my movements. Unfortunately he happened to be there the weekend I came up to collect the stuff. I was walking the dogs and there he was in the lane. I was aghast to see him, said hello and hurried away.

Terrified that he would appear, I took both dogs to bed with me that night and lay there in a blue funk, jumping at the night noises of the house. Every time the tree branches banged on the roof the dogs barked and growled, which did not help. I was certain the man was about. Maybe in the woods outside? Maybe even in the house? It was stupid to be so scared – I am sure he was not dangerous – but as the house itself was spooky it was easy to let my imagination run riot. The final straw was when the catch on the bedroom door gave way and the door burst open. I gasped out loud and sat bolt upright, where I remained totally paralysed with fear until I found the courage to slide down under the bedclothes.

Later I told my father about the dreadful night I had had.

'This is going too far,' he said grimly. 'I'll put a stop to it.'

He telephoned my persecutor and told him that enough was enough. He must take the pony away from Rose Hill and leave me alone. What else he said I do not know, but whatever it was it seemed to work and I never saw or heard of the man again.

I sold the house in Wales. It took a while, but we finally found a place in Cornwall I could afford, a house called Killivose just outside Camborne. It was a long Cornish cottage – two joined into one – with outbuildings, and three fields across the road and one adjoining. There were nine acres in all and it had been a smallholding. I thought this would suit Malcolm. The house was quite pretty and we were not fussy. There was an old dealer in animals who still used the stabling and the fields. He asked us if he could continue to keep his granddaughter's show ponies in the fields. Being me I said yes. This was another of my many mistakes. It did not take him long to work out that if he came in with a poor, downtrodden animal I would buy it, sucker that I was. I ended up with three mares in foal and two ancient, mangy donkeys. I started with just the one donkey, but took on the second because I felt sorry for the one on its own. I also kept chickens. I liked having the animals, but they were a responsibility as they kept getting out of the field. The old dealer kept bringing more until I could not afford to buy them.

'Please don't bring animals that need help,' I would say, but he took no notice and every time I capitulated. Then to my fury, when I wanted to sell the place, he insisted he was a sitting tenant and I was forced to take him to court. I hired a London lawyer, which did not go down well with the local magistrates. I won, but I had to pay all the £3000 costs.

We muddled along running the smallholding. Malcolm was meant to do most of the work. It did not take a lot of time and I thought it would be something productive for him, but he was by nature neither practical nor productive. We had been together for four years, and I was beginning to worry about how we were going to live: certainly not off the smallholding since it did not produce a living wage. I was thirty-three and knew modelling was finished – Portugal had taught me that. I had a panicky feeling about the future and what was going to happen to me and I started going to bed every afternoon.

The days seemed endless. That old depression was creeping back again.

On a low day I would go and see Di, who always made me welcome and cheered me up. She was warm and giving and, best of all, chirpy. One day she said: 'You should start an antique shop, my love. You've got a good eye.'

'I don't know enough about it,' I said.

'You'll learn. I'll help you.'

She nagged until I decided that perhaps it was a good idea. Like Felice before her she saw that I needed to work, and stepped in to save me from drifting back into depression again.

I rented a shop at Marazion and stocked it with stuff from my own home. I went round the salerooms and bought a few things, and Di loaned me stuff from her shop on sale or return. I ran the shop myself and enjoyed it. Buying antiques is an obsessive business and I am an obsessive person. I had a lot to learn. If anyone brought in anything to sell I would ask them to leave it, and then trot round to Di for her opinion of what it was worth. As well as occupying me, the shop helped me earn a bit of money – though not, unfortunately, enough for our needs. I enjoyed the peace of sitting in the shop reading a book, surrounded by all the things I had acquired. I only bought things I liked and I sold most of the stock to the trade, giving everyone trade discounts before they even asked for them. I suppose I did not like selling – I was a funny sort of shopkeeper.

It was during that time at Marazion that I first met Michael. I looked up from my book to see this tall, blond man hurrying into the shop. He had seen a pair of jade bangles in the window which had taken his fancy as a present for his wife.

He bought them quickly and without any haggling over the price. Later he told me he wasn't wasting time because he wanted to go to the loo. It was a brief encounter, but we had registered each other. He went out of the shop thinking I had a wonderful smile (I always thought I had a dreadful smile) and I thought he seemed honest. He looked very straight – the

Guards officer type that every mother wants for her daughter. I did not see him again for another year.

Marazion was a mad place to have a shop; it was too small and there was no passing trade. People barely knew it was there. Eventually I took some premises in Truro which were better situated. It was about then that something happened which was to prove of great significance to my life. In rural Cornwall, just up the road from our smallholding, a Buddhist Centre opened.

Malcolm had always been interested in meditation and Eastern philosophy, and he saw it as a good omen that the Buddhists had virtually come to him.

'I'm going up there to talk to them,' he announced.

I was happy to see him do this. Anything that would steer him to a calmer life could only be good.

He went off to spend a weekend with them, but he could not stand the soul-searching that was required of him. It was too much for his fragile sensibilities and he returned home deeply depressed. He knew that he wanted to join them and was strongly drawn to the religion. He persisted with the Buddhists and practised the meditation they taught him. The form it took caused him to behave strangely. He would go upstairs and sit in a small room until he reached what he called a trance level and then 'let through' whatever needed to 'come through'. This basically consisted of making the most peculiar groaning and moaning noises, sometimes shrieks, which would fill the house. He would walk around the room, bent double, his hands clutching at his ankles, declaring that he was bound hand and foot to his mother.

I became resigned to all this odd behaviour and did not take much notice. I just got on with my own life until he started pressing me to get involved.

'Why don't you join me?' he asked.

I was interested in what he was doing, but the groaning and moaning had put me off. I could never have let myself go to that extent.

'I'd feel silly,' I told him.

It would not have worked for me. I am far too

western in my outlook. I would have been bored sitting there meditating, though I do not doubt that meditation is beneficial for those who have the temperament for it. It certainly worked for Malcolm. It supported him and brought out what was productive in him, and that is the best you can hope for from anything. As for me, I could not understand why I was surrounded by broken people and broken animals.

Even more negative was the knowledge that my relationship with Malcolm was coming to an end. This was exactly what I wanted on many levels, but despite that the prospect of being on my own again was frightening; however, I encouraged Malcolm's association with the Buddhists. I could see no future for us together and I wanted to get on with the shop, hoping that it would lead me to a new career. Even Malcolm, in the midst of all his own confusion, could see that all was not well. One day I said to him rather sadly that I felt my life was going in circles and I wished I understood myself better.

'I think you should go into Jungian analysis,' he said.

I took time to consider what he had suggested. I had a friend in London who was being analysed and she suggested that I visit her analyst who had a practice in Plymouth, just about driving distance from where I lived. I rang and made an appointment.

I was not in the least anxious about going: it was a new experience and I was interested in the prospect. The analyst first asked me why I was coming to him, what I hoped to gain from seeing him, and what was troubling me. He then had to decide whether there was any therapeutic value to be gained from my seeing him. Jungian analysts often work through one's dreams, and he told me to get a notebook and jot mine down. When I protested that I could never remember them, he assured me they became easier to remember in time.

After my first visit to him I had a clairvoyant dream which I took to be a good sign. I was on a boat going along a river and Bailey was taking photographs. There was a male model on one side of me and we were both holding up a megalithic stone. The water was dark and murky and I was afraid of falling into it. On the bank was an ox that had been skinned – which I took to be a symbol for my going into analysis and stripping myself bare.

I told the analyst about the dream.

'What shape was the stone?' he wanted to know.

'Sort of triangular,' I told him.

He looked at me, his expression quizzical. 'Come with me,' he said. 'I want to show you something.'

He took me into his garden and there were two stones, both exactly like the one in my dream.

I took this as further confirmation that I had done the right thing in coming to analysis. And the experience did help me. The fifteen or so sessions that I attended clarified an awful lot of my behaviour patterns. This did not mean that I stopped behaving in that way, but it meant that to some extent I knew *what* I was doing and *why* I was doing it. Being analysed showed me that I did not stand on my own two feet enough; that was another failing of my personality that I had to learn to come to terms with. But I did discover that much of the power of fear is taken away by knowledge of oneself.

I do think, however, that being analysed for years must be counter-productive. It is such a self-indulgent process and can be enormously destructive to a relationship. All resentments are brought bubbling to the surface. Malcolm could cope with its effect on me because he had been through it all himself. He allowed me not to talk about what had happened if I did not want to, and when I came home resentful he understood.

But being analysed did make me angry with him. His rages were distressing for both of us and I felt a lot of buried anger myself. In one of my dreams I was driving the Mini and I had this wooden Christ figure in my passenger seat with me. It was symbolic of Malcolm, the passenger on my back. I do believe that if I had not met Michael I would have gone slightly crazy myself and finished up with a house full of animals and probably drinking a fair amount of whisky.

But maybe I underestimate myself. I did not let life

get completely out of control. I always fell very low in my relationships and then rose again. The trouble was that it always took such a long time before I set the upward trend in motion. Now that my life is so much happier, it is odd for me to remember how I took everything that happened to me and just shrugged it off. I must have been very confused, and my way of dealing with the confusion was to suspend all critical faculties.

In July 1977 Malcolm learned that the Buddhists were moving from Camborne to Cambridgeshire, and the news distressed him terribly. He was determined to join them – for good. I encouraged it. I could take no more.

'What will you do?' he asked.

'Something,' I said.

'Why don't you become an analyst?'

I laughed at the time, but began to think seriously of studying. I doubt, though, if I would ever have gone through with it. It would have been necessary to go to Zurich and live with people whom I did not know, and I find that so uncomfortable. It would also have been like going back to school, and I had not enjoyed that the first time round.

Then I saw Michael again.

He came into the shop in Truro without knowing that it was mine and we recognized each other immediately. We started talking. Most customers are a nuisance, but I thought he was terribly nice. He took to calling in, even if he was not looking for anything. I sometimes offered him a cup of tea and we just talked and talked. I knew he had a wife but, though he never said so, I felt that perhaps all was not well with the marriage.

One day he came to ask if I would be interested in buying some pine furniture he wanted to sell. He did not think highly of antique dealers generally and thought I might be fairer than most.

'There's rather a lot of it,' he said. 'Would you mind coming out to the house?'

Malcolm came with me and we drove to Mylor where Michael and his wife, Caroline, lived. She was waiting with him, tea was prepared and we all sat and chatted. I liked his home; they had some very nice furniture and it had a warm atmosphere. We all seemed to get on well. Caroline was attractive – fairish with her hair cut in a fringe – and she had a good body.

I was aware that Michael was a remarkably handsome man, but this I disregarded. Respectable blond men were not my type – I had always gone for oddities. My problem then was that I equated neurotic with interesting when in fact such people were often a pain in the neck. But as I talked to Michael I kept coming up against an enormous integrity – a quality lacking in the people with whom I had been surrounding myself. He never treated me as Jean Shrimpton. He knew who I was but had not the slightest interest in my fame. Though he was five years younger than me he seemed much more mature. We got on well. Talking to him I realized that he was fascinating, and that he was not at all as he seemed while he was exactly as he seemed.

Slowly the friendship grew, and it was wonderful. I had not felt so easy and comfortable with anyone for years. Michael does not fear anyone or anything and can be brutally frank. He said to me one day, 'You can't stand your own ordinariness.' He was right, and it was a revelation. Having been told that I was special for so long, it was quite a shock to discover not only that I was not special, but that it did not matter. He made me understand that it was no bad thing to be ordinary, and that most of us waste time and effort trying to escape from our own ordinariness.

His marriage was not a problem one – Michael would not have a problem marriage – but it had gone stale. There was no excitement. We were both carrying a load and were relieved to talk to each other. Then we started to see each other as a foursome. He and Caroline asked us over for dinner, we asked them back, and the friendship took root. Michael and Malcolm were interesting together because they were so different, and yet they got on well. Michael has a very good mind and an amazingly wide range of knowledge. He reads constantly, from utter junk right through to the classics and strange cryptic literature. He cannot leave a bookshop without at least six books.

When he and his wife began to go around with us I was just starting my trips to Plymouth, and he found it fascinating that I was being analysed. He enjoyed the company of both of us, and while he found me attractive he did not dwell on it. It was Michael's wife who felt more threatened by the friendship – quite rightly, as it turned out.

Malcolm was aware there was an attraction between us, but it did not bother him terribly. He and I were not in love. He was too fractured to be in love with anyone. I was replaceable by Buddhism or another woman; Buddhism was about to claim him and I suspect he had other women while he was with me, yet I was never unfaithful to him. God knows in the early days I could have been – with Jack Nicholson and lots of others.

The money problem was raising its head yet again and I had to move somewhere cheaper, so I bought a dear old farmhouse at Hayle which had not been modernized. I put Killivose on the market, and by coincidence Michael and his wife were selling their house at Mylor. Caroline decided she wanted to buy Killivose because she liked it. Michael did not – he felt the atmosphere depressing – but Caroline wanted it so he bought it. They did not want the fields over the road, so I was able to leave a lot of furniture stored in the barns there. And so the friendship went on.

Without us realizing it, my life and Michael's were becoming intertwined. We both drove around a lot and we were always passing in our cars, usually just waving at each other but sometimes stopping for a chat. I drove around because I liked the countryside, and if I did not do that I went to bed. And I knew that was not good. Michael was taking photographs – he had just discovered photography and took pictures all the time. That was something else we had in common. There were never any people in his pictures and there was a sense of isolation about them. I once showed them to Bailey, who said they were good.

223

August came, and Malcolm went off to train at the Buddhist centre in Cambridgeshire. He left cheerfully enough, clutching his few possessions and leaving me alone in the new house, sad but resigned. Happily my mother, sister and nieces came to stay for a few days.

Michael popped down to see me while my mother was there. After he had gone, Mum and Chrissie looked at me with raised eyebrows.

'Not my type,' I said hastily.

'Who does she think she's kidding?' said my sister.

Mum went home, and after being alone for about a week I found I was coping better than I had thought I would. It was a lovely sunny morning and I was pottering in the kitchen, not long having finished breakfast, when suddenly Michael came in through the open back door. He was wearing jeans and a light shirt and had a camera bag slung over his shoulder.

'Anybody home?' he called.

I was childishly pleased to see him, but tried not to show it. 'Where did you spring from?' I asked.

'I've been photographing round here. I thought I'd just drop in and see how you are.'

'I'm fine,' I said, thinking I was all the better for seeing him. 'Would you like a cup of tea or coffee?'

'Whatever you're having.'

I busied myself putting the kettle on. I had never been shy with him, but suddenly I was. I was vividly aware that Malcolm had gone and I was free.

'How's Caroline?'

There was a brief silence, then he said: 'She's gone away for a month.'

I felt a little jolt of excitement. 'Oh?' It was a question.

'To think about things,' he explained. 'We haven't been getting on very well. The marriage is a bit rocky.'

I was uncertain of what else to say, and I kept my back to him as I waited for the kettle to boil. I did not want him to see my face.

'Do you miss Malcolm?' he asked abruptly.

224

I considered the question. 'No,' I said, and turned to face him.

I thought he seemed relieved, and when the fresh tea was poured we began to talk more seriously than we had ever done before. We found there was a mutual feeling of being able to discuss our situations and our partners, and it brought a great sense of relief. We seemed to be finding a closeness which came from being able to talk honestly and freely about our problems. I am sure we were both aware we were in love, but it was not yet the moment for any declarations.

When we had talked ourselves out, he said abruptly: 'Let's go out. Let's do something.'

We were both wondrously free. Michael had a month of freedom; I was totally uncommitted and ready to start life all over again. The world was our oyster. But all we did was drive twenty miles up the road to Truro, making the excuse that I must check on my shop.

It was a wonderful day. Michael bought me twenty-six bunches of mixed flowers, an extravagant armful of bold colour that I could barely hold. 'What will I do with them all?' I protested. I was flushed, excited and happy. We were having fun. Spontaneity was back in both our lives.

Back home I scattered the flowers the length of a big refectory table – there were not enough vases in the house to hold them all. We were both ravenous and I cooked us some food. We ate it quickly and then without any discussion we went upstairs to bed together. There seemed no point in attempting to deny what we both felt, and this *was* the time for declarations. When I woke in the night to find Michael beside me I moved closer to him, and sleepily decided it had been the best day of my life.

In the morning we had breakfast together as naturally as if we had been a twosome for years.

'I'll just go and collect some things from Killivose,' Michael said on a rising note, and I nodded. No answer was required. It seemed the most normal thing in the world that he should come to stay with me.

For the next two days I felt bathed in happiness. Michael and I made the most of every instant of his freedom. We were doing nothing more than enjoying ourselves together. There was no conversation about what the future held or what we should do when Caroline came back. We just snatched at the chance to be together while it was there.

It was another hot and sunny afternoon when, after lunch, we went up to bed. We seemed to need each other physically at the most inopportune times, and this time proved inopportune indeed. Suddenly we heard someone calling Michael's name from downstairs. I froze and clung to him.

'It sounds like Caroline,' I whispered.

'It *is* Caroline,' Michael said grimly.

She was back – almost three weeks early. The sense of horror and embarrassment I felt is indescribable. It was bad enough for her to have caught us in bed together, but the small detail uppermost in my mind was the flowers. The twenty-six bunches of flowers everywhere in the house – in vases, scattered on the table. Fading a little, maybe; but I had not wanted to throw them away. Caroline would guess he had bought them for me and it would be so hurtful. Perhaps more hurtful than the fact that we were lovers. In a panic I pulled the sheets higher up around me.

'My God!' I said. 'What shall we do?'

'It's all right.' He sounded totally calm. 'I'll deal with it. You stay here.'

Michael has no fear of situations. He went downstairs and faced her where she stood in the hall. He said without preliminaries: 'I'm sorry, but it's all over. Our marriage has come to an end. I've fallen in love with Jean. There's no point in going on, but I'll do everything I can to make it easy for you.'

She was very brave, though shocked and a little frightened at the thought of the unknown and the sudden loss of her security. But there was no anger or animosity. It was just sad. They were fond of each other, but while neither had ever admitted it both knew that the end had come.

The confrontation took barely ten minutes – ten minutes which seemed like ten hours to me crouched in the bedroom and waiting for Michael to return. Downstairs Caroline turned on her heel and went. I heard her footsteps outside the house, her car starting, and she was gone. Then Michael came back upstairs, looking amazingly composed.

'What happened?' I asked.

'It's all right,' he said, collapsing back on to the bed.

'Was it awful?'

'Not good, but it's better that things are in the open.'

I clung to him for a moment and we did not say any more. Then we went downstairs and put the kettle on and over cups of tea sat and talked the situation over. We both felt a slight sense of panic. Events had taken over and catapulted us into this situation without any preparation or discussion. We were thrown together much more strongly than either of us had intended at this point. There was no doubt about it. We were in love and that was frightening. We had both wanted space and time to be on our own. I had been in compulsive relationships too often and I needed to live alone. Michael felt the same way, but it did not work out like that. It was obvious that our feelings for each other were strong, and I knew I had met someone who was really important. This frightened me because I had never thought it would happen.

'We have to tell Malcolm now,' Michael said.

'I suppose so.' I didn't relish the thought, and Michael could see it.

'You have to face it,' he said gently. 'It's the honourable thing to do.'

It was about time I started facing up to things, so I dealt with it myself. I rang the Buddhist centre in Wisbech where Malcolm was, and asked to speak to the Thai man who ran it. I had met him a few times with Malcolm and liked him. I briefly told him what had happened.

'. . . so I need to know what sort of psychological state Malcolm is in, because I have to tell him that I'm with someone else,' I explained.

He said that Malcolm was pretty disturbed at that time, and that they would let me know when the time was right for both Michael and me to go and see him to break the news.

That time eventually came, and Michael and I travelled first to London, where we stayed at the Blenheim Crescent flat for the night before driving on. The scenery did nothing to lift my spirits at the thought of the confrontation ahead: it was a flat, depressing journey through flat, depressing countryside. I was in a state of nerves, shredding paper handkerchieves and dreading seeing Malcolm.

When we got to where the Buddhists had set up home I went into the red-brick building alone, full of apprehension, while Michael waited in the car. The Thai man took me to Malcolm, explaining on the way that everyone there had a simple room with no more than a bed and a chair.

Malcolm was sitting quietly in his monastic room reading, and as I came in he smiled his slightly embarrassed smile. He looked well but subdued, and he seemed pleased to see me.

'Hello,' he said. 'You look very pretty. I always forget how pretty you are.'

I could have cried. There was not the slightest sign of animosity. What I had come to say I said in a rush. I finished my confession by saying diffidently: 'Michael's outside in the car.'

Malcolm listened to me quietly and then said, 'I'm not exactly surprised. But why don't we all go and talk about it somewhere? I want to know all about it.'

He came out to the car. I was now tearful, but Malcolm seemed to understand the situation and he and Michael were much stronger than I was. We were able to talk about it in a way that was not destructive. The two men had always got on well, and we were all on a quest to work things out for ourselves in our own ways. We went for a walk on a sparsely wooded common. It was a pleasant, sunny day and there was something good about the meeting. Malcolm wished us well. There were no recriminations. But, in fairness, I did not owe him anything. I had not treated him badly, and it was he who had left me. He had been difficult to live with. In the six years we had been together I could never show any rage or pain of my own for fear of increasing his rage and pain. For all that time I had been bottled up.

It proved to be the most tidy of break-ups. Three days after we had said our tearful farewells, Malcolm telephoned my mother. He wanted her to tell me not to worry. He had met someone else in the Buddhist community who attracted him: an American heiress, no less. Caroline had taken herself to Michael's parents' house after she caught us together. They were sympathetic and supportive and took her with them to a cottage they owned in Somerset. They stayed with her for a while and then left her there on her own. Happily, a week or two later she formed another relationship with an older man. It worked very well. They are still together and have a young family.

No one was desperately upset, but then I believe that if things are meant to be there are not too many broken hearts.

Caroline came back to Cornwall to discuss financial matters. Michael being Michael, he gave her the house and most of the furniture. He kept a small amount of money. He would probably have given her the lot, but he felt he did not want to come to me with nothing.

Caroline's untimely return had left Michael homeless, and he talked of renting somewhere to live. 'I'd better start looking for a cottage to rent for myself,' he said.

It was not the best time of year to find a vacant cottage in Cornwall and it seemed unfair that he had lost his own home because of me.

'That's ridiculous,' I said. 'You know you're not going to stay in the cottage for long. Let's see how we get on together.'

We lived together straightaway in my house and that felt comfortable. What was uncomfortable for me was making any commitment, even though I knew I was in love with Michael. I knew I had a great chance of happiness and that I had met the right person. Curiously, that seemed like a great responsibility as I took the idea of marriage so seriously. I could not commit myself totally without believing I could be completely faithful to my own idea of marriage, and I was not sure if I could do that.

Michael was wonderful. He made his will over to me about the second week we were together.

When he told me what he had done I was appalled. I said: 'But how can you be so sure?'

He just looked at me and said: 'I will never leave you.'

That was something so easy to say and so difficult to mean, and yet I knew he meant it.

The freedom of leaving one's options open seems like a luxury, but it is not. It took me a long time to make a commitment to Michael. Once I did, I found that so much was cut through. When I settled for permanence I could give my attention fully to my life and to Michael's, instead of being distracted by the allure of freedom. Other people are so insecure that they will not commit to anything for fear of being hurt. Michael is not like that. While I vacillated, he set about talking me into it and showing me that life could be light-hearted. We were terribly happy. We did exactly what we wanted. Michael did not know London, and while at the flat I was able to show him my favourite places; I loved being his guide. We did all sorts of things. We went and bought a pair of red high-heeled shoes for me at Gamba. We scraped up enough money to go to L'Etoile, where the waiters greeted me like an old friend. I showed him my alternative London of fascinating backstreets and old-fashioned shops. Back in Cornwall we converted the barns and improved the house. Michael dug out the courtyard to make a garden. We were building our home, but most of all we were building our relationship and Michael was certain that we were right for each other.

He accepted all my reservations and hesitations. He had anticipated how I would react and just said: 'It's all right.' Most men would have been made insecure by my apparent doubt, muttering to themselves, 'She hasn't committed to me even though I've committed to her.' When I finally knew

I would marry Michael I found it very uncomfortable. I never thought I would marry anyone. I knew he was right for me, but it was out of character for me to behave sensibly. The strength of my feelings frightened me. I had never felt like that in my life before.

I was still visiting the analyst and my dreams were strange, mirroring my confusion. About a fortnight after we had started living together I had a dream that I felt was important, and I was anxious to tell my analyst about it without delay. In my dream there was a photograph of my parents, but instead of holding me they were holding my niece, Clover. She seemed to be about two. The dream was no more than a man and a woman holding a child. I watched them, and then went out into the garden to pick flowers. The flowers were ice – frozen. I knew that as I picked them they would thaw, and this seemed to be important.

Michael drove me to Plymouth and waited for me while I went in for my appointment. He was quite apprehensive about the influence the analyst had over me, feeling that the man might try to persuade me against marriage or any steady relationship.

'If he reacts negatively,' Michael said, 'I shall go in to talk to him myself.'

I told the analyst about my dream, and when I had finished he said, 'It is a hopeful, good dream.' But I wanted more response.

'You know I'm in love with this man,' I said. 'But I feel so guilty. He's married. And while I feel so lucky I wish it were not me who has this wonderful love. I wish it were my sister, or someone else I care about. I feel other people need love more than I do. It doesn't seem right that it should be me.'

Then he told me a Greek myth about a king who came to an island, and the island was in a most unhappy state. But when the king took over and ruled wisely and well everything flourished and people became wealthy and the island prospered. But then the people accused the king of the sin of hubris and said that he was equating himself with

231

the gods. They demanded that he must make a sacrifice to the sea to humble himself.

So as an act of humility the king took his biggest diamond and cast it into the sea. Then he continued with his work.

Later came the time for the island's yearly banquet, when the farmers harvested their land and the fishermen worked day and night to catch food for the feast. The produce was piled before the king for his approval, and the fishermen laid their catch before him; the biggest fish was to be his. As he cut it open he fell back in amazement. There in the fish's belly was the diamond he had thrown into the sea, returned to him.

'Why shouldn't this happen to you?' the analyst said. 'I'm telling you it is your right to have this happiness. For the moment, just don't tell anyone. Don't go babbling to friends. Don't dissipate what you have. Put the situation in a retort and let the chemical change take place. Go back to Michael and get on together. Don't see people. Shut yourself away and don't let your happiness be tarnished by the reactions of other people. Be your own judges.'

I was so grateful. I left his consulting rooms and went to tell Michael what he had said. Michael was grateful, too. He had been certain the man was going to tell me I was doing the wrong thing and had been prepared to fight to change his mind. Although I was still afraid, I did what he had said, and from then on I was on the way back to some kind of normality.

Arising from all this, Michael decided to go into analysis for a while himself – just so that he could understand what I was doing and what was happening to me. He only went a few times, but it clarified things for him. He came to understand that he had taken his father as a role model – which was no bad thing; but, of course, he was not his father.

Michael has always had the courage of his convictions. He is better able to cope with life than I ever was, and yet he did not mind the instability in me.

232

Michael likes his food and gets very grumpy when he is hungry. Being a pragmatist, when he left school he decided that he would go into something where he would be fed so he chose catering college. He had also been impressed by a hotel where his parents once took him on holiday. It gave him the idea that it would be good to work for himself and be fed and looked after by staff. When he was twenty-two he sold his flat and, with the help of his parents, bought a little hotel in Somerset which he and his wife ran. He did well and built up a faithful clientele; he encouraged a funny cross-section of people and it worked. If several people whom he liked were coming he would not take any other guests. It wasn't a way to make much money, but people enjoyed staying at his hotel.

In those days, however, he was ambivalent about running a hotel. What he really liked (and still likes) is restoring things. When he sold his hotel in Somerset he and his wife bought the shell of a little old cottage that was falling down. He and a couple of helpers rebuilt it from scratch. He found he could make money from doing up a house and moving on – just as I had been doing myself in London.

And that was only one of the many things we found we had in common as we got to know each other better.

— 10 —

There was never any proposal. Neither of us ever said: 'Will you marry me?' or even 'Shall we marry?' Those questions were not necessary. Without any kind of formal discussion we both knew it was the right thing to do. I did not need to be married. It was not and never had been a priority in my life. In truth I still don't *need* it. I have no doubts that Michael and I would have been equally happy even if we had never troubled to make it legal. But I did feel that I wanted the ceremony as an expression of how serious I was about him. This time I knew I was not going to bolt as I had done in the past. Marriage would mean that I had committed myself. I was thirty-five years old and had never been certain enough to take such a step. I take the concept of marriage incredibly seriously, and can see no point in not doing so. I rarely make big gestures, and when I do I make them with complete sincerity.

Obviously we could not marry immediately; Michael had to wait for his divorce to come through. But it did not matter to us *when* we married. We knew we would, and the timing was irrelevant. Then, having made the romantic decision to marry, we made another romantic decision. We decided to have a baby. I had never wanted children before, but now I believed there was nothing more significant that I could do. It seemed to be the biggest commitment that I could make, and I wanted to do it more than I have ever wanted to do anything in my life.

When I made this momentous (for me) decision we had been living together for about a year. I stopped all

234

contraception and waited to see what would happen. I was certain I would have difficulty in becoming pregnant but, surprisingly, quite quickly I did.

I was three months pregnant when we were finally free to marry, in a quiet ceremony on Friday, 12 January 1979 at Penzance register office. I was not worried that I was pregnant, since I felt it was our wedding and nobody else's; an act between Michael and me. My personal view is that a marriage should be private, so we made no fuss about it. I did not need a crowd around me and would have preferred that no one knew. It even annoyed me that we had to make our plans public by posting the banns. Michael asked a couple of his friends to come along as witnesses, but I would have been quite content to grab two strangers off the street. I wore a black skirt and grey jacket; we drove from our home outside Penzance, parked the car and walked up the road hand in hand to the register office. The ceremony took no time at all which, since I felt surprisingly nervous, was just as well.

It was a quirk of fate that we chose the Abbey Hotel – the place Michael and I loved best in Penzance – for our little wedding celebration. At that time I had no idea that a year later we would be buying this old Gothic-fronted house overlooking the harbour. It had not even come on the market, and there was no reason to think that it would do so. In those days the mildly eccentric Mrs Clifford ran the hotel with a highly eccentric staff. Most of the guests were elderly residents and the place had a time-warp quality. It was more like a big, rambling town house than a hotel, and at lunchtime was full of old ladies in hats conversing in gentle, hushed tones. The furnishings were good antique pieces, lovingly polished, and there was always a pleasant smell of beeswax and lavender in the rooms. Elegant but faded, it matched the people who chose to live there. It fascinated me, and at one time I managed to get a good look round the entire building. My excuse was photographing one of the waitresses who lived in. I talked her into letting me photograph her in several of the hotel's rooms. It was a perfectly valid excuse – the girl had a most unusual face. But then nothing about the Abbey was ordinary.

The wedding ceremony over, the four of us sat down by the huge open fireplace in the hotel dining room to a wedding banquet – the dish of the day, fish and chips, washed down with champagne. Mrs Clifford did not normally serve chips, but on this Friday, by luck, she did. We happened to mention that we had just got married. She was delighted and she and her staff joined in the celebration. They are all in our wedding photographs, and some of them still work with us.

I had difficulty eating my fish and chips. The pregnancy was beginning to get to me and I felt queasy. It took a lot of HP sauce to help the food down. Then I began to feel really ill.

'I'm sorry, Michael,' I said, 'but I'm going to have to go home.'

I finished the day tucked up in bed, but not for the usual wedding night reasons. I felt very poorly indeed.

The following six months were a nightmare. In the first eight weeks of the pregnancy I had felt a bit sick, as women generally do. Everyone assured me it would get better after three months. It did not. It got worse. As the months went on I vomited all the time. I could not face food, and when I did manage to eat something I was unable to retain it. All that would stay down was the occasional banana sandwich. I marvelled at how little it is possible to eat and still live. I couldn't even keep water down. Many times I think Michael regretted our romantic gesture. I don't know how he stood my pregnancy. I don't know how I stood it myself.

I had a condition called hyperemesis-gravidarum – a little-known but quite dreadful illness which apparently caused the death of Charlotte Brontë. In the past any pregnant woman unfortunate enough to suffer from it died an exceedingly unpleasant death from dehydration. I was alive and starving, but the really serious problem was the dehydration brought about by the sickness. I was carted off to hospital in Truro on five different occasions to be put on a drip, and every time I went back they kept me in for several days for observation. Michael was driving back and forth to Truro two and three times a day while I was there, but without this treatment I would have died.

I was also given a transfusion of iron on a drip, and that was something else that went wrong. I had my usual bad reaction to drugs, and there was a lot of panic and running about because my blood pressure was dropping rapidly and there were fears for the safety of the baby. Once that problem had been dealt with, I found the iron in my system made me desperately thirsty. A few hours after I had been taken off the drip I would have killed for a drink: I had to keep ringing the nurses for more jugs of water. When I got home again, Michael brought me eight litres of Corona lemonade each day and I drank the lot. The hiss of the lemonade bottle being opened woke him up at all hours of the night. I also had to collect my urine at this time. Other mothers had half a jug; I had jugs and jugs of the stuff.

This iron treatment also had a bizarre side effect – it temporarily turned me into what we called Wonder Woman. All my wrinkles disappeared and the bags under my eyes went. My skin was perfect, quite flawless, and my eyes were as blue as blue. It was as if someone had magically cropped ten years from my age. I quite liked the effect and it temporarily cheered me up, but Michael hated this strange phenomenon. The sight of my rejuvenation unnerved him.

'You look as if someone from another planet has taken you over and crept into your skin,' he would say, giving me uneasy looks. But after thirty-six hours all these weird effects vanished and I was back to looking exhausted and thin again.

Michael looked after me morning, noon and night. When I dragged myself out of bed and went to the doctor's surgery, we constantly had to stop the car at the kerbside for me to be sick – and I had to watch the way the wind was blowing or it was all over me. It was disgusting. I was so ill that as the pregnancy advanced I did nothing but sleep. I only woke up to throw up. I reached a stage of nonbeing, where I was not even in pain any more. Michael was stunned by the whole experience. Indeed, we were both in a state of shock. Michael felt as if the woman he loved was dying before his eyes and he was responsible. And I found it hard to believe that he could go on loving this creature who did nothing but throw up and burp all day. It was a grim start to our marriage.

In the midst of all this horror I met the waitress from the Abbey Hotel at the maternity clinic. She, too, was expecting but her pregnancy, happily, was rather less dramatic.

'Did you know the Abbey is up for sale?' she said as we sat waiting to see the doctor.

'It is?'

She nodded. 'Mrs Clifford wants to get out. She says she's had enough and it's time she retired. The residents are starting to die off. There's hardly anyone left.'

I was sad to hear of the demise of the behatted old ladies, but the news that the Abbey was up for sale was the first thing that had sparked any enthusiasm in me for months. When I had seen the doctor I left the clinic and hurried as fast as I was able to where Michael was waiting in the car.

'The Abbey's for sale,' was the first thing I said as I got into the passenger seat.

'Oh, yes,' he said, rather cautiously.

'Wouldn't it be wonderful to own it?'

My excitement did not communicate itself to him. He was silent as he manoeuvred out of the parking space and then he said: 'I suppose it would.'

I was aware of a lack of enthusiasm – a certain air of non-committal – but took no notice.

'Let's go and look at it,' I said.

'Now?'

'Why not?'

He did not argue, and we drove straight there. The old house was as lovely as I remembered it as we walked in through the door into the flagstoned porch. A rather surprised Mrs Clifford showed us round – she could not think why we should be interested. Michael did most of the looking as I was too weak to see every room. I could not get up to the top floor and barely made it up the fine flight of wide stairs to the superb first-floor drawing room. The house had been built in the seventeenth century, the Gothic frontage added in 1820, and from that time on little had been done. Nothing having been altered meant that nothing had been spoilt. The hotel was not large – eight bedrooms – but they were all spacious enough to take bathrooms in due course. Its greatest asset was the exceptional charm of the building itself.

There were problems. There were only two bathrooms, no central heating, and Michael's quick eye registered that the whole house not only needed rewiring but required an enormous amount of structural work as well. This, he pointed out, would be tedious as well as expensive.

'We have had an offer,' Mrs Clifford told us. 'A rather curious one. The Kentucky Fried Chicken people are interested in buying it.'

'Kentucky Fried Chicken!' I said, appalled.

'Yes,' she nodded. 'Odd, isn't it?'

Odd! It was sacrilege. No way would Kentucky Fried Chicken get their greasy fingers on the Abbey. Not if I could prevent it.

I was instantly obsessed with owning the hotel, for the thought of seeing this elegant old house changed into a fast-food venue was very distressing. I wanted to restore it to its past glories, and could picture how it ought to be. Michael and I went home and discussed the prospect for hours whilst I lay in bed. We had finished the work on our own home and it was beautiful, but its completion had left us without anything to achieve. We had the time to work on the Abbey. Neither of us was doing anything else, and we needed some form of serious livelihood.

'I think it would be lovely to run a small hotel,' I said tentatively, since I could sense Michael was not that keen.

Having experienced the reality of running a small hotel he was anxious for me to understand the nitty-gritty of the profession rather than the fantasy.

'It's hard work, demanding, and it never stops,' he warned.

'We can get good staff,' I said blithely. 'And you know all about it.'

'That's true,' he said rather ruefully, and capitulated. It was agreed that we would buy the Abbey.

My dream was an expensive one. We would have to sell everything we had, borrow money and work like mad. It was a wrench to sell our beautiful farmhouse that we had worked on so lovingly, but there was no choice. When I look back I understand Michael's hesitation. It was a bold decision that we made, but a decision which has proved to be the right one.

It was also madness to be thinking about moving while I was so ill. In the fortnight before Thaddeus was born I ate only a few cherries, but at least I managed to keep them down. I seemed to be feeling just fractionally better. The baby was already late, and I felt it would help me to give birth if I was induced while I had this unexpected bonus of a little strength. I suggested this, and the doctors took me into the hospital for two days before inducing me. First they gave me an enema which, as I had not eaten anything much for months, Michael regarded as a form of madness.

If the pregnancy had been a nightmare, giving birth was almost worse. Michael was with me when they hooked me up to a machine which recorded the baby's heartbeat. When the nurse had finished fiddling with the machine, she turned to Michael and said cheerfully: 'Let us know if anything goes wrong.' And left the room. I have rarely seen a look of panic on Michael's normally confident face, but I did then. There was one good thing about that machine – Michael could see when a contraction was coming and warn me. This was very necessary, as the contractions were terribly painful and the gas and air cylinder they had supplied did not seem to be helping. This was not surprising. Michael was peering at it when he suddenly said: 'The bloody thing's empty!'

Furious, he went looking for the nurse. 'My wife is in great pain,' he said, 'and the gas-air cylinder that you gave her is empty.'

'Oh, really?' she said. 'Go and see if you can find another one.' And again she scurried off.

There was hardly anyone about while Michael searched the empty corridors for a full cylinder. The hospital, like me, was half-dead. Eventually he found one propped in a corner. He also found a trolley to put it on and wheeled it back to my room for the nurses to connect up. The relief! The birth was proving so difficult that towards the end they gave me pethidine. I am very bad on drugs, and the pethidine confused me and made me push in the wrong direction. I was using my neck and shoulder muscles instead of the abdominal ones. The problem was that, though Thaddeus was an emaciated little baby at birth, he had a large head. Michael, who was still sitting with me, could see his head beginning to appear and then disappearing again. It became obvious that the only thing to do was to cut me.

They took me off to another room, where a doctor came in holding what looked like a pair of garden shears. Michael was sent off to the waiting room. He was pacing up and down when he noticed a telephone. On it was written in bold letters, 'If you have a flat baby, pick up this phone.' Michael reasoned that a 'flat' baby was one that was very poorly indeed, and he was devastated when a few minutes later a nurse rushed out and picked up the phone. The call immediately produced a rash of doctors, white coats flapping, stethoscopes dangling, running down the corridor. Michael sank his head into his hands, convinced that our nine months of misery had been for nothing. But Thaddeus was not the 'flat' baby. Two minutes later a nurse appeared, beckoning Michael.

'Mr Cox,' she beamed, 'you have a son.'

They led him back into the room to see this thin little 6lb fellow who had finally made it into the world. I was woozy and exhausted. It seemed to me they had stitched me up terribly badly. I sensed that the doctor was doing a bad job, but I was too weary to complain. The birth had been horrendous from start to finish.

Thaddeus was a big surprise to both of us since we were convinced he would be a she. We even had a name: we were going to call her Mimosa.

Perhaps because it had all been such a nightmare at first I did not seem to have much maternal instinct. There I was with this baby, and I did not know what to do with him. He cried because he was hungry, but I did not know what was the matter and could not calm him. I was determined to breast-feed him, but my milk did not come. Thaddeus wailed and I panicked and kept asking myself: What have I done? I've done it again. I have this baby to look after and I don't know how. What have I done to my life?

Four days later, when he started to lose weight because my milk would not come, I cried and cried and I broke through. My maternal instincts asserted themselves. I knew I desperately wanted this baby to live. Suddenly my milk came, and ever since then I have been on the motherhood hook. I have never faltered, not for a minute. I breast-fed Thaddeus for nine months in the daytime and for fifteen months at night. I was being extreme again, but I was certain it was good for the baby. I was amazed I had milk at all as I had been starved for so long. It was also astonishing how fast I recovered after not eating for all those months, though I was tired and wiped out for a year.

We do not talk about that terrible birth. It has paled into insignificance against all the joy that Thaddeus has given us.

We came home with the baby and had three months at our farmhouse before we moved to the Abbey. It was a lovely hot summer and I dozed in the afternoons while Thaddeus slept in an old pram under the lilac in the garden. Our next-door neighbour had five daughters and he was pleased that a boy had come to the farm. He was a wonderful old man, always with a pipe in his mouth. On wet days, to keep it dry he smoked it upside down. He cultivated a field of vegetables for his huge family and he let us help ourselves to anything we wanted.

We had to leave all this when we moved into the Abbey on a beautiful sunny October day. We had sold what we had, begged and borrowed from wherever and whoever we could, and we knew that the debts would be a millstone. But we were confident it would all be worthwhile. We had two weeks in the hotel completely on our own before we started work on the alterations, and we explored the place from attics to cellar. As we did not really know exactly what we had bought this was exciting. Quite a lot of furniture had been included in the sale price, including the tables and chairs in the dining room where we had eaten our fish and chip wedding breakfast. We had furniture of our own, including the pieces that I had stored in the barn when Michael bought my house; Michael had other things in store. Furnishings were the least of our problems.

There was so much to be done. There was no liquor licence – it had expired eight years previously. We also wanted a restaurant licence, which meant putting lavatories in the cellar – and the cellar was in bad shape. It had to be dug out with a pneumatic drill, and the noise was indescribable. It was not the best start for a three-month-old baby. Floor-boards were up everywhere and I was forever stepping over joists with the baby in my arms. Workmen arrived at eight in the morning and left at ten-thirty at night. We never had a minute's peace. It was eight months before we could take guests, and when the the first arrived Michael was laying the carpet on the back stairs as I was showing them up the stairs at the front.

At first we rented a little house across the road to get away from the noise, but that was not ideal as it was another financial outgoing. We eventually settled in part of the Abbey complex which we had bought along with the main building. We should not really have been living there – the property was so dilapidated and damp that it had a council closing order on it. Everything in there went mouldy. Our clothes grew a pretty green fungus, and the two rooms were littered with bowls to catch the raindrops as they poured through the ceiling. Furnished with some nice old pieces it looked

243

good, but it did not bear close inspection. As winter came on, the place was freezing cold. When they show television programmes of places where people should not be living I often recall that once we, too, lived in awful circumstances.

We stayed in those rooms for eight years and it was quite a strain to have a child, the mess, and water dripping down as we struggled to get the hotel looking as we wanted it to while running the place at the same time. One of the television companies asked us to do the *Through the Keyhole* show, on which a panel has to guess from pictures whose home it is. We should really have agreed. Nobody would ever have guessed the owners, what with all that damp and mould in a room set about with elegant furniture and an authentic Buddha or two. That derelict apartment is now our home, and charming, but it took a long time before we could afford to get it right.

I managed for a while to hang on to the London flat in Blenheim Crescent, which served us as a bolt hole. Eventually it had to go in order to pay for more work on the Abbey. But while we had it, it did at least mean we could occasionally break away from the squalor of the way we were living.

But our life was not all hard grind. In London we would see friends like Francis Wyndham, Geoffrey (Michael loved his shop), Valerie and Carina. We led the social life for a day or two while Mum looked after Thaddeus.

On one of these trips Carina invited us to join a small party to see the State Opening of Parliament. As Britain's premier duke, her father, the Duke of Norfolk, was officiating. We decided we should go as it was a rare opportunity, but I had nothing suitable to wear. Valerie lent me a black suit and a pair of black suede shoes, but I still needed a hat.

'We'll buy you one,' Michael said.

We went to Peter Jones in Sloane Square and I was trying on these little eight- or nine-quid numbers until Michael brought over a small black velvet hat with a spotted veil. It was a Freddie Fox creation from the

couture department. I looked at the price tag. It was
£70.

'I am not buying a £70 hat,' I told Michael as he held it
enticingly in front of me.

'Try it on.'

I sighed and put it on. It looked wonderful. 'No,' I said
firmly, taking it off.

'It's perfect and it's near your birthday,' he reminded
me. 'I'll buy it for you.'

I put the hat back on and faced the mirror. I did look
good in it. Even I could see that, and other customers were
eyeing me.

'No,' I said again, but with less conviction.

'You haven't spent any money. You've borrowed everything else.'

'W-e-l-l?' I said.

We bought it.

The day before the State Opening I went to my bank
and took out the beautiful necklace which I keep there. It
is a mourning piece with a design of skulls and skeletons
and dates back to about 1680 – which is why I keep it
in the bank. I wore the necklace with Valerie's suit and
Michael's birthday-present hat, and I looked good. Carina
had some friends called Dot and Barry from the film world
who had arranged the party. They got their old Bentley out
and we sailed off to Westminster in style. It was all swank
and great fun. For the first time in my life I was walking
round London wearing a hat with a veil, looking truly chic
and thoroughly enjoying myself.

The Westminster ceremony was impressive and interesting, though the place smelt a bit gamey. Afterwards we
went to one of London's most expensive restaurants and
drank wonderful pink champagne. Stupidly I ate oysters
followed by steak tartare. A few hours later, on the street
near Charing Cross Station, done up like a dog's dinner, food
poisoning struck. Again I was throwing up and again Michael
was wonderfully supportive, holding up both me and my veil.
The hat was fastened on with pins and we could not get it

off. Because the shoes were not mine I had to step out of them, kick them out of the way and stand there in my stockinged feet. As awful as I was feeling, I was miserably aware that the clothes I was wearing were borrowed and I was terrified of damaging them. It was ironic. The one time in my life when I had actually dressed up, I was so ill – and so publicly. It is terrible enough throwing up when you are normally dressed, but looking as I did made it all the more embarrassing.

Fortunately we were near the office of the friends we were on our way to visit, and we went there to borrow a plastic waste-paper bin for me to be ill into. All I wanted to do was get home.

'I *am* sorry,' I said to Michael when we were indoors and I was able to mop myself up. 'And thanks for holding my head.'

'It's all right,' he said with a grin. 'I'm used to it. I've had practice. Remember?'

I was ill for twenty-four hours and not displeased to get back to Penzance, even as uncomfortable as our home then was.

Being puritanical in some ways, I do not think those years of hardship did us any harm. Today the Abbey is as I visualized it, and a statement I wanted to make of how things should be. I feel that the hotel is something we have created, but more important it is something that has its own identity. It is not dependent on my being beautiful or a top model. For years I was told that I was beautiful, but being beautiful is something uncontrollable. It was chance, luck or fate that gave me my looks. They were a gift, but I can be proud of the Abbey because Michael and I are its creators. We have spent an enormous amount of money, but have also expended a vast amount of effort and thought getting it all together. Places do not have character if they just reflect chequebooks, and the Abbey has character.

It will be years before the hotel pays for itself, and in the early days, when guests were few and far between, the worry was awful. I am immensely intuitive. I know which guests are not going to turn up; I look at their name written in the book and I think to myself, 'They're not gonna come', and I'm always right. It used to drive me barmy when we were beginning. These days we do not have the same worries. The hotel is a success, though being such an old building it is expensive to keep in trim. It says much for my devotion to the place that every now and then – usually when the roof starts to leak – I have reluctantly come out of retirement to earn the money to pay for the repairs.

The roof was causing problems a few years ago when out of the blue Bailey rang up.

'Do you want to earn some money?' he asked.

'Doing what?' I said cautiously.

'It's a commercial,' he explained, and went on, sounding faintly apologetic, 'for hair that's going grey.'

I burst out laughing. 'Bailey,' I said, 'I've retired.'

'It's very well paid,' he coaxed.

I remembered the roof and groaned. 'OK,' I said. 'I'll do it. But I want you to know you have just ruined my day.'

Bailey has always come up trumps when I have been in dire straits. He is a naturally helpful person. A year or so ago when I was staying with my mother I rang him up because a friend of mine who was a neighbour in Wales had a beautiful daughter who wanted to be a model. He was not in, so I left a message for him to ring me. It just so happened that he was filming in the studios at Beaconsfield, just down the road from Rose Hill Farm, when he rang back.

'What are you doing up here?' he asked.

'I'm just staying with Mum,' I told him. 'Michael's holding the fort.'

'Shall I come over?' he asked.

He had not seen my mother since all those years ago when we split up and he came running to cry on her shoulder. They were thrilled to see each other again and we had a perfect hour and a half, the three of us together. It must have been funny for him sitting there looking at us both. I was pleased to see him – I am always pleased to see him. There is always a lingering spark, the collective memory of

247

shared experience and that *frisson* that comes from seeing someone you once loved and still like. Bailey and I are both happy. He has a lovely wife and two children, being a father has brought so much to his life.

Today, now I have Michael, I am a great deal more confident and I can handle life so much better. I would never stay in the desperate situations that I stayed in in the past.

I have a good life. I love my husband and my son above all else. My few friends from times past are still friends, and with Michael I have made more. When I was famous it was hard to find real friends at any level: being wealthier than most of the people I liked set up a barrier.

Death has claimed some of the people who were important to me. Di Cottrell and Geoffrey Bennison both died some years ago and are much missed. But the most poignant loss was that of my father.

He died on 16 December 1987. He was very ill, and I was glad that I was able to help nurse him. I found I could touch him, undress him and comfort him and I was not embarrassed. He was emotional and he cried all the time but I understood – the tears represented many years of repressed emotion.

He told me before he died that if he had his life to live over again he would not change a thing. I said: 'How can you say that?' But I have come to terms with the fact that he lived his life to his own satisfaction, and that cannot be a bad thing. All I have of him now are the time sheets he used to give his workmen, full of homely sayings that are so indicative of his beliefs. I have a character assessment of his handwriting by a graphologist, his best wallet and a poem that my brother, Dan, wrote about him. These were all I wanted of his personal possessions, as they seemed to me to hold the essence of my father. There is one special memory I cherish of him. We were walking round the farm together when I was at my lowest, at the time when I was breaking away from Heathcote. We looked at all the animals together (animals had always been our bond) and, although nothing was said, I knew that he felt for me, loved me and wanted the best for me, though he would have found it hard to articulate his feelings.

My mother is still the tower of strength that she always was. She lives on the farm and latterly she has taken up bridge and golf. She is a resolute lady, my mum. She has an enormous capacity for happiness and she is at her happiest when all her family are around her. Of course, the sadness of my father's death is always with her, but she is strong and has come through what was an emotionally draining period and managed to create a new life for herself.

My life is happier now than it has ever been. There is not one picture of me as a model in my home – nor was there even when I was famous. Modelling was a strange career for me. Looking back, I realize that I was never really comfortable with the fame that came with it.

We never told Thaddeus about my work until Harry Secombe came to Penzance with his *Highway* programme, and, as publicity for the hotel, I agreed to appear.

Thaddeus could not think why the producers of the programme should be interested in me. 'Why do they want you on the programme, Mummy?' he wanted to know.

Without making too much of it, I tried to explain that I was once a well-known model. He refused to believe me. He was convinced I was pulling his leg.

Then, a couple of days later, my picture was in the local paper with an article about my modelling days.

'Oh, golly, it's true then,' he said in tones of deep disgust. 'You really were famous, weren't you? I can't bear it.'

'And neither could I, darling,' I told him. 'Neither could I.'

Index

Sphere now offers an exciting range of quality titles by both established and new authors. All of the books in this series are available from:

Sphere Books,
Cash Sales Department,
P.O. Box 11,
Falmouth,
Cornwall TR10 9EN.

Alternatively you may fax your order to the above address. Fax No. 0326 376423.

Payments can be made as follows: Cheque, postal order (payable to Macdonald & Co (Publishers) Ltd) or by credit cards, Visa/Access. Do not send cash or currency. UK customers and B.F.P.O.: please send a cheque or postal order (no currency) and allow £1.00 for postage and packing for the first book, plus 50p for the second book, plus 30p for each additional book up to a maximum charge of £3.00 (7 books plus).

Overseas customers including Ireland, please allow £2.00 for postage and packing for the first book, plus £1.00 for the second book, plus 50p for each additional book.

NAME (Block Letters) ....

ADDRESS ....

....

☐ I enclose my remittance for _____

☐ I wish to pay by Access/Visa Card

Number ⬚⬚⬚⬚⬚⬚⬚⬚⬚⬚⬚⬚⬚⬚⬚⬚⬚

Card Expiry Date ⬚⬚⬚⬚